Sensation, perception and action

Sensation, perception and action

An evolutionary perspective

Johannes M. Zanker

Professor of Neuroscience and Head of Department of Psychology,
Royal Holloway, University of London

First published 2010 by
PALGRAVE MACMILLAN

Palgrave Macmillan in the UK is an imprint of Macmillan Publishers Limited, registered in England, company number 785998, of Houndmills, Basingstoke, Hampshire RG21 6XS.

Palgrave Macmillan in the US is a division of St Martin's Press LLC, 175 Fifth Avenue, New York, NY 10010.

Palgrave Macmillan is the global academic imprint of the above companies and has companies and representatives throughout the world.

Palgrave® and Macmillan® are registered trademarks in the United States, the United Kingdom, Europe and other countries

ISBN 978–0–230–55266–1   hardback
ISBN 978–0–230–55267–8   paperback

This book is printed on paper suitable for recycling and made from fully managed and sustained forest sources. Logging, pulping and manufacturing processes are expected to conform to the environmental regulations of the country of origin.

A catalogue record for this book is available from the British Library.

A catalog record for this book is available from the Library of Congress.

10 9 8 7 6 5 4 3 2 1
19 18 17 16 15 14 13 12 11 10

Printed in China

This book is dedicated to my parents, who allowed and encouraged me to be curious.

Contents

List of Figures

List of Table

List of Colour Plates

Preface

Why another textbook on perception? This question has been nagging me for many years, and I was reluctant for a long time to add something to a long list of excellent, and well-established, introductions to this topic. And yet, during almost a decade of teaching Sensation and Perception to Undergraduate Psychology students I noticed, from many enquiries of my students and my own efforts to cut through a jungle of knowledge and to organise my thoughts, that many textbooks covering the field in a more traditional way, while presenting an extensive collection of perceptual phenomena and relating them to brain function, are missing two aspects. On the one hand, the close connection between perception and action is often treated like a non-essential extra, even though perception serves a central task in organising behaviour – and therefore its function is driven by what is needed to guide a person safely through a dangerous world. On the other hand, the focus on humans, which is rather understandable for psychologists, can obscure the view on a wide range of alternative perceptual systems that can be found in other species that have to solve similar tasks, such as detecting and recognising objects, communicating, or navigating, but do so in different environment. Also, the full range of different senses is not always fully appreciated. Taking these aspects into account leads to a more radical 'evolutionary perspective' of perception, which looks at external drivers that led to the evolution of biological sensory systems, including humans, in a particular ecological niche. We can compare the evolutionary process to the problems and solutions for the design of artificial sensory processing mechanisms that an engineer would have to ponder when building an agent that is highly adapted to its environment and its task space. This context is the essence of this book, which talks about perception in close connection to action and about evolution as the underlying principle that shaped sensory systems.

Like a developing engineer, but much less constrained and far more effective, the evolutionary process changes and adjusts sensory processing mechanisms (e.g. colour vision) to solve a problem (e.g. breaking camouflage or living underwater). Perception is the interface between the physical and the mental world, full of scientific puzzles and philosophical challenges. To understand how sensory systems work, this textbook adopts a – now generally accepted – information processing paradigm that interprets the brain, and its input and output, as a colossal data processing machine, or in other words as a computer, which allows us to precisely describe what kind of information is collected and how it is used by the perceiving individual. Such an approach allows us to assess the costs and benefits of a particular sensor or processing design, and why a specific design would help an organism operating in a particular task space. All of this may sound rather technical and theory-heavy, but it is surprisingly accessible to students at all levels, just by using common sense, when rigorous mathematical treatment is replaced by intuitive descriptions and supported by everyday examples from our IT-dominated world as illustrations. The core 'functional' question is no more than asking what we need to do in order to achieve a certain goal. This question may be quite straightforward when we want to make a sandwich for lunch, it could be slightly more challenging when we want to construct a bicycle from scratch (after all, we would need to invent the wheel) and can be rather complex if we want to design an intelligent camera, such as the eye. In each of these cases, however, asking the functional question helps us to understand the specific appearance of the final product: why there is butter between the slice of bread and the ham, a handle bar attached front wheel of your bike a flexible lens at the entrance of the eye. Given the diverse and sometimes puzzling nature of the phenomena we want to understand, this treatment of the topic can be experienced as both intellectually challenging and entertaining. In consequence, this book may serve as an introduction not only to students of Psychology, but equally to those of other disciplines such as Biology, IT and Robotics, Medicine, and possibly even Philosophy.

So much about designs, perspectives, paradigms, ideas. Alas, there was a long, long way from the conception of this book to its actual realisation. Writing this book at times was a struggle, when the world outside of my study offered much better things to do than looking at an apparently comatose computer screen; it often was exciting and entertaining, when making headway into fields unknown to me and discovering new aspects of the amazing world of sensory systems; and it always was a challenge to try making complex phenomena accessible to a wider readership. After going through a much too long and often interrupted stream of activity and procrastination, however, my recollection is dominated by a sense of enjoying this search for clarity. Countless mugs of coffee fuelled the process, and kilograms of chocolate kept me going, as did the fabulous editorial team that guided me through what sometimes felt like a never-ending uphill struggle. My thanks go to Jamie Marshall and Anna van Boxel for picking up on my initial ideas and reassuring me to follow them up, and to Jamie Joseph for keeping up my spirits and guiding me through some more mundane aspects of the editorial and production process. Equally, I am indebted to a number of colleagues who helped to nurture this book by getting drawn into many discussions, just being around to keep my spirits up, listening to crazy ideas over lunch, challenging me with critical questions and commenting on various aspects of the manuscript – in particular Szonya Durant, Tim Holmes and Marina Rose who patiently scrutinised selected chapters of this book. Special thanks go to Ulrike Siebeck for introducing me to the wonders of UV vision in the coral reef and providing illustrations of this strange world, and to Alexandra Stanton for sharing with me her skills in BSL. Furthermore I am indebted to my students who gave me the inspiration and kept up the motivation to write this book, and always bring me back to planet earth with their questions when I go off on tangents. Last but not least, I want to thank my family for their patience, allowing me to withdraw from the chaos of real life to my study for (sometimes) undisturbed reading and writing, and for picking up my chores in house and the kitchen – they had to put up with quite a few follies. Without the support from all these individuals, and many more, the idea for this book would never have turned into reality!

Johannes M. Zanker
London, Summer 2009

Acknowledgements

The publisher and author would like to thank the organisations and people listed below for permission to reproduce material from their publications:

Figure 10.3a © Newspix/News Ltd.

Figure 10.3b © Getty images.

Figure 9.5b: Macmillan Publishers Ltd: *Nature Neuroscience* 10, 27–29: 'Mechanisms of scent-tracking in humans', Jess Porter et al. (2007).

Figure 11.6: Macmillan Publishers Ltd: *Nature Reviews Neuroscience* 4, 26–36 'Non-spatially lateralized mechanisms in hemispatial neglect', Husain, M. and Rorden, C. (2003).

Figure 11.7: Macmillan Publishers Ltd: *Nature* 398, 34 'Change-blindness as a result of "mudsplashes"' O'Regan et al. (1999).

Elsevier for Figure 11.8. Original source is Gustav Kuhn and Michael F. Land (2006) 'There's more to magic than meets the eye', *Current Biology*, 16 (22): R950–R951.

Elsevier for Figure 12.5a. Original source is Marc O. Ernst and Heinrich H. Bülthoff (2004) 'Merging the senses into a robust percept', *Trends in Cognitive Sciences*, 8 (4): 162.

Alexandra Stanton for Figure 12.7a.

Lawrence Erlbaum Associates, Inc. for Figure 13.7. Flowfield redrawn from figure published in J. J. Gibson (1979) *The Ecological Approach to Visual Perception*.

Elsevier for Colour plate VIII, Figure 2. Original source Ulrike E. Siebeck (2004) 'Communication in coral reef fish: The role of ultraviolet colour patterns in damselfish territorial behaviour', *Animal Behaviour*, 68 (2): 273–282.

Every effort has been made to obtain necessary permission with reference to copyright material. The publisher and author apologise if, inadvertently, any sources remain unacknowledged and will be glad to make the necessary arrangements at the earliest opportunity.

1 PERCEPTION AS GATEWAY TO THE WORLD

OVERVIEW

Why is perception such an important topic of study for psychologists? Throughout every single day of our life we incessantly and effortlessly solve complex tasks related to the collection and interpretation of sensory input, and the planning and execution of action based on what is perceived. We (usually) experience little difficulty in preparing a sandwich, catching a ball, riding a bicycle, or crossing a busy road – but each of these seemingly simple tasks requires a huge amount of sensory information processing! Only when we observe the hopeless efforts of robots facing much, much simpler challenges (like walking up a step), do we start to appreciate how difficult it is to navigate and coordinate movements in a group of independently moving individuals, for instance, on a crowded dance floor. To address these questions, and to understand more generally how a person collects knowledge about the world and acts in the world, the information processing paradigm is introduced, together with the computer metaphor for the brain. This approach is closely linked, through the specific relationship between brain and perception, and more generally the relationship between brain and mind, to the study of brain function, which embeds perception in a variety of scientific disciplines that help us to analyse and conceptualise human behaviour. The attempt to localise mental functions in the brain is an illustration of how the information processing approach, and neuroscience, are highly relevant to gain some deep understanding of psychological phenomena. Sensory systems usually are treated as information processing channels that are tuned to particular signals (such as sounds, or odours) and used to solve particular tasks (such as communication). Studying such mechanisms from a scientific and/ or engineering perspective allows us to tackle questions of how their designs are optimised in the context of evolutionary adaptation and ecological constraints. In this framework, perception can be described as the window between the physical world and mental states.

WHAT IS THE PURPOSE OF THIS BOOK?

In a time of rapidly growing competition for resources, be it the time invested by a student in reading a book (as well as the time spent by the author writing it), or the timber harvested from shrinking forests and processed into printing paper at high costs in terms of energy and water pollution, the first question when picking up a book and beginning to turn the pages is 'why should I read this book?' The most simplistic answer for the Psychology student, 'because it will help me to get my degree', is certainly insufficient, and not a good reason to dig into hundreds of pages about phenomena and contexts that sometimes even present some challenge to understand. The reason for writing and reading this book, and for seriously engaging with its topic, is the fact that sensation, perception and action have a fundamental relevance for all aspects of human behaviour and thinking. How can you prepare your tea and sandwich in the morning? How do you coordinate getting dressed, picking up – and keeping hold of – your bag? How do you cross the road without getting run over, ride your bike without falling over, or steer your car through dense traffic without getting involved in an accident? How do you find your favourite cereal in the supermarket and pick it off the shelf? How do you follow, throw or catch a ball? How do you communicate with the people around you? And how do you actually read a book?

In all our daily activities we need to interact with the world surrounding us, and for any interaction we need to use our senses to collect information and control our actions. And yet all of these processing steps are happening completely unaware and effortless! Without being equipped with a sensory system and perception, however, no autonomous agent would be able to act, nor survive, in its given environment. The little sketch in Figure 1.1 illustrates this crucial role of sensation and perception: the presence of an apple in the environment is picked up by the sensory system (through the eyes, or possibly by smell) and recognised as a real instance of the concept 'apple', which can trigger the behavioural response of grasping and eating (or avoidance, if the apple turns out to be rotten).

The purpose of this book, therefore, is to provide a basic introduction to the function of sensory information processing in the context of action control and of a particular lifestyle and environment, and to give some clues about how evolution shaped these systems to make them efficient and reliable, so that an agent (such as a person) can safely navigate in a complex environment and survive. It is important to note that the phrase 'function' has a dual meaning. On one hand this word relates to a specific mechanism, i.e. to the question 'how does it work?', which will be touched mainly in an abstract way in this book, because the actual workings of the neural machinery is the topic of more specialised neuroscience textbooks. On the other hand the word 'function' relates to a purpose, i.e. to the question 'how is it useful, what is it made for?', which relates much more closely to the behavioural and ecological context. In this distinction, however, one should not forget that through evolutionary mechanisms the actual design of mechanisms is closely linked to its role in behaviour and environment, similar to the slogan of the Bauhaus arts and design school 'form follows

Figure 1.1

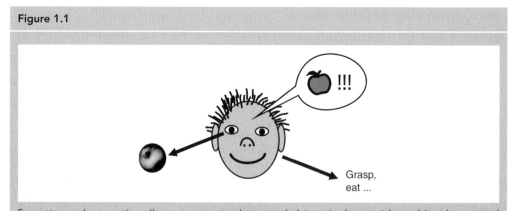

Sensation and perception allows a person to detect real objects in the outside world and to control the appropriate action in response to objects and events. In this example an apple is picked up by the visual system of our little egghead, recognised as an instantiation of a highly relevant class of objects (the thought 'this is an apple'), and the appropriate response will be triggered and again guided by sensory information (grasp, eat ...).

function'. As a result of this conceptual framework, the current text differs from many other textbooks on the topic of sensation and perception by going beyond the mere description of perceptual phenomena, and focussing on the adaptation of particular perceptual mechanisms in the context of their use to solve tasks that we are facing in our everyday 'struggle for survival'. As such this textbook, whereas mainly directed at students of Psychology and in its level of detail written for psychologists with limited previous exposure to an engineering perspective, can also serve as introduction to the topic for computer scientists, engineers and biologists.

REPRESENTING THE OUTSIDE WORLD

So how do we perceive the outside world? What initially seems to be a straightforward question turns out to be a rather tricky philosophical problem. How do we know where we are, what is in the space surrounding us, what the effects of our actions are, how do we communicate with others and understand messages in a complex society? The answer seems to be very simple: we use our senses. We see the furniture, the walls, the trees in our environment, we hear birds, cars and airplanes, and what other people are saying to us, we smell burning toast, and sense the heat (and sometimes the pain) when trying to remove it from the toaster, we feel the knife in our hand and taste the melting butter and the flavour of the jam. Very simple, and yet quite complicated when you think more thoroughly about it – there are myriad tricky questions lurking behind these everyday perceptions and actions, some of which will be answered in this book. How do we steer clear of furniture, know the distance away of walls and trees, how can we judge the speed of an approaching car? How do we recognise the voice of a friend, the face of our grandmother? What makes us smell the toast burning? When do we feel the heat and when does it turn into pain? How do we know how to grasp the knife at its handle and not at its blade? What makes us discriminate the taste of strawberry and raspberry jam? The common theme behind these questions is the collection of information about the outside world, in order to know, to understand and to act. It could be argued that through our senses we are building a representation of the outside world in our mind. Although this concept is contested by some authors (such as Gibson 1979), we will accept this notion as a simple description and revisit its limitations later (see Chapters 12 and 13).

The guiding question towards the understanding of the visual system therefore is: what are the fundamental steps of information processing to convert the outside (physical) world into internal (mental) events? This question – perhaps not surprisingly, because it touches on one of the most fundamental aspects of the human condition – has been raised by many philosophers for many centuries (see, for instance, Wade 1998). An early description of the fundamental principles of optical projection, (neural) transmission and (cortical) mapping can be found in Descartes (1664) the French philosopher, scientist and mathematician who often is called the 'father of modern philosophy'. René Descartes (1596–1650) is regarded as key figure in the 'Scientific Revolution' (Kuhn 1962), which replaced previous belief systems and speculations with observations and experiments. Figure 1.2 summarises his dualist attempt to describe how images of the external world (an arrow) are formed and processed in the visual system, leading to an internal representation in the brain, more specifically in the pituitary gland, where it becomes accessible to the mind. We can therefore regard this figure as one of the roots of our understanding of sensory information processing, as we interpret it in the twenty-first century through the methods of science – and science is what we are interested here.

Figure 1.2

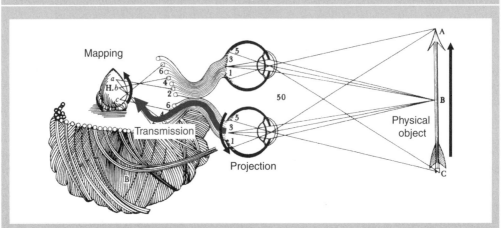

Representing the outside world in the brain (adapted from Descartes 1664). The arrow is viewed and inverted through the eyes and the image is transmitted through the optic nerves to the brain, where it is mapped on the pituitary gland (which Descartes believed to be the seat of the soul). Whereas some anatomical and physiological features are recognised correctly, such as the inversion through the eye's optics, there are other aspects in this sketch, such as the reversion of the image in the optic nerve and the mapping on the pituitary gland, that are not supported by modern science (see Hubel 1979).

From Descartes' sketch of the visual system in Figure 1.2, we can already recognise a number of important questions to ask about the relationship between the physical world surrounding us and the internal, mental world:

- Why do we think that the mental world is located in the brain?
- How do we 'read' the mental map, and what turns it into a percept?
- Why is the perceived world not upside down after the optical inversion in the eye?
- Is the internal representation a veridical picture of the world?
- Is the perceived world the same for each of us?

Some answers to these questions will be given in the course of this book, others are challenging enough to be still disputed by philosophers. When Descartes claimed the pituitary gland to host the 'soul', which today we would call the mind, he showed himself as a representative of a philosophical position called 'dualism' – the coexistence of a material body and a non-physical mind. Contemporary scientists, in contrast, tend to support a 'materialist' position, according to which only the physical world is accessible to scientific method which can offer a comprehensive explanation of all phenomena in this world, and the mind is an emergent property of the body (see Valentine 1992). The key scientific approach to investigate perception was defined as discipline by Gustav Theodor Fechner as 'Psychophysics' – as the study of 'functional or dependent relations between body and soul, or more general between material and mental, physical and psychological world' (Fechner 1860). Many clues on the relationship between the physical and the mental world arise from looking at visual illusions (Gregory 1968): what you see is not what you have!

SENSATION AND PERCEPTION – AND NEIGHBOURING DISCIPLINES

In many cases when you hear about Perception, you are confronted with a sibling term, Sensation, and indeed many books on the topic are entitled 'Sensation and Perception' (Goldstein 2007).

What makes these two terms such close companions, and what are they referring to? They belong together because they are regarded to be two important steps in human information processing, from the raw data in peripheral sensory organs, such as images in the retina, to the central extraction of features or categorical information, such as objects or faces. Sensation, on the one hand, is traditionally believed to be related to low-level signals, which undergo only basic, unaware processing and are not easily accessible to others. Perception, on the other hand, refers to high-level 'stuff' that is available to consciousness, and therefore can be communicated to others. It is immediately clear that it would be very difficult to exactly separate such two processing levels, and that the low/high-level boundaries between sensation and perception might be even impossible to define. As a matter of fact, there is a continuous processing stream from the signals captured by the sensory organs to the point where we recognise objects and events in our environment. Furthermore, we would end up struggling with giving a precise and comprehensive explanation of terms like 'awareness' or 'consciousness' (Crick 1995), and we cannot deny that we are able to build high-level representations of the outside world without being aware of their contents (Koch and Crick 2001). Just imagine how safely you can navigate a vehicle through dense traffic without being aware of most of the scene around you (Land 2001)! To avoid such theoretical and practical difficulties, the distinction between sensation and perception will be largely abandoned here, and the term 'perception' will be used at all stages of the processing stream. The benefit of this approach will become obvious when the information processing paradigm has been introduced later in this chapter.

Why is perception so important for psychologists? Psychology is the study of human behaviour and thinking, or more specifically 'the science of the nature, functions, and phenomena of the human mind' (Oxford English Dictionary). Thinking is an extraordinary phenomenon: we spend all our life thinking (which doesn't mean, obviously, that we always produce clever thoughts) and would find it very difficult to switch it off – which is fundamentally different from most kinds of other activities. Therefore it is one of the most exciting challenges for contemporary science to find out about the machinery of thinking. The mechanisms of thinking are studied in cognitive psychology, and its biological substrate – commonly assumed to be the brain – is studied in neuroscience. Some core thought processes, related to the acquisition, handling, storing and application of knowledge, can be grouped as 'cognition', and Cognitive Sciences comprises a multidisciplinary group of scientific approaches (psychology, linguistics, artificial intelligence, neuroscience, philosophy) with the common goal of understanding the human mind (Eysenck 2006). Some authors regard the study of perception as part of (experimental) cognitive psychology, because it is the starting point for acquiring knowledge about the world, for all higher thought processes, and for the control of behaviour. Just think about language – communication is based on reading text, watching signs, or listening to sounds and spoken words. Even if one doesn't want to treat perception as part of cognition, it is obvious that thinking and behaviour is based on a chain of information processing in the nervous system that starts with the collection of sensory signals and perception. As illustrated in the simple block diagram of information flow of Figure 1.3, it might be better to talk about a network rather than a chain of information processing, because bottom-up processes transmit information from the sensory organs into higher areas of the human nervous system, while at the same time lower areas are modulated through top-down connections. This design of recursive information flow is called by engineers a 'feedback loop'.

To fill the abstract block diagram with some specific meaning, let's run through a rather trivial, everyday example, which illustrates different aspects and levels of processing – demonstrating how little effort is needed for a lot of simple and complex processing tasks.

Figure 1.3

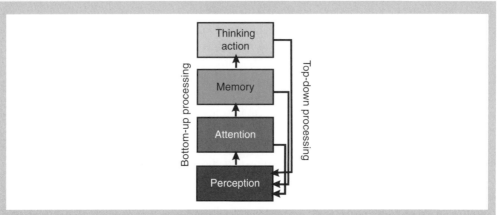

Perception is the starting point for higher cognitive processes: the selection ('attention'), storage and retrieval ('memory') and reorganisation of knowledge ('thinking'), and through this the control of behaviour ('action'). Whereas the initial flow of information is 'bottom-up', from lower processing levels of sensory to more higher processing levels handling more complex and abstract representations, there are 'top-down' mechanisms which modulate early processing.

Figure 1.4

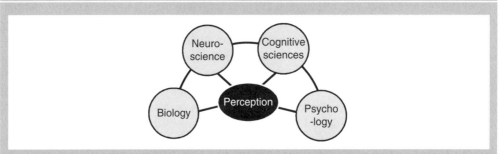

Perception, the 'window' between the outside (physical) world and inside world (mental states), is studied in the context of a variety of overlapping disciplines: biology, neurosciences, cognitive sciences and psychology. All of these disciplines are concerned with the question of how information about the environment is collected, stored, interpreted and used to control behaviour.

Imagine you meet your friend in the café to work on your statistics exercise – what are the necessary processing steps in your brain? Perception: you enter the café and look around, identify tables, desks, the people populating the place, smell the coffee; attention: you ignore almost everything and find your friend; planning and control of action: you approach the table without knocking over chairs; learning and memory: you find the problem sheet in your bag; language: you start a conversation; knowledge handling: you try to memorise the contents of the lectures; reasoning: you select the right equation and compute the result.

Because perception is the starting point for all other areas of psychology, and is equally relevant for our understanding of how the brain works and how behaviour is organised in a wide range of animals, the study of perception is closely linked to, and overlapping with, other disciplines, including neurosciences and behavioural biology (see Figure 1.4).

As a result, this book on perception will make repeated references to crucial topics from neuroscience, and even will offer an excursion into some exciting areas of biology – with the goal to extend our understanding of the crucial design features of perceptual mechanisms and their limitations.

THE INFORMATION PROCESSING PARADIGM

You may be surprised how often words like 'signals', 'information' or 'processing' were used in the preceding paragraphs, and might be puzzled about this rather technical language. This terminology reflects the scientific paradigm – information processing – that guides our current understanding of perceptual and cognitive systems, as well as the control of behaviour. Whereas early studies of perception focussed on phenomena, such as illusions, and led to abstract explanations in terms of 'constructing' perceived representations (Von Helmholtz 1924), the contemporary approach is dominated by major conceptual and technological developments in the mid-twentieth century. During this dramatic period of scientific progress, the American mathematician Norbert Wiener (1894–1964) founded the discipline of Cybernetics (Wiener 1948), which enabled us to systematically describe basic control systems and in the last decades has been successfully expanded to the mathematical modelling of complex systems, artificial as well as biological (Marr 1982). Based on these advances of information theory, the first powerful digital computer was developed by John von Neumann (1903–57). This revolutionary design was the foundation for modern microprocessors and computers that nowadays populate or world in astounding density – you find them in cars, washing machines, iPods, digital watches, mobile phones, laptops and all other fancy gadgets that you are accustomed to, and which continue to flood the market place with growing speed. Perhaps more importantly, digital computing changed the way we are thinking about things.

In particular, information theory and digital computing changed our understanding of how the brain works. The central scientific approach to describe nervous systems, perception and cognition pivots around the acquisition, selection, storage, recall and processing of data, which is called the 'information processing approach' (Lachman et al. 1979). Correspondingly, although there are wide-ranging differences between the brain and man-made IT devices, most obviously in relation to the underlying hardware and plasticity, an often used metaphor for the human brain is a computer. As a natural extension of this approach, we can test our explanations of perceptual or cognitive processes: if we can build a machine that does exactly the same as the brain, then we are successful in understanding the underlying processes (Braitenberg 1984; Minsky and Papert 1988). In order to appreciate the progress made by applying the information processing paradigm, we should have a brief look at some historical metaphors of brain function, keeping in mind that identifying the importance of the brain for thinking and control of behaviour was a scientific achievement in itself. Descartes (1644), inspired by the first micro-anatomical descriptions of nerve fibres, suggested that information is transmitted in nerves by fluids travelling through these fibres – a 'hydraulic' model of brain function! In the nineteenth century, the mathematician and self-made mechanical engineer Charles Babbage (1791–1871) designed a mechanical computer at a gigantic scale, driven by a steam engine, to calculate astronomical tables. He compared this 'difference engine' to the workings of the brain, leading to the label 'cogwheel brain'. A partial reconstruction of his ingenious machinery can be seen, sometimes even in action, in the Science Museum in London (Swade 2000). It is worth noting from these examples that the understanding of brain function is related to the lead technology of the period: hydraulics, mechanics, IT. Try to image yourself in a fifty or hundred years time, when digital computing might be replaced by a new advanced technology – what do you think the metaphor for brain function will be?

THE WORKINGS OF THE BRAIN IN PERCEPTION, COGNITION AND THE CONTROL OF ACTION

When lecturing perception, cognition, action control, or neuropsychology to Psychology students, one often is confronted with the expectation, or angst, that these areas are difficult, irrelevant and not really a part of psychology, and possibly even boring. Part of these concerns might be generated by the discrepancy with the common image of Psychology as a discipline that often looks at topics like the interaction of humans in groups or the patterns and causes of 'abnormal' behaviour, as well as the rigour and technical challenges imposed by methods of natural sciences imposed on the study of the human mind. Some readers will still be sceptical at this stage about the relevance of perception and the value of an information processing approach and ask themselves whether a psychologist should really need to be exposed to all this technological jargon and would gain anything from the understanding of brain function. Although the full benefit of this – let's call it, for want of a better word, 'science-engineering pursuit' – might only be clear at the end of the book, the strength of such an approach will be illustrated with some examples in the following (for a wider view of such evidence, see Blakemore 1977).

Is the science-engineering pursuit difficult? It certainly will be outstandingly difficult to fully understand how the brain, or the mind, works; and many scientists argue it would be impossible as a matter of principle (Gierer 1983). However, complex systems can be approached at difficult levels of understanding, and science offers theoretical frameworks to describe them in compartments or reductions (Valentine 1992). We are used to operating machines (like cars or computers) and understanding their function, even if they are quite complex – so why should we not look at the brain in action and try to understand it? The validity of such attempts obviously needs to be carefully evaluated; but if we can build a simple contraption or 'model' that generates the same behaviour as the system we want to explain, we have come a long way! A straightforward and simple approach to understanding how the brain or mind works is to divide processing into functional units (or components), or to identify brain regions that are responsible for distinct operations. This approach has a long history, going back to scholars like Albertus Magnus (*c.*1206–80) who localised mental functions in the ventricles, the cavities in the brain filled with fluid, which were believed to be the 'animal spirit'. Although there is some dispute about the exact nature of the three basic functions (Stratton 1931), in general sensory analysis (*sensu communis*), reason (*ratio*) and thought (*cognatio*), and memory (*memoria*), were attributed to the three respective compartments (see Figure 1.5a). Emerging from a scholastic background, this figure has little support from what today would be accepted as 'scientific evidence', but it demonstrates a clear attempt to break a complex problem down into simpler components. Exploiting the dramatic progress in neuroscientific imaging techniques, most notably magnetic resonance imaging (MRI), during the last two decades (Le Bihan 2003; Salvador et al. 2005; Tootell et al. 1995), we can now advance from speculation to hard scientific evidence, and draw up a coherent, and rather detailed, picture of the functional architecture of the brain (as sketched in Figure 1.5c). In various imaging studies it has been shown in great detail, for instance, which different brain areas are active

Figure 1.5

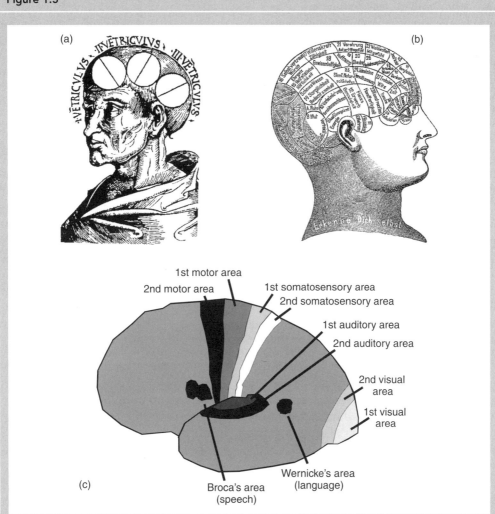

Understanding the brain in terms of compartments. (a) At the outset of a long tradition; it was generally believed that the three ventricles host sensory analysis, reason and thought and memory, respectively. From the 1506 edition of Albert Magnus' 'Philosophia pauperum' (after Blakemore 1977). (b) The 'Phrenology' map of human brain areas that were believed to be responsible for individual attributes (including personality traits) and for organising behaviour this map, originating from Franz Gall but shown here in a version by E. F. Bill (1990), is a historical – and seriously flawed – document, which nevertheless demonstrates the relationship between the mind and the brain as its substrate which therefore will set constraints to the working of the mind. (c) The distribution of activity in the human brain during various activities can be determined with modern imaging techniques, which allow us to assess the 'functional architecture' of the brain (Zeki 1993), as illustrated in this rough sketch.

when a participant is communicating with others by means of language, demonstrating the different and shared networks in the brain that are activated during reading words, listening to spoken words, or speaking (Price 2000).

Is the science-engineering pursuit irrelevant for Psychology? On the contrary – it is fundamental to other areas of psychology! Perception is crucial for many other aspects of human life because these are mediated through the brain and its sensory systems: how we interact with the world, how we select, store and retrieve acquired information, how we communicate, how we organise our social life, how we maintain mental health, how we plan actions, make decisions. More generally, neuroscience today is believed to be the key to understanding the processes underlying mental events (Kandel and Squire 2001). Once again, the historical fascination with brain maps (see Figure 1.5b) reflects this important relationship between our understanding of human mental capacities, the subject of Psychology, and the understanding of the brain, the subject of Neuroscience. Charting the human brain into maps of regions that were believed to determine individual attributes and behaviour was the ambition of 'phrenologists' (Zola-Morgan 1995). These maps were based on data collected by methods that today are recognised as seriously flawed – generating ideas that were much closer to fiction than to science! However, the idea of functional components in the brain is now supported with a wealth of hard scientific evidence (Gross 1998; Zeki 1993), and there is a growing variety of human behaviour, such as the rapidly growing field of 'Neuro-Economics' (Sanfey 2007), that is studied with neuroscientific methods. Although there are sceptical voices that speak of a 'new phrenology' (Uttal 2003), it is becoming increasingly obvious that the science-engineering pursuit provides a solid scientific basis for understanding issues in social, personality, occupational, health psychology, etc.

Is the science-engineering pursuit boring? Obviously this is a matter of taste, and readers will have to answer the question themselves. Just as a taster to help with the decision, here are some typical questions (for a more comprehensive list, see Lewin 1992) that are tackled in such an endeavour:

- How do we know that what we see (hear, smell, etc.) is actually out there? Do two individuals always/ever see the same? How do you compensate for the loss of sight? How does a magician make us not see things that are out in the open in front of our eyes?
- How do we plan and coordinate complex motor patterns? Why does it sometimes go wrong? (for instance in Parkinson's disease, after stroke, when you are exhausted, or drunk).
- What is the basis of addiction? What happens in the brain? How do drugs affect perception? What makes drugs feel pleasant? How do they change our consciousness?
- What is consciousness? Does it depend on the brain? How is it related to neural activity? How does it interact with perception? Why do we need it? Are animals conscious? How can we know this?
- How is memory organised? How much can we memorise? Do memories reflect perceptions or ideas of objects? Are some things easier to remember? Why do we forget? Can you train your memory?

Most importantly, the science-engineering pursuit is addressing some of the most exciting questions of mankind, such as: How do we think? What constitutes the mind?

To conclude, there are three main reasons why it is important for Psychologists to engage with the scientific study of the brain, and study perception, and cognition: (i) Pure scientific curiosity: the aim to understand the human mind as such; (ii) The wish to design 'intelligent' applications: the objective to implement knowledge in thinking machines (Artificial Intelligence); (iii) The search for a theoretical basis to understand pathology and manage impairments (as investigated in Cognitive Neuroscience). To indicate the relevance and scope of the clinical aspects, just think of one prominent example, the memory loss in Alzheimer Type Dementia, which is expected to affect six million individuals in the US population in 2020 (Hebert et al. 2003) and currently has no treatment.

PERCEPTION AS INITIAL 'DATA MINING' TO FEED THE HUMAN MIND

We need to navigate through and operate in a dangerous world and we need to collect 'intelligence' (knowledge) in order to 'make sense of' (understand) the world. There is no computational work, no controlled behaviour, no knowledge, no decision-making, without sensory input. Sensory information, just as any information, needs to be accessible, manageable and reliable in order to be useful. Whenever you search the Internet for some topic you want to learn something about, you are facing two basic problems: Firstly, your search engine may return too few or too many hits, which makes it difficult to select from the vast amount of information that is available on the web those entries that seem to be most relevant. Usually you would respond by refining your search profile or making sure that the list of information returned from your search is ordered (according to popularity, relevance, chronology, etc.). Secondly, having selected the relevant pages, you need to consider the reliability of the particular source – you don't want to draw conclusions about the best beaches in your holiday destination from some questionable comments released on the Internet by someone who happens to runs a bar on a particular beach, would you? To reiterate, information needs to be accessible, manageable and reliable, otherwise it is useless. Similar to you depending on your Internet access, which opens for you the window to the outside digital world the human mind is depending on the sensory systems to open the window to the outside physical world. Interestingly, unlike you browsing the Internet, sensory information processing is completely incessant and effortless. Whereas you can shut down your browser and load it again when you want (at least one would hope so), you don't need (and you can't) switch your senses on or off, and you are not getting exhausted from the unbelievably vast amount of sensory signals streaming through your nervous system. Given the sheer amount and variety of input information processed by the sensory systems, together with its automaticity, computer scientists would talk about 'data mining' – we are steadily digging through all these visual, auditory and chemical signals that are continuously bombarding our sense organs.

The comparison with searching the Internet for information highlights two issues that are central to all information processing (illustrated schematically in Figure 1.6) and will accompany us through the following chapters. (i) Each system, be it technical, sensory or cognitive, has capacity limits of data flow (a 'bottleneck'), which call for intelligent coding strategies to minimise information loss. Similar to measuring flow capacity of a water pipe in litres per minute, transmission capacity in digital systems is expressed as bits per sec [bps], which can

Figure 1.6

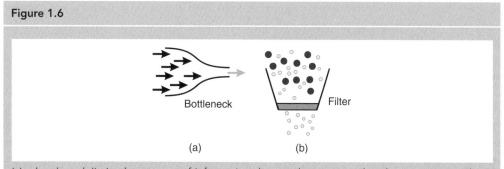

(a) a bottleneck limits the amount of information that can be processed at the same time within a channel; (b) a filter selects the type of information (a particular grain size in this 'literal' example of a filter) that is to be processed in a given channel, which helps to optimise processing performance.

be used for all kinds of information channels, such as a printer or a WiFi connection; (ii) In order to make optimal use of the available capacity, irrelevant data is removed from the information stream, whereas relevant data are retained – such selection mechanisms are usually called 'filters', defining an information processing channel.

In a computer, information is entering the system through devices such as a keyboard, a webcam, a microphone, a modem, etc. In the nervous system, information is collected to be processed in the brain through the senses – these sensory channels are the topics for the next chapters. Following the ideas of the Greek philosopher Aristotle (384–322 BC), there is a tradition to distinguish five senses (Everson 1997): vision, touch, hearing, taste, and smell (Gonzalez-Crussi 1990). However, closer inspection reveals that there are additional senses in humans, such as temperature, pain or balance, and further senses can be found in other animals, such as infrared vision, ultrasound, magnetic or electric sense. We will return to this question in Chapter 13, illustrating the wide range of sensory channels in the context of evolution. A cursory assessment of the human sensory channels illustrates that despite the huge differences between the specific designs of particular sensory systems, the information processing paradigm offers a conceptual framework, which emphasises unifying principles that hold the key to the understanding of the function of sensation and perception. More specific aspects of these and other sensory channels will be discussed in relation to the information processing paradigm in the following chapters.

Hearing (auditory perception) is used to pick up acoustic signals about events in the environment; it is crucial for communication and orientation, and it mediates emotional responses such as relaxation or stress – the ear is, as we shall see later, an intelligent microphone that employs a number of filter operation to maximise the information that can be transmitted through the auditory nerve to the brain while capturing a wide range of acoustic information.

Touch (somatosensory perception) is essential for detecting and recognising objects through physical contact, for maintaining the position and integrity of the body, and for controlling movements. This channel depends on mechanosensors distributed all around the body, which define the type and amount of information that is made available to the control circuits in the brain. It is a very powerful and highly adaptive system we are usually completely unaware of – can you feel the glasses on your nose or the shoes on your feet?

Smell and Taste (olfactory and gustatory perception) are very basic sensory systems that are often forgotten, but help us importantly to keep us safe in a complex and dangerous world, and are crucial for our well-being and emotional balance. These channels are defined, and their capacity is limited by the kinds and numbers of molecules that can be absorbed by the sensory epithelium to assess the chemical composition of the air, or food, respectively.

Sight (visual perception) is often regarded as the most important of the senses, because it is an immediate and very rich source of information. In a technical sense, it is most impressive for its large channel capacity. With 100 million receptors in the retina of each eye, 1 million nerve fibres transmitting the information from each eye to the brain, where it is processed in about 30 brain areas, which amount to more than 20% of the brain and contain some 10 billion cortical neurons (Wandell 1995), the visual system is unparalleled in its processing power and richness of output information by any technical system built so far.

Take Home Messages

- studying perception, together with cognitive psychology, is part of a multidisciplinary attempt to study the human mind: how do we think?
- the central scientific paradigm is the information processing approach: the brain is interpreted as a computer dealing with huge and complex data sets
- by localising and modelling brain function we can address a number of interesting questions with great cultural and practical importance
- perceptual processes are required as input for the neuronal machinery, providing the information necessary for a wide range of vital functions
- perception is both a bottleneck reducing the amount information and a filter selecting relevant information – we speak of channels, tuning, capacity

Discussion Questions

- Describe the relationship between the physical properties of the outside world and its internal representation.
- What is the information processing approach?
- Describe the historical development of understanding the functional architecture of the brain.
- What are the main channels of the human sensory system?

2 THE MACHINERY: UNDERSTANDING THE NEURAL CODE

OVERVIEW

In order to understand sensory information processing, we need to know some basic facts about brain function – the machinery of the mind. Neural encoding – converting what we see, hear, smell, etc. into the activity of nerve cells – is the fundamental process that allows the internal representation of the outside world. This chapter will run in some detail through one well-understood example of sensory encoding, the representation of visual information by neurons in the 'visual system': the parts of the nervous system that are dedicated to the processing of information captured by the eyes. Vision starts with the conversion of light into neural signals, called 'transduction', similar to the encoding of a digital picture by electrical signals in a mobile phone, which then can be stored and transmitted to (and seen by) others. By studying the behaviour of single neurons and simple networks we can understand how some basic computations are used to process sensory information, thus generating 'receptive fields'. The electrophysiological analysis of receptive field structure and location (leading to maps, similar to pixel images on a screen) opens the door to studying advanced properties of neurons, which can be understood as filters for extracting higher-level image features (for instance, contours, textures, shapes). How receptive field organisation can be regarded as the basis for understanding perception is demonstrated by opponent mechanisms that can explain simultaneous contrast illusions: the shade of grey of an object can be profoundly misinterpreted, depending on its background. A brief survey about how receptive fields act like filters for other properties like spatial detail ('spatial frequency channels'), colour, orientation, depth or motion is used to highlight some general principles of information encoding, in particular 'tuning', 'contrast enhancement' and 'redundancy reduction'. All these different analysis mechanisms operate simultaneously, and in parallel at a range of scales, thus creating a rich, highly efficient and accurate representation of the environment, which then feeds into high-level processing mechanisms. This intelligent combination of serial and parallel processing steps in sensory systems leads to a performance in biological systems that is unparalleled in artificial systems, and allows us to operate fast and safely in dangerous environments.

ENCODING OF INFORMATION

Have you ever wondered how you can speak with a friend who is miles away when you use your mobile phone? Perhaps not, and you may even think this is a silly question! In fact in this form of communication, information is exchanged through a technical device that converts, encodes and transmits signals from a sender to a receiver (Bradbury and Vehrencamp 1998). Let's start with a simpler device, which you may remember from your childhood, a tin can telephone (if you don't know this low-tech phone, you should try it!): two empty tin cans are connected by a piece of string, and you whisper into your tin can while your friend holds the other tin can close to their ear. As long as the string is pulled straight, the friend can understand each word you whisper whereas nobody else can hear what you are saying – you have established a secure, albeit somewhat pointless, communication channel! How does this work? The sound waves generated by your voice are captured by the tin can, which starts to move ever so slightly along with the sound waves, and sets the string that is connecting the two tin cans into vibration in the same way as your sound waves; the tiny vibration of the string generates small movements of the second tin can in front of your friend's ear, which generates sound waves, which can be picked up by the ear, and your friend can hear what you are saying. In this purely mechanical system, illustrated in Figure 2.1a, sound waves are converted into mechanical oscillations of the first tin can, the string, the second tin can and back into sound waves, so we have mechanical signals all along the way and there is no encoding of information into another medium. In contrast, your mobile phone, which obviously works over much longer distance and without a physical connection between sender and receiver, picks up sound waves through the microphone and encodes them first into electrical, and then into radio signals (electromagnetic waves), which are transmitted 'wireless' (no strings attached), as illustrated in Figure 2.1b. The mobile phone of your friend then decodes the radio signals into electrical signals and converts them into sound waves by means of a loudspeaker, which through these mechanisms of transduction and transmission eventually can be heard by your friend. Never forget that this information can be also be picked up by the telephone company and MI5, who easily can tap into the encoders, decoders or the radio waves.

The important aspect of this technical example is that signals (which are carrying messages, or 'information') are converted (or, in other words, are 'encoded') from one physical medium (or 'communication channel') into another, to be transmitted from the sender to the receiver. In this process signals (i) can be sent along long distances, and (ii) can be processed in such a way that maximum use is made of the communication channels. They also can be encrypted, that is, encoded, in such a way that nobody else, including MI5, can listen into the conversation! In the same sense, the brain encodes information, thus converting physical

Figure 2.1

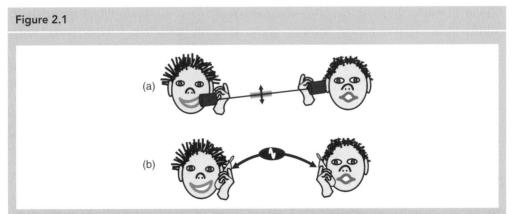

Transduction and transmission. (a) In a children's tin can telephone, the sound is captured, transmitted, and replayed by the mechanical oscillations of the first tin can, the taut string and the second tin can, respectively. (b) In a mobile phone sound signals are encoded (transduced) in electrical signals and electromagnetic waves in the sender and transmitted via radio waves to the receiver, where they are decoded into sound.

Figure 2.2

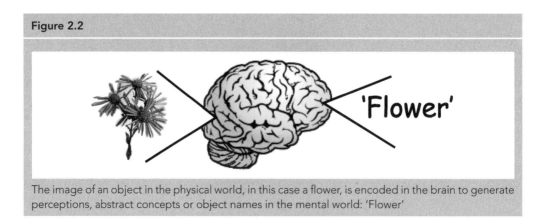

The image of an object in the physical world, in this case a flower, is encoded in the brain to generate perceptions, abstract concepts or object names in the mental world: 'Flower'

events (like the image of a flower, as shown in Figure 2.2) into mental events (e.g. the conscious experience, abstract concept or name of a flower). It is worth noting that conscious experience resembles an encrypted channel, because it is a private experience that may be shared to a certain degree, but is difficult if not impossible to be accessed by others (see Wandell 2008).

This technical analysis of a routine information encoding process in the brain raises a number of questions about the nervous system, which will provide important clues to understanding how perception works.

- What is the neural code? Your mobile phone is using analogue and digital electric signals, and in transmission electromagnetic waves, to encode sound, text and pictures. The nervous system is using biological electric signals – action potentials, or spikes, carry information along the axon and dendrites (communication lines) of a neuron, and information is encoded as graded voltage change or spike rates (Rieke et al. 1996). The communication between neurons is often sustained by chemical signals – neurotransmitters are used to carry information across synapses between neurons, with the concentration of these molecules reflecting the level of neuronal activity.
- What are the constraints and strategies of encoding information in nervous systems? Your mobile phone contains a lot of electronics and a microprocessor to send packages through the ether, which are densely packed and retain all the relevant information while removing all unnecessary junk, to make the communication as efficient as possible (Bellamy 2000). This method saves time, energy and bandwidth in the channel, and thus makes your call as cheap as possible (or maximises the profits of your service provider). Throughout this book, we will ask whether the brain uses similar strategies to compress information and make optimal use of the nervous system's capacity. Obviously, a fundamental constraint is the need to avoid any loss of crucial information.

STUDYING SINGLE NEURONS

So far we have looked at the neural code in rather abstract terms of information theory, but we need to take into account some basic knowledge about brain physiology to understand how encoding is implemented in nervous systems. The common way to analyse the function of nervous systems is by means of 'electrophysiological' recordings: electrodes are inserted into

Figure 2.3

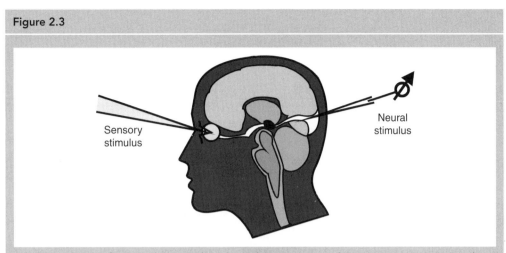

Schematic sketch of a typical electrophysiological experiment in the sensory system: A stimulus is presented to the sensory organ (here the eye) and electrodes are located in the nervous system (here: early visual cortex) to record the response to this stimulus, which is the activity of neurons in the corresponding region.

the nervous system, on the surface of neuronal tissues, in nerves, or in the proximity or inside of individual neurons. This allows the experimenter to observe the activity of individual or groups of nerve cells in animals (Hubel 1979). Pioneering work in this area has been carried out by Kuffler (1953), and Hubel and Wiesel (1962) who received the Nobel Prize in Physiology or Medicine in 1981. In such experiments (illustrated in Figure 2.3), the stimulus–response relationship is analysed to characterise the function of neural processing. The stimulus needs to have the adequate modality, that is, the stimulus attributes have to match the sensor, such as light for visual system (or sound for auditory system) and the stimulus has to originate from a restricted location (e.g. a particular region in the visual field). The responses, that is, the activity of neurons reflecting their 'neural code', are recorded as graded electric potentials (voltage changes) or as action potential (spikes), for which the activity level is reflected by frequency of spikes – this 'rate code' was originally discovered in the somatosensory system (Adrian and Umrath 1929).

Sensory information is processed simultaneously as collected from many different locations in the surrounding world, which technically are referred to as 'sampling points', with the help of a huge number of sensory neurons. This kind of 'parallel processing' is most conspicuous in the visual system (imagine the optic nerve like a big fat telephone cable with hundreds of thousands of parallel lines), leading to 'retinotopic maps' in the visual cortex, which conserve the neighbourhood relationships between retinal sampling points (see Figure 2.4). This mapping of the environment onto cortical projections was already speculated about by Descartes (see Figure 1.2), albeit without the corresponding experimental evidence. We now have a huge amount of neurophysiological data that show how visual neurons in many brain regions are organised in large arrays to sample the complete visual field, point by point, creating such maps in which neighbouring points in the visual field, and therefore in the retina, are represented in neighbouring neurons. This representation, which can be distorted considerably depending on how much cortical area is dedicated to different regions in the visual field, is sometimes referred to as a 'neural image' (Wade 2007).

Figure 2.4

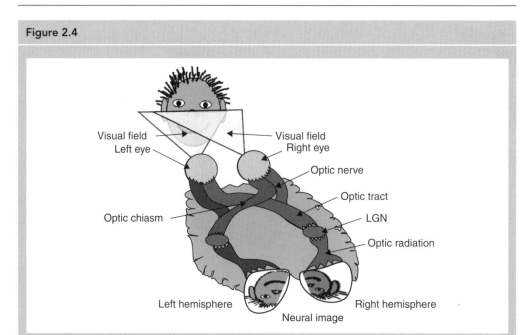

Schematic sketch of the visual stream. The visual scene (in this example a face) is creating an image on the retina inside of the left and right eye, each of which has a slightly different field of view. From here the information is transmitted through the optic nerve and the optic chiasm (where the outside parts of the visual fields are crossed over) and optic tract such that in the Lateral Geniculate Nucleus (LGN) the left visual field is processed on the right side of the brain and the right visual field on the left side. From the LGN the information is transmitted point by point through the optic radiation to the cortex, still conserving neighbourhood relationships. This parallel and serial architecture leads to (partially distorted) 'retinotopic' maps in cortical representations of the visual field at several stages of the processing stream, as indicated by the caricature of the neural image in the left hemisphere (right visual field) and right hemisphere (left visual field). For details see text (cf. Frisby 1979).

At the same time, the visual image is processed in successive steps in the visual stream that leads from the eye to the subcortical and cortical areas dedicated to different aspects of vision (see Figure 2.4). This 'serial processing' starts in the retina of the eyes, which contain an array of fine-grain receptor cells, rods and cones, which are sensitive to the brightness and the colour of light, respectively, and some initial processing between these receptor signals in a dense network of retinal ganglion cells. These retinal signals are transmitted through the optic nerve and optic tract to the thalamus region of the brain, where the so-called P-cells project to the 'parvo' regions of the Lateral Geniculate Nucleus (LGN) that are sensitive to spatial detail and colour information. Furthermore the so-called M-cells project to the 'magno' regions of the LGN, which are more sensitive to motion and brightness information. From the LGN the visual signals travel through the optic radiation to the cortex, where the information is further processed in a series of visual areas, V1, V2, V3, V4 and V5. Some of these appear to have specific functions, such as colour vision in V4 that projects to the inferior temporal cortex, and motion vision in V5 projecting to the parietal cortex (Zeki 1993). The specialisation for different aspects of the visual information led to the notion of two pathways (Mishkin et al. 1983), the 'ventral stream', which is mainly dedicated to the form of objects, including colour ('what'), and the 'dorsal stream', which is mainly dedicated to the spatial properties of objects, including motion ('where'). The consideration of the anatomical and physiological details of the visual stream will only serve as background in the following sections, which will largely focus on the fundamental processing mechanisms without taking account of the particular neurons that are involved in such processing.

In generating a 'neural image', the human visual system shares some similarity with the operation of a digital camera, which can be very instructive to understand its function (for the history of such comparisons, see Wade 2007). The image is encoded in an array of points, which are called picture elements, or 'pixels' in the camera, to capture the visual field of the eye, or field of view in case of the camera, in one shot. In both the biological and the technical system the number of encoded image points limits the spatial resolution of the representation, which is the amount of detail that is contained in the image. The picture taken with a cheap digital camera, or a mobile phone, may look rather grainy when enlarged, because it is based on no more than 1 million pixels (1 megapixel, approximately the resolution of a standard computer screen or HDTV). More advanced cameras now have 8 or 12 megapixels, but for high-resolution cameras speed and storage space becomes a problem. The reason for this limitation is the transmission of the image data into the memory. In contrast to the eye, which transmits data to the brain in parallel, the data from the digital camera chip are conventionally processed in a serial manner, one pixel after the other. Although the resolution of the eye, with about 1 million fibres in the optic nerve, is no more than 1 megapixel, and its bandwidth is estimated to be comparable to a very fast Internet connection with approx. 1 GB/sec (Koch et al. 2006), it is superior to all existing technical systems, not only by virtue of this parallel architecture, but also through its much higher overall sensitivity – we can see reasonably well at low brightness levels such as moonlight without the need of a flash light – and its wider operating range, giving it the ability to capture a much larger number of light intensity levels than a digital camera. Most importantly, the eye employs 'intelligent' processing mechanisms to maximise the information transmitted through the optic nerves, as discussed in the following sections, and combines an area of high resolution, the fovea, with scanning eye movement strategies to make maximum use of the overall number of pixels available. Note that you see, that is perceive, the world around you, with much larger spatial detail than you would expect from a 1 megapixel neural image: if your computer monitor would cover your whole visual field, you would clearly see the boundaries between individual pixels.

NEURAL COMPUTATION: CONVERGENCE, EXCITATION AND INHIBITION

The very first step of neural encoding is the conversion of a physical or chemical stimulus into electrical signals. Different sensory systems use different 'receptors' to achieve this goal, usually classified as mechano-, chemo- and photo-receptors. Nevertheless after this initial step all the different information about the environment is encoded in exactly the same neural code: using the electrical signals of neurons, all sensory systems speak the same language, and therefore can 'talk to each other' (see Chapter 12 on sensory integration). In the visual system, this initial step happens in the dense layer of photoreceptors, the photoreceptor mosaic, which is the first processing stage of the retina – the light-sensitive lining of the inner surface of the eyeball (Boycott and Wässle 1974). Light, which in physical terms is an electromagnetic wave, is converted by means of photopigments in the outer segments of the photoreceptors into changes of the potential (electrical voltage) across the cell membrane, a process that is called 'transduction'. The photoreceptor mosaic is composed of two kinds of photoreceptors, rods, which are sensitive to low-light intensities and insensitive to colour, and cones, which operate at higher light intensities and are responsible for colour vision (see Chapter 4). The graded

Figure 2.5

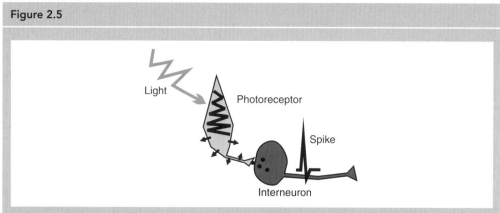

In the visual system, the electromagnetic waves that are seen as light (zigzag arrow) are converted in photoreceptors by photopigments (folded structure in grey cone) to changes of membrane potential (small black arrows); the graded potential resulting from this transduction is communicated through neurotransmitters (black dots) to sensory neurons; after some processing in interneurons these signals are integrated by ganglion cells that generate action potentials (spike) to be transmitted to the brain.

potentials in the inner segments of photoreceptors control the release of neurotransmitters that are picked up by interneurons, called bipolar cells, and after some interaction with similar signals in the neighbourhood the resulting potential is relayed to the ganglion cells, from where short pulses of electrical activity, action potentials or 'spikes', are transmitted through the optic nerve to the brain (see Figure 2.5). It is important to note that only after conversion from light to electric signals in the photoreceptor mosaic is the information contained in the retinal image ready for computation – it is encoded in the responses of the array of ganglion cells.

This brief summary of how the first steps of visual information processing are carried out in the retina, as the interface between the physical world and its neuronal representation, sets the scene to describe some simple principles of information processing and their relation to perception. Visual neurons sample sensory space – the light from the visual field, for instance, is captured by the photoreceptor mosaic in an ordered manner, and engineers speak of an 'array of sampling points' like the pixels of a digital camera. At the same time, and different from a digital camera, neurons interact with each other, thus integrating the information collected at a number of sampling points. The type of lateral interaction with signals from other sampling points determines the properties of such an integrating neuron, and the type of information conveyed to the next processing level. The spatial response properties of a neuron that result from lateral interaction are often described as 'receptive fields' – how these are generated will be explained schematically, without any consideration of the specific underlying neuronal hardware.

The simplest case, the *absence of any lateral interaction* similar to a digital camera, results in a direct representation of each sampling point: each receptor signal is encoded in a single neuron (see Figure 2.6). The response of this neuron is the same for small and extended patches of light, because it can only respond to the input from a single photoreceptor and is blind to neighbouring regions, which may be excited as well. In other words, stimulus size is not encoded in such a neuron, and it has a low sensitivity because it only can respond to light that is hitting its own receptor. On the other hand, an array of such neurons has a high spatial resolution because the maximum possible number of image points are sampled separately.

The simplest interaction, and the most simple neural computation, is a 'summation', or spatial pooling, of the inputs of neighbouring photoreceptors (see Figure 2.7). The fact that a

Figure 2.6

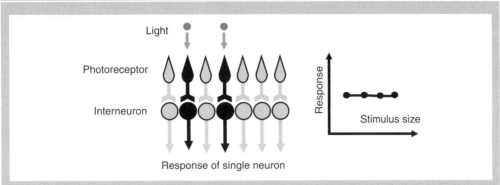

A (one-dimensional) array of visual interneurons (light and dark grey discs and arrows) sampling a horizontal section of the image *without any lateral interaction*, i.e. with a one-to-one connection to individual photoreceptors (light and dark grey cones, providing synaptic input to interneurons). These neurons are only active (dark grey) if their photoreceptor is excited by a light stimulus (small dot and small arrow), but are silent (light grey) if no light hits the photoreceptor. This connectivity leads to high spatial resolution and low sensitivity, and it does not encode stimulus size ('size tuning' curve on right side).

Figure 2.7

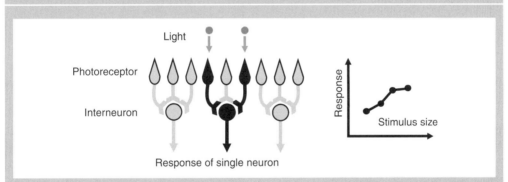

An array of visual neurons sampling a horizontal section of the image with *summation*, where several photoreceptors (cones) converge on a single neuron (discs). These neurons are active (dark grey) if any of their photoreceptor is excited by a light stimulus (small dot and arrow), and their response grows with the number of stimulated photoreceptors up to the point when all input photoreceptors are stimulated. This connectivity reduces spatial resolution but increases sensitivity, and it does encode some measure of stimulus size ('size tuning' curve on right side).

number of inputs are projecting to a single neuron is referred to as 'convergence'. In this case the response of the output neuron is proportional to the size of the stimulus, because it grows when an increasing number of photoreceptors are hit by light, and its sensitivity is high because the overall probability of catching some light is increased. The price for this kind of integration is a reduced spatial resolution, because the information from a reduced number of effective sampling points is transmitted to the next processing stage. This loss of resolution could be compensated for by increasing the number of neurons with overlapping regions of spatial pooling (not shown in the image), which however still would lead to a blurred neural image. In such a case, a single photoreceptor would feed several neurons, a process referred to as 'divergence'. In the human visual system, we find many instances of both convergence and divergence.

Figure 2.8

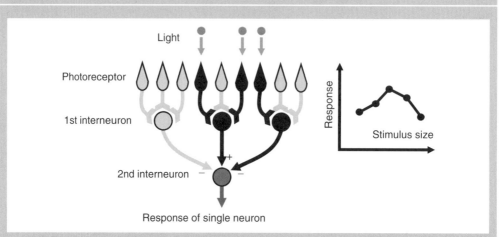

An array of visual neurons sampling a horizontal section of the image with summation and subtraction, where several photoreceptors (cones) converge on each interneuron (light and dark grey discs and arrows). The interneurons are active (dark grey) if any of their photoreceptor is excited by a light stimulus (small arrows and dots at top of the image), but are silent (light grey) if no light hits their photoreceptor, and their response grows with the number of stimulated photoreceptors. The second-stage neuron (medium grey disc) is excited by the centre interneuron (+) and inhibited by the neighbouring interneurons (−) that may be stimulated by light (small dot and arrow, top right) through *lateral inhibition*. This connectivity makes the second-stage neuron generating the biggest response for a particular stimulus size (size tuning curve on right side).

A more sophisticated type of integration involves the subtractions from neighbouring regions, 'lateral inhibition', which can be achieved by a set of interneurons that are integrated with different signs in a second processing stage, producing excitation or inhibition (see Figure 2.8). In the second-stage neuron, the response grows until an optimum stimulus size is reached, but is reduced when the stimulus grows further in size and stimulates photoreceptors that feed neighbouring interneurons and thus lead to inhibition. It is worth noting that in this pattern of connectivity we added a simple arithmetic operation, subtraction, to the summation used before – and generated a completely new feature, the 'tuning' to a particular size. In general, lateral inhibition (see Hartline and Ratliff 1957) leads to opponent behaviour, or 'opponency': signals from neighbouring regions are weighed up against each other and the difference between these regions determines the final output. This is a very simple form of neural computation that leads to surprising results.

RECEPTIVE FIELD FUNCTION

After this schematic illustration of the basic principles of how simple computations can generate a range of properties in visual neurons, we now turn to spatial integration in a more general and more realistic case, considering two spatial dimensions. From the extent of the visual field, each neuron samples the stimulus within a restricted region – its receptive field. In the simplest case, a neuron would just add up the signals from all photoreceptors covering its receptive field. As early as in retinal ganglion cells and similarly in LGN neurons, however, the typical receptive field is structured, with excitatory and inhibitory regions, where a small light spot

Figure 2.9

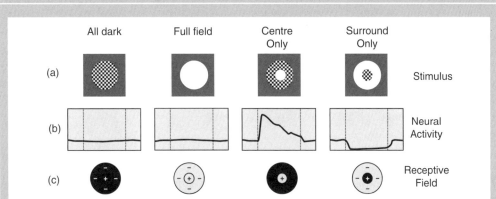

Responses of retinal ganglion cells, shown as time course of neural responses (b: 'neural activity' indicated by black line, stimulus onset and offset indicated by vertical dotted lines), for four different stimulus conditions, shown systematically in top row (a: 'stimulus'; white areas within receptive field, indicated by chequered region); bottom row illustrates schematically the activation of the ON centre (+) and OFF-surround (–) of the receptive field (c). No stimulation ('all dark') is the control condition with spontaneous activity, in which centre and surround are not activated. During illumination of the entire receptive field ('full field') spontaneous activity is maintained because the excitation from the centre is cancelled by inhibition from the surround (c: light grey in all regions). A light spot confined to the centre region of the receptive field ('centre only') leads to very high neural activity (c: light grey in the centre indicates full excitation, dark grey indicates no inhibition). A ring of illumination in the surround region of the receptive field ('surround only') abolishes spike activity because there is no excitation in the centre (c: dark grey) and strong inhibition from the surround (light grey).

would increase and decrease the neuron's activity, respectively. The standard way of investigating receptive field structure is to point a small spotlight at different locations and record the activity of the neuron. Using this technique, Kuffler (1953) plotted the receptive fields of retinal ganglion cells (see Colour plate I, Figure 1). He identified a general pattern where the centre of the receptive field is integrated with the opposite sign from the surrounding region, by systematically shining a small spot of light on different locations on a screen in front of the animal's eye. Some of the ganglion cells are excited by the spotlight stimulating the centre and inhibited by the spotlight stimulating the surround ('ON-centre cells'), and others are inhibited by centre stimulation and excited by surround stimulation ('OFF-centre cells').

Lateral inhibition, as illustrated in Figure 2.8 for one spatial dimension, is the key to understanding the function of such centre–surround, or 'concentric', receptive field structures in two spatial dimensions. When the signals from the two regions within the receptive field are integrated with opposite signs, a property emerges that is called 'opponency' – the amount of light stimulating the central disk is balanced against the light stimulating the ring-shaped surround. For instance, an ON-centre cell, which without stimulation generates a small number of spikes ('resting' or 'spontaneous activity') is activated to produce much higher spike rates if the centre receives more light than the surround, and it is silenced to very small or zero spike rates if the surround receives more light than the centre. Lastly it returns to ticking along in spontaneous activity when the same amount of light falls on the centre and surround. The best way to demonstrate this opponency is by making electrophysiological recordings from such neurons with different stimulus configurations, which stimulate the centre, the surround or the complete receptive field (see Figure 2.9). The optimum stimulus for a receptive field of a given size is a light beam that just covers the ON-centre of this receptive field; larger light beams reduce the response to spontaneous activity; and exclusive illumination of the OFF-surround of the receptive field inhibits all neural activity. This neural response tuning to a particular stimulus size, similar to the one-dimensional case considered above can be understood as the integration of excitation from the centre and inhibition from the surround of the receptive field (Colour plate I, Figure 1). Such a simple balancing of stimulation of different inputs is a fundamental function of neural information processing that we will encounter time and again in our journey through the field of sensory perception.

FEATURE EXTRACTION IN HIGHER-LEVEL NEURONS

By combining such simple steps of information processing, the brain encodes a range of stimulus features – for example, some neurons respond preferably to a specific orientation of boundaries or lines (Hubel and Wiesel 1962). This property is achieved by structured receptive fields, which are more sophisticated than the uncomplicated concentric receptive field structures (Colour plate I, Figure 1). When plotted in electrophysiological experiments with a light spot, such receptive fields reveal particular arrangements of excitatory and inhibitory regions, as shown in Colour plate I, Figure 2a for two exemplary cortical neurons (Hubel 1963), which respond preferentially to luminance edges and lines of particular orientations. Such orientation tuning (Colour plate I, Figure 2b) is not only measured in electrophysiological experiments but can also be demonstrated in perception (Campbell and Kulikowski 1966). Colour plate I, Figure 2c shows a simple model of how such receptive field structures can be constructed by the convergence of several concentric receptive fields such as those found in retinal ganglion cells (Hubel 1988). Since the original discovery of these receptive fields by Hubel and Wiesel, scientists have made great progress in the experimental characterisation of a wide variety of receptive field structures (DeAngelis et al. 1995; Watson et al. 1983) and the mathematical modelling of their computational properties (Daugman 1988; Freeman 1993).

It is important to note that the hierarchical integration of neurons, each with its own receptive field, can be used in a systematic way to generate novel receptive field properties (Hubel 1988). As illustrated in Colour plate I, Figure 2, the orientation tuning of a cortical simple cell is derived by simply integrating concentric receptive fields arranged in a linear array – the optimum stimulus now is a line of a particular orientation! In a similar way, we can understand the visual system, as well as other sensory systems, as a cascade of divergent and convergent integration steps that enables sensory neurons to encode specific features. Returning to the retinal image of the environment (see Figure 2.10), this means that each image point is analysed in parallel by neurons to represent a variety of local features such as brightness or colour, as well as size, which are then recombined to encode orientation, texture, motion or stereoscopic depth. Such 'intelligent' encoding of local features and recombination in serial processing steps to more sophisticated advanced features is the basis for perception, as will be discussed in the following chapters. Similar processing steps are used for early image analysis in machine vision systems (Watson 1993).

Going through these consecutive steps of the visual stream, we encounter another fundamental principle of neural information processing, which is important for all sensory systems: parallel and serial processing. The brain can be decomposed into a hierarchical network of brain regions that communicate with dense arrays of nerve fibres, which transmit information from many image points in parallel and are analysing different properties in parallel (van Essen et al. 1992). The design of this network can be summarised as follows (Figure 2.11):

Figure 2.10

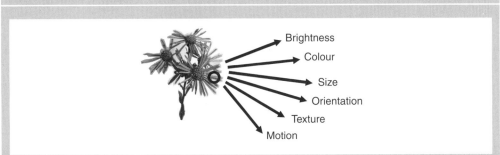

For each location of a retinal image, a large number of neurons in the visual system analyse a range of stimulus features in parallel, such as brightness, colour, size, orientation, texture and motion. Increasingly sophisticated receptive fields are created by hierarchical networks of serial processing steps to encode advanced stimulus features at higher processing levels. At some point all of these local features need to be joined together to recreate a coherent neural representation of objects in the environment, such as this flower.

Figure 2.11

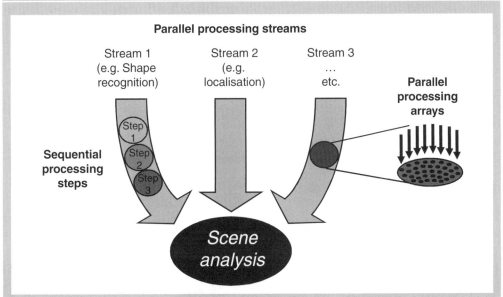

A schematic picture of parallel and serial processing in the brain. Visual information is processed in parallel in several streams that may be dedicated to different image properties and may feed into different aspects of thinking and behaviour, which are eventually combined again to create a coherent representation of the scene (dark oval); within each stream we find sequential processing steps that extract the image properties required for scene analysis; within each processing step a large number of image points are processed in parallel by arrays of neurons organised in maps.

- The retinal image is sampled at a large number of image points, which are processed simultaneously, in parallel, generating retinotopic representations in the early visual system – this requires information transmission in the visual stream in many parallel nerve fibres with high bandwidth.

- Advanced features are extracted through sequential, or serial, processing – this leads to characteristic channels carrying specific stimulus information: perceptual filters.
- Parallel processing streams are specialised for particular aspects of the image – it is separated into functional components, which correspond to individual brain regions.
- Perceptually, we experience the combination of stimulus features in a unitary representation of our environment – this means that at some higher stage of the visual system the different streams are merged to a coherent scene analysis, sometimes referred to as 'cue combination' or 'sensory fusion'.

FROM RECEPTIVE FIELDS TO PERCEPTION

At this stage, you may wonder whether and why you need to know anything about all this neurophysiological machinery. To get an idea about the benefits of knowing the basic principles of neural processing of sensory information, have a look at the contrast illusion shown in Figure 2.12. The vertical bars seem to have different shades of grey, and yet they have exactly the same intensity. The intensity of all vertical bars is the same intensity that covers the horizontal bar in the middle of the pattern, which again seems to change from a darker shade on the left to a brighter shade on the right. You can convince yourself that the horizontal bar is of uniform grey by covering everything above and below.

The central claim of this chapter is that we can explain such brightness illusions in terms of neural encoding, linking perception to the information processing mechanisms in the brain. As we have seen in the previous sections of this chapter, in concentric receptive fields (Hubel 1963) excitation and inhibition are operating in opponency, weighing up the amount of light falling on the centre and the surround, respectively. An ON-centre–OFF-surround receptive field balances the excitation by light from the centre with the inhibition by light from the surround, and therefore responds best to bright spots (and the inverse response is found in OFF-centre–ON-surround receptive fields). 'Looking through' such a centre–surround receptive fields explains simultaneous contrast illusions, because the amount of light captured by the centre determines the amount of neural excitation, while the amount of light captured

Figure 2.12

An example of a simultaneous contrast illusion. Compare the brightness of the vertical bars – are they identical? Yes – but they don't look like this! In fact they share the same brightness as the big horizontal bar in the centre, which in itself seems to get brighter from left to right. This effect demonstrates how local brightness is perceived relative to its surroundings.

by the surround determines the amount of neural inhibition, and together they generate the final output of the sensory neuron – and this final rate of activity corresponds to perceived brightness. Therefore, if an ON-centre receptive field is positioned over a patch of grey that covers its centre, leading to a certain level of excitation, is surrounded by a lighter shade of grey there is more inhibition, and therefore less final activation, than if it is surrounded by a darker shade of grey, which leads to less inhibition and therefore a higher final activation (see Colour plate I, Figure 3). In consequence the patch of grey is presented in a bright surrounding, and thus should appear darker than he same patch of grey surrounded by a bright surrounding. This simple consideration – which actually is oversimplified, as will be discussed in Chapter 3 (Fiorentini et al. 1990) – shows how simple receptive field properties can account for the basic illusions seen in Figure 2.12 and Colour plate I, Figure 3. Receptive fields serve multiple functions; apart from the *contrast enhancement* demonstrated here, they serve *spatial filtering* and *redundancy reduction*, as will be shown later.

Another consequence of the centre–surround receptive field is that such a neuron will respond preferentially to stimuli of a particular size. We already encountered this property called 'size tuning' in Figure 2.8: similar to when you are tuning your radio to your favourite station, a receptive field is tuned to an optimum size stimulus. In other words, the receptive field acts like a *spatial filter*. As illustrated in Colour plate I, Figure 4, the optimum stimulus size matches the size of the receptive field centre because in this configuration the excitation is maximised while the inhibition is minimised. For smaller stimuli the excitation is reduced, and for larger stimuli the inhibition is increased, which in both cases would reduce the final activity level of the neuron.

In other words, the size of a receptive field determines the spatial detail that is visible, and different images are visible at different spatial scales of the receptive fields. You will read more about the effects of such spatial filtering in Chapter 3. As used by artists to great effect, we can actively select levels of spatial detail in images, which we are attending to, while ignoring others, presumably by attending selectively to spatial filters of different size tuning. In fine-grain etchings, such as the self-portraits of Rembrandt van Rijn, we construct the image from a pattern of very fine lines, and in a similar way we can see a gentle flow of colour in some paintings of Paul Klee, which are actually composed of small rectangles of uniform colour and fine colour borders. On the other hand, in some broad-brush or block-structured paintings, such as Salvador Dali's famous 'Lincoln in Dalivision', we cannot ignore the coarse structure and the forms are hidden in strong contours – we need to blur the image in order to experience a second layer of meaning.

Finally, let us take a brief look at what happens to concentric receptive field outputs at a luminance border (see Colour plate I, Figure 5). In regions of unchanging luminance (i.e. in the middle of dark or bright regions) excitation and inhibition cancel each other out to a large degree. At the boundary excitation and inhibition are not balanced and thus increase the relative difference in the neural response – the transition between the dark region on the left and bright region on the right is 'sharpened' in the filter output. The opponency incorporated in concentric receptive fields, which is generated by the lateral inhibition that determines the receptive field structure, enhances the perceived contrast at a luminance border which is the relative difference of bright and dark patches.

The contrast enhancement at a luminance boundary, which resembles the contrast illusion demonstrated in Figure 2.12, goes along with a reduction of response in regions without change in stimulus intensity: redundant signal components are removed. 'Redundancy reduction' is referring to the removal of parts of a message without losing essential information, and we will encounter it time and again when we will go through the various senses in the following chapters. It may seem to be a rather theoretical concept from information theory, and indeed can be challenging in its mathematical description (Shannon and Weaver 1949), but it is not difficult to understand intuitively: when you pause in a conversation on your mobile phone, the silence does not need to be communicated, and the transmission line can be used for someone or something else. Such methods are used by communication service providers to save bandwidth and storage space, to avoid loss of speed in heavy information traffic, which actually saves such companies millions of pounds. In the same way, one of the functions of concentric receptive fields is to transmit no signals where and when there is no change in the input, which helps the nervous system to remove redundancy, to reduce noise (the meaningless components of a signal, which makes a telephone call sometimes so difficult to understand), and thus to achieve efficient and economical encoding.

Image compression resembling that of the visual system is a technique commonly used in contemporary IT: redundant signals are not transmitted by applying clever encoding strategies, so that expensive equipment and networks can be used for something else in the meantime. There is a wide range of standard methods of data compression, such as JPEG (an example is shown Figure 2.13) for images or MPEG for movies. We all encounter these file types when browsing the Internet, but usually would not think about their purpose. The direct impact of these methods is that you can download pictures and movies much, much faster – WiFi and YouTube would never have taken off without image compression.

After all these technical considerations, even an engineer would benefit from a reality check. So what do you see, let's say, when you are looking at a painting, such as Leonardo da Vinci's *Mona Lisa* (*La Gioconda*, 1503–6, Louvre, Paris)? At lower levels of analysis the visual system encodes local features, such as brightness, colour, contrast, spatial detail, orientation, texture or motion. At higher levels of analysis the visual system needs to combine features and create coherent representations of shapes, objects and surfaces, and their relations to each other. And finally the combination of all these jigsaw pieces needs to be put together by the brain to grasp the meaning of images – such as the mystery of Mona Lisa's famous smile.

Figure 2.13

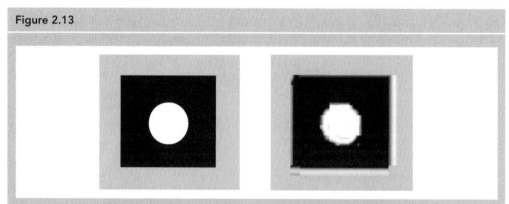

Images contain large amounts of information because they are two-dimensional arrays of luminance and colour information, and data compression therefore is vital to save time and bandwidth in telephone and Internet communication lines. In the most common compression methods redundant signals are removed by means of various types of opponency operators, resembling those we know from receptive fields in nervous systems. The original image (left: 110 × 100 pixels RAW file) has a size of 37 KB, whereas the compressed image (right: same size JPEG file) is reduced to a size of 1 KB. Note that in this extreme example it is very obvious that spatial resolution is lost.

Take Home Messages

- the sensory system makes the physical world accessible to the brain and the mind
- the basic unit of brain function is the neuron; sensory neurons are characterised by their receptive field, which has a structure reflecting their function
- signals arising from sensor arrays are analysed in a complex network of parallel and serial processing in the brain
- receptive fields encode specific image features, which is the basis of visual perception
- smart techniques of image encoding that are used in highly evolved brains are cheap, fast, robust, reliable – and they resemble those applied by IT engineers

Discussion Questions

- Describe the basic principles of information encoding in the nervous system.
- What are the simple mechanisms to generate receptive fields with a distinct structure?
- How can concentric receptive fields be used to explain brightness contrast illusions?
- What is meant by redundancy reduction in the sensory system?

3 VISION 1: BRIGHTNESS

OVERVIEW

The physical luminance of the light emitted or reflected by an object or surface is converted into perceived brightness in the visual stream. This conversion of the outside world into mental representations is the result of neural encoding strategies that reduce redundancy and enhance local contrast. Such processing mechanisms lead to illusions, which often are interpreted as 'errors' of representation, but equally can be used as a tool to understand the workings of the brain. Brightness contrast illusions are revisited as a starting point to look at the encoding of light intensity in static images as basic visual processing – seeing bright and dark is arguably the most ordinary task for the visual system. Perceived brightness serves as an input to many other steps of visual information processing, and as such has a fundamental importance for more complex tasks like three-dimensional shape or face perception. Neural encoding through opponency filters explains the resolution of spatial detail in spatial frequency channels, and also gives initial clues for the function of contrast enhancement, redundancy reduction and image compression. These filters therefore can be well understood as a product of the evolution of optimal filter mechanisms. More complex brightness phenomena, such as the conservation of uniform shades of grey perceived within regions enclosed by uninterrupted boundaries, give some initial indication about higher-level processes beyond the initial filtering stage, in particular a filling-in mechanism that is needed to reconstruct the brightness for uniform surfaces. Finally, it will be shown that in less trivial configurations, including the appearance of transparent surfaces and shadows, the visual system provides effective tools to extract the information from images, which is most relevant for meaningful interaction with the surrounding world.

SIMPLE VISUAL STIMULI

Many readers, I presume, would be most interested in questions about perception that are related to high-level interactions of humans, like the one raised at the end of Chapter 2: how can we perceive, interpret and understand the mysterious smile of the Mona Lisa? We have seen in Chapter 2 that a dense network of serial and parallel information processing is the basis of visual perception, converting images of the visual field to retinotopic representations of image features ('neural images'): the three-dimensional environment is captured as flat two-dimensional (2D) images in two eyes, and then the information is processed along the visual stream in a set of brain regions (see Colour plate II, Figure 1). The various analysis steps in the visual stream, in the eyes of an engineer, reduce the information in the stimulus and extract the relevant aspects for any particular task, such as face perception and the recognition of facial expressions. In this framework, the retina works like a digital camera with some initial data compression, the optic nerve serves as highly parallel data bus, and after a relay station in the LGN the information is distributed across at the early areas of the visual cortex for initial image analysis and storage (Hubel and Wiesel 1979; van Essen et al. 1992). In particular, area V3 is generally thought to be concerned with the representation of form, area V4 serves the representation of colour, and area V5 is specialised for motion processing (Zeki 1993).

Given the complexity of the underlying information processing stream, and of the inter-actions between the brain regions involved in such processing, searching for an understand-ing of how we can read the Mona Lisa's smile is like searching for a needle in a haystack. In Chapter 1 it was argued that the key to understanding perception and brain function is to dissect complex problems into simple steps. A quick look at image reproduction technologies can give some clues to how the richness of a visual scene can be reduced to simple represen-tations, thus providing less information while retaining the core of an image. Line drawings or etchings (each image point is black or white, carrying 1 bit of information) were the tradi-tional means of picture reproductions in books. Photography started with greylevel pictures (in digital images usually encoded with 8 bits per image point, or pixel), went on with colour images (usually 24 bits per pixel), and led to cinematography, with sequences of moving images (whereas a still photograph can be stored using a couple of hundreds of kilobytes in compressed format, a movie requires a many megabytes, and a high-capacity DVD as storage medium). Therefore, in an attempt to reduce the complexity of image processing under inves-tigation, in the first instance (i) we restrict our analysis to static images (motion will be cov-ered in Chapter 6) and (ii) focus on greylevel images, ignoring colour (covered in Chapter 4).

Op Art paintings, such as Bridget Riley's (Riley 1995) geometric black and white patterns (e.g., Tate Gallery, London), give an indication of how rich perceptual experience can be in absence of colour or movement. In Akiyoshi Kitaoka's collection of simple static patterns (Kitaoka 2002) you can admire the many facets of such images, how they trick the eye, and see how they are augmented by the addition of colour. When studying the perception of brightness, we therefore will have another, and a closer look at a number of illusions. Illusions are often regarded as failures of the sensory system to provide a veridical representation of the outside world – but we will see that they do provide crucial pointers towards understanding the mecha-nisms of its information processing mechanisms. In this context, illusions are a key to reality!

DESCRIPTORS OF GREYLEVEL IMAGES

Let us start with a brief look at the physics of the intensity of light entering the eye. Light can either be emitted by an object, such as a candle or a light bulb, or it can be reflected from a surface, such as a sheet of paper in sunlight. The amount of visible light that comes to the eye from a surface is called 'luminance', whereas the amount of light that is shining on a surface is called 'illuminance', and the proportion of light reflected from a surface is called 'reflectance' (see Figure 3.1). These purely physical properties can be measured using physi-cal devices, such as a luminance metre that measures light intensity, or tallies the number of light particles arising from a small region of a scene. Perceptually, there is an interesting difference between the direct appearance of a surface and its physical properties. Perceived luminance, or the perceptual correlate of the light that arises from a surface, is referred to as 'brightness', whereas perceived reflectance, or the perceptual correlate of the light that bounces back from an illuminated surface, is referred to as 'lightness'. A piece of white paper looks white in the sunlight, and it also looks white in moonlight, despite the fact that there is much less light coming from its surface to enter the eye. There would be no difficulty for a human observer to notice the difference of brightness under these two illuminations, and

Figure 3.1

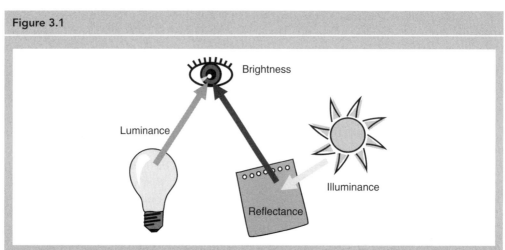

The physics of light intensity, as seen by the eye. Light emitted from an object (light bulb) or reflected by a surface (sheet of paper in sunlight) is entering the eye, giving rise to a luminance distribution which is perceived as brightness; the object property that determines the relationship between illuminance – the amount of light that falls on a surface – and the amount of light reflected from this surface, its 'reflectance', is perceived as lightness (white or grey paper).

still the piece of paper would be recognised as white rather than grey – which is a surface property independent of illumination (Gilchrist 1979). We will return, at the end of this chapter, to this interesting aspect of the visual system, which is referred to as 'brightness constancy', when looking at shadows.

When it comes to perceiving brightness, perhaps the most basic question is how many different shades of grey a human observer can discriminate (see Figure 3.2). The answer commonly offered to this question, based on discrimination thresholds for boundaries between similar shades of grey at different base levels, is that we are able to discriminate about 5000 shades (4096 different levels could be encoded with 12 bits of information). Notably, this is much more than the 256 grey levels provided by a typical computer screen, or an 8-bit digital image, the typical bitmap format.

This observation raises a number of scientific questions. What is the best description, and neural representation, of a greylevel stimulus? In Chapter 2, we saw that neural encoding strategies emphasise luminance changes. Indeed, the most efficient description of brightness does not relate to absolute levels of grey, but to differences between neighbouring regions, or contrast. It will be shown in the following pages how these mechanisms affect brightness perception. We will ask what the relationship is between objective (physical) luminance and subjective (perceived) brightness, and ask whether we can interpret the visual system as measurement device similar to a ruler that is used to measure length. The simple statement about 5000 discriminable levels of brightness is an oversimplification because brightness is not perceived in a linear fashion, which means that equal steps of luminance do not lead to equal steps in brightness. Instead, larger luminance differences are needed at high average luminance levels than at low average luminance levels, in order to perceive a difference in brightness. This fundamental relationship between the intensity of a stimulus and the smallest difference between two different intensities that can be discriminated, is a very common property for all kinds of sensory systems and can be generally described by 'Weber–Fechner Law', which claims that the proportion of change needed to detect an

Figure 3.2

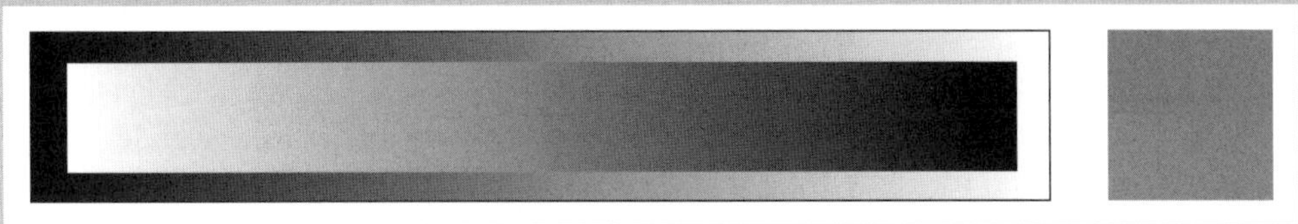

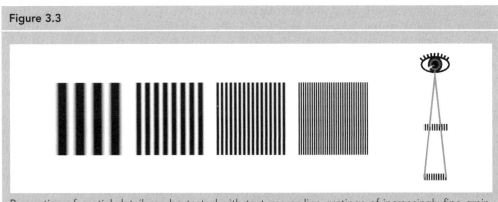

Perception of brightness. In the grey wedge on the left side, ranging from white to black (surrounded by a frame of opposite polarity) a human observer can discriminate approximately 5000 shades of grey, about 20 times more than the levels provided by a typical 8-bit image: boundaries between areas of a single unit difference (1/256 of range) are visible, as can be seen by close inspection of the set of four squares on the right.

Figure 3.3

Perception of spatial detail can be tested with textures or line gratings of increasingly fine grain, usually measured as spatial frequency (number of lines, or grating cycles per degree of visual angle). Looking at the page from a distance of 80 cm, at which each of the four squares (14 × 14 mm) covered with gratings has the angular size of c. 1 deg, the 4 gratings have a spatial frequency of 4, 8, 16 and 32 cycles/deg. If you increase your viewing distance further, at some point the fine gratings blur into a grey field and are no longer visible: this is your resolution limit. The sketch on the right shows how spatial frequency of a grating image increases with viewing distance: the 10 degrees of visual angle between the two grey lines is filled with 5 grating cycles (i.e. 5 cycles/deg) at the smaller viewing distance, and 10 grating cycles (i.e. 10 cycles/deg) at the larger viewing distance.

intensity step is approximately constant, later refined as 'Stevens' Power Law' (Stevens 1961; Stevens 1970). Based on this observation, we can get a better idea about the metrics of brightness, that is, how the 5000 visible shades of grey are mapped on a luminance scale. Because the smallest visible steps do not have the same size, such a scale is non-linear, unlike the linear scale of a ruler, where a millimetre covers exactly the same distance at 1 cm as at 1 m, for instance. Such scaling extends the overall range of luminance levels that can be discriminated, the so-called operating range. In many technical devices, such as video monitors, this non-linear behaviour is incorporated in the display by means of 'Gamma-correction'.

The next basic question is related to the spatial resolution of the human visual system: how much spatial detail can we see? Usually, you would not be able to see individual pixels on your computer or television screen (typically 1028 by 768 pixels), but if you use a lower screen resolution (640 by 480 pixels) or a larger screen, you will see that it is made up of small image points, or pixels, if you get close enough. This 'spatial resolution' of the visual system can be investigated systematically by line patterns, or gratings (see Figure 3.3). It is important to note that increasing or decreasing the viewing distance changes the number of lines that fill a degree of visual angle. The number or grating cycles in a degree of visual angle (cycles/deg) is called by physicists and engineers 'spatial frequency'. The reason why you take a closer look of an image or an object when you attempt to see its fine spatial detail is that the visible detail is limited by resolution of the visual system, in points per degree (or cycles/deg), and by reducing viewing distance you are growing the size of the image (or the cycles of a test pattern), as sketched on the right of Figure 3.3. When our eyesight gets worse, for instance in old age, it means that the resolution is reduced, and we need magnifying glasses to recognise fine detail, or read small texts. An optometrist or ophthalmologist uses standardised tests to measure visual acuity, and 100% visual acuity corresponds to the resolution of approximately 50 cycles per degree (Adams et al. 1988; Westheimer 1984).

Again, there are a number of scientific questions to be asked. How can spatial detail be described, and what is the metric of such detail? As mentioned above, for simple gratings a straightforward measure of spatial variation is the number of cycles per degree, or spatial frequency. It turns out that this is a very general and useful measure because physicists use a mathematical framework, Fourier Theory (Bracewell 1986), to compose arbitrary spatial patterns from a combination of sinewave gratings. Whereas a Psychology student not necessarily needs to understand workings of Fourier Theory, it is important to note that it is very common to investigate the function of the sensory systems with sinewave gratings and to express performance in terms of frequency. In the case of spatial vision this is spatial frequency, measured in cycles/deg (Campbell and Robson 1968; Watson et al. 1983). What are the experimental approaches to investigate the spatial properties of the human visual system? For instance, we can measure detection thresholds for gratings at different contrasts, or how well different gratings can be discriminated. Starting from this, the performance of less simple stimuli can be determined, and by applying Fourier Theory mathematical models for the processing of arbitrary patterns can be developed (Wilson 1991). In the nervous system, the tuning of individual neurons to spatial frequency can be determined and compared for a range of neurons and brain regions (Tootell et al. 1981). This brings us back to the simple receptive field structures of retinal ganglion cells introduced in Chapter 2, which already show size, or spatial frequency, tuning. Each neuron in the early visual system has characteristic spatial frequency tuning, where the optimum frequency corresponds to the receptive field size (cf. Colour plate I, Figure 4). Groups of neurons with different optimum frequencies cover the full range of spatial frequencies visible to the human observer, the so-called Contrast-Sensitivity Function (CSF, see Figure 3.4). The universality of such neuronal properties, and the power of this approach, led to scientific discussions whether this is a complete picture of early visual processing, and whether the visual brain can be understood as a 'Fourier Analyser' (Maffei and Fiorentini 1973; Ochs 1979).

THE FUNDAMENTAL CONCEPT: FILTERING

Whether or not the brain can be regarded as Fourier analyser, there is a bulk of experimental evidence (Campbell and Maffei 1974) that visual function can be explained to a large degree by *spatial frequency channels* that transmit and represent fine- to coarse-grain versions of an image, which are processed, stored and used in separate neurons. Such filter mechanisms are interpreted as a property emerging from the receptive field structure of sensory neurons, which are organised in parallel sets not only for spatial frequency (Figure 3.4), but equally for other properties, such as colour, orientation or velocity (see Chapter 2). When the action of sensory neurons is described as such filtering, what does this mean in more conceptual terms? The parallel sets

Figure 3.4

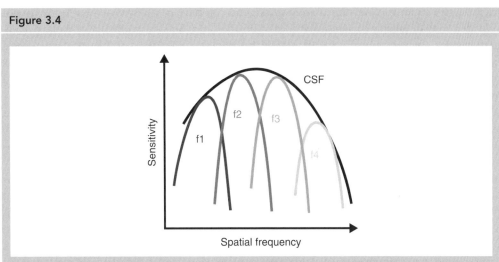

Schematic sketch of the contrast sensitivity function (CSF, black curve), which represents the sensitivity of the human visual system for gratings with variable spatial frequency. It can be understood as the combination of a set of neurons tuned to different optimum spatial frequencies, f1–f4 (curves with different shade of grey), or spatial frequency channels.

of neurons are interpreted as pattern analysers, which are organised as filter banks operating in the visual stream. The size and structure of receptive fields determines the optimum size, or spatial frequency, of the encoded stimulus, which is then described as the filter mechanism processing only a selection of the information available. To understand the function of such spatial frequency channels at an intuitive level, they can be compared to a simple mechanical system – a gravel pit. In the sorting engine of the gravel pit, mixed sediments that were dug up from a riverbed are separated into materials of different grain: sand, pebbles and rocks. A simple way of doing this is involves sets of sieves, which allow material of a particular grain to pass (i.e. filters), whereas larger grains are retained in the flow (see Colour plate II, Figure 2 left). At the end of such processing the different components included in the original mix can be collected in separate containers, which then contain material of a particular grain.

In the same way, in the visual system parallel sets of receptive fields are operating to separate different spatial frequency components from those that are contained in the retinal image. Through this filtering the visual scene is analysed and represented in a set of different spatial frequency channels (see Wilson 1991): Fourier analysis. At some later stage of the visual stream the information from these separate representations needs to be combined, together with other image features such as colour or motion, to deliver a unitary and rich percept – therefore, as will be discussed in the final section of this chapter, such Fourier analysis is a good description of the early stages of visual systems, but does not capture all aspects of visual perception.

ILLUSIONS AS KEY TO REALITY

When was the last time you were sitting on the train, waiting for it to leave the station, and looking out of the window at the train right on the next track you got the impression that your train had started moving – only to notice a few seconds later that you were still waiting at the platform, and that it was the other train that had started to move? Quite often, probably, as your eyes are tricked when looking at the surrounding world, and you have to realise that your senses do not provide you with reliable or veridical information about the outside world, but generate perceptual illusions. Painters, when trying to provide 'realistic' representations of the world, are using a bag of tricks to create such illusions. For instance, in order to create an impression of depth on a flat canvas, the theory of geometric perspective and shading has been systematically developed and exploited since the Renaissance in Western Visual Arts (Gombrich 1977). Op Artists in the second half of the twentieth century started experimenting with 'optical illusions' created in simple line drawings or colour patterns (Riley 1995; Wade 2003). With the introduction of computer-aided editing and animation techniques, in the twenty-first century the art form of cinematography reached new levels of presenting augmented, puzzling or impossible – but visually absolutely convincing – worlds (just think of the special effects in movies like *Harry Potter* or *Lord of the Rings*). Even live television broadcasts should be watched with a certain level of scepticism (remember the fireworks in the opening ceremony of the Beijing Olympics?). Furthermore, illusions and other visual puzzles are frequently used in advertising, which may be less surprising in view of the fact that the reality of a product is rarely what customers want to buy.

The important thing to notice is that we are constantly exposed to illusions, and that our senses do not tell us in a reliable way what exactly is out there (Gregory and Gombrich 1973). Whereas we usually think that we should only believe what we see, we could also arrive at the conclusion that we never should believe what we see (Coren and Girgus 1978; Marshall 1987). Although this suggestion may be rather sobering, or perhaps even irritating, there is something very exciting about illusions: while puzzling our minds, these phenomena tell us a lot about how our brain works. In fact, visual illusions are rarely 'optical', and don't trick our eyes, but reflect how our brains are processing visual information – and for the very same reason illusions play a major role in the scientific study of sensory systems. So what can we learn from illusions about visual information processing? In science, minimal stimulus configurations are essential to study perception. Figure 3.5 shows a famous example of a very

Figure 3.5

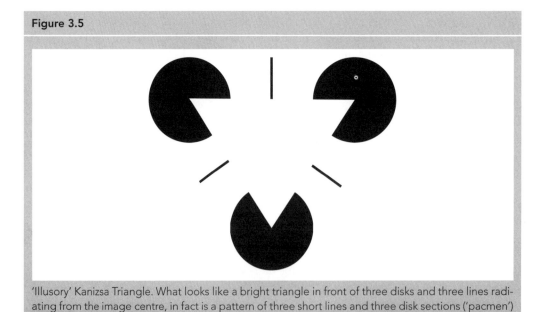

'Illusory' Kanizsa Triangle. What looks like a bright triangle in front of three disks and three lines radiating from the image centre, in fact is a pattern of three short lines and three disk sections ('pacmen') oriented towards the centre.

simple drawing that generates an illusion, the 'Kanizsa triangle'. We see a white triangle in front of three lines and three discs, and sometimes perceive the triangle as brighter than the background – this is referred to as illusory or 'subjective' contours (Kanizsa 1976).

Using illusions generated by such simple stimuli as a guide to understand the visual system, two fundamental approaches to understand illusions have been proposed. On one hand, we have supporters of 'Gestalt Psychology' who interpret illusions as a reflection of perceptual organisation (Kanizsa 1979; Koffka 1935). Within this conceptual framework, perceptions are understood as unitary experiences emerging from and going beyond the components of a stimulus: 'the whole is more than the sum of parts'. In cases like the illusory triangle, the perceptual system chooses the best, simplest and most stable shape, according to the Gestalt law of '*Praegnanz*'. More about this can be found in Chapter 13. On the other hand, illusions are understood as by-products of the processing mechanisms underlying perception (see Chapter 2), which under some specific conditions lead to discrepancies between the physical stimulus and its mental experience that could be regarded as representation 'errors'. In recent decades a wealth of evidence has been accumulated of properties of individual cortical neurons that can account for the perceived illusion of subjective contours (Paradiso et al. 1989; Peterhans and von der Heydt 1991). This physiological approach is complemented by computational modelling, formalising the operations carried out

Figure 3.6

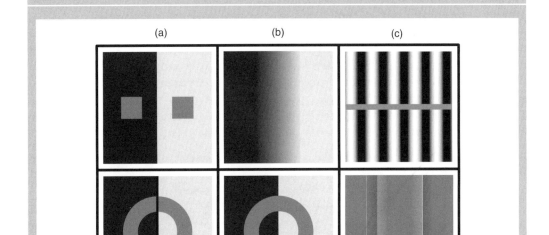

A zoo of brightness illusions. Top row: (a) simultaneous contrast – the brightness of the square is influenced by the shade of grey in the background, see Chapter 2; (b) Mach bands – a dark vertical line and a bright vertical line are perceived when luminance starts and ends to increase gradually from one low level to high level; (c) grating induction – the grey horizontal stripe in the centre appears to be modulated in brightness in reverse to the vertical gratings above and below. Bottom row: (d) partitioned Koffka ring – simultaneous contrast; (e) open Koffka ring – in a single object crossing the background luminance border, simultaneous contrast breaks down and a unitary brightness is perceived for the whole object; (f) Craik–Cornsweet illusion – the vertical region in the centre looks brighter than the left and right regions, although they only differ in the boundary regions but not in the middle.

by the neurons along the visual stream (Marr 1982). Illusions tell us a lot about the mechanisms of visual information processing.

Some of the challenges for such an information processing approach are illustrated by some examples from the 'zoo of brightness illusions' shown in Figure 3.6. In the top row of this figure some examples are shown of how the perceived brightness at a given location depends on its neighbourhood, like the simultaneous contrast illusion presented in Chapter 2, and similar effects in Mach bands (Ross et al. 1989) and grating induction (Blakeslee and McCourt 1997). The bottom row of this figure shows some examples of how the perceived brightness of a clearly outlined surface tends to be uniform, such as the Koffka ring (Koffka 1935) or the Craik–Cornsweet illusion (Cornsweet 1970). The functional significance, and the cooperative relationship between the processes of contrast enhancement and filling in, will be discussed in the two next sections.

CONTRAST ENHANCEMENT IN BRIGHTNESS ENCODING

In Chapter 2 it was demonstrated that opponent filtering, as generated by the lateral inhibition mechanisms of centre–surround receptive fields, generates minimum and maximum responses at luminance boundaries and discards average luminance. This phenomenon of contrast enhancement is illustrated schematically in Colour plate II, Figure 3: the perceived brightness profile at a luminance boundary is generated through the opponent integration mechanism between the excitatory centre and inhibitory surround of a concentric ON-centre receptive field.

The same action of opponent receptive fields can account for illusions with less simple patterns, like the multiple luminance step function shown in Figure 3.7a. Although each of the five vertical bars has a constant luminance, they are perceived as darker on the left than on the right. This can be easily understood as the influence of the contrast enhancement at each luminance step as illustrated in Figure 3.7b.

The very same organisation of receptive fields, which can be interpreted as coding strategy to amplify luminance differences across contours, also operates in two spatial dimensions. The

Figure 3.7

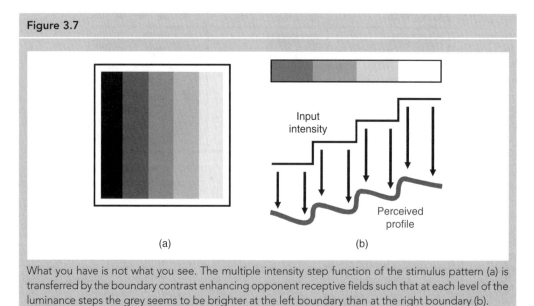

(a)   (b)

What you have is not what you see. The multiple intensity step function of the stimulus pattern (a) is transferred by the boundary contrast enhancing opponent receptive fields such that at each level of the luminance steps the grey seems to be brighter at the left boundary than at the right boundary (b).

famous 'Hermann Grid' shown in Figure 3.8a is made up of a regular pattern of black squares separated by small white regions ('edges'). At the intersections of vertical and horizontal edges grey blobs are perceived, as long as they are not in the centre of the visual field. In the visual field centre the intersection is projected on the fovea, the retinal region of highest spatial resolution, where receptive fields are smaller and do not match the size of the white edges as is necessary for the explanation of the perceived grey blobs suggested in the next paragraph.

In Colour plate II, Figure 4 a neural explanation is provided for the grey blobs appearing in the intersections of the white edges. In opponent filters (ON-centre–OFF-surround receptive fields), larger parts of the inhibitory surround are stimulated in the intersections of the edges, as compared to the white edge regions between the intersections, which explains the apparent reduction of brightness seen as grey blobs. This simple, schematic consideration demonstrates how the contrast enhancement delivered by opponent filters operates in two spatial dimensions, leading to a strong brightness illusion in the Hermann grid. An interesting amplification of this illusion is the 'scintillating grid', a quite recent discovery that raises interesting new questions about the underlying brain mechanisms (Schrauf et al. 1997). Obviously the explanation put forward here is a very idealised picture, and despite the simple explanation of the illusory grey blobs, there are other aspects that await an explanation: The opponent filter mechanism would predict darker regions close to boundaries of the black squares than in the middle of the squares, but each square appears constantly black. Additional aspects of image encoding that can explain this effect will be discussed in the next section.

IMAGE COMPRESSION IN BRIGHTNESS ENCODING

Revisiting the variety of simultaneous contrast illusion between regions and at luminance boundaries (see Figure 3.6) in the context of the observation made for the Hermann grid (Colour plate II, Figure 4) that each black square appears uniformly black, leaves us with a small paradox. The simple opponency mechanism discussed so far explains how the luminance of the background affects the brightness of the grey square in the foreground of Figure 3.6a, and the underlying lateral inhibition would predict a particular contrast enhancement of luminance borders, because the modulation of activation from nearby regions should be largest at a luminance step. However, while such a contrast enhancement is perceived for the multiple luminance step pattern shown in Figure 3.7, it is not visible at the boundaries of the squares in Figure 3.6a or Colour plate II, Figure 4 – the squares clearly have the same brightness in the complete area surrounded by the luminance border. A similar uniform level of grey is perceived in the open Koffka ring shown in Figure 3.6e, where the simultaneous contrast illusion that is visible in the partitioned ring (Figure 3.6d) breaks down for a coherent shape crossing a luminance boundary in the background. This discrepancy suggests that the operation of simple receptive fields does not provide a full explanation of how we perceive brightness, and perhaps – not surprisingly – some additional, higher-level mechanisms need to be considered. Considering the limitations of the most simple models will bring us back to the fundamental questions of how perceived features reflect physical properties, and what the function ('purpose') of opponency encoding might be.

This discrepancy between the filtering expectation and the observation of uniform grey levels inside borders can be best seen for the dark–bright–dark profile shown in Figure 3.8: the expectation for the encoded profile, if the neural image is generated by opponency filtering, would show strong contrast enhancement at the luminance boundaries, and very

Figure 3.8

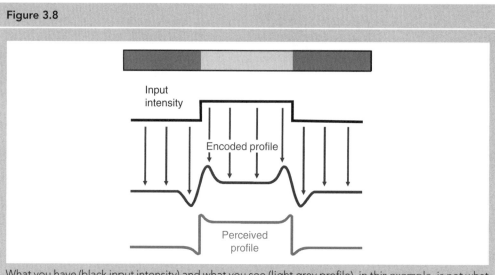

What you have (black input intensity) and what you see (light grey profile), in this example, is not what you what you should see if simple opponency filtering (symbolised by dark grey arrows) would be the only encoding mechanism in the visual stream (dark grey, encoded profile) – a region of uniform luminance embedded in dark background should have enhanced contrast in the border regions and reduced brightness in central region (compare with Colour plate II, Figure 3 and 3.7, for instance).

similar activation levels in the inner regions of the brighter and darker sections. Because the exclusive encoding of spatial changes through opponent processes removes redundant image components that do not contain information, it can be interpreted as an effective image compression strategy. When no signal is transmitted for regions without luminance change, and information is only encoded at luminance boundaries, the information about the uniform luminance level between such boundaries is no longer represented. The fact that for the stimulus illustrated in Figure 3.8 perception is dominated by a clearly outlined region of enhanced brightness therefore raises the question of how the average luminance level of objects is reconstructed in the brain. There could be various possible mechanisms, such as combining information from different spatial scales, which could support such a reconstruction process. The observation that the enclosure of an image region is so important for performing uniform brightness (see Figure 3.6d and e) led to the proposal of a cortical 'filling-in' mechanism by which regions that are surrounded by clear boundaries assume the same brightness (Pessoa et al. 1995). The result of such a reconstruction mechanism, which can also account for the uniform black squares in the Hermann grid (Colour plate II, Figure 4) is illustrated in Figures 3.8 and 3.9.

In essence, a filling-in mechanism reconstructs the redundant image regions by assuming that regions enclosed by contiguous boundaries originally have the same intensity. In view of such processing one could expect a stimulus that has a physical profile, which looks like the encoded profile that only indicates luminance borders without any change of average luminance, would lead to a very similar encoded profile and after the reconstruction should be perceived as a change of mean brightness. This effect is nicely demonstrated by the Craik–Cornsweet illusion (Cornsweet 1970) illustrated in Figure 3.9b. The central area appears brighter than the regions on the left and right, although the physical luminance

Figure 3.9

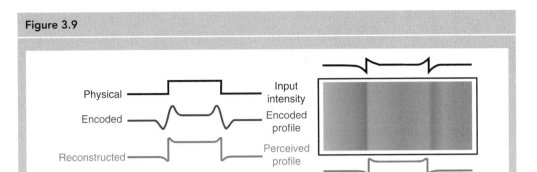

(a) The discrepancy between physical luminance profiles (black line) and activity profiles as encoded by opponent filters (dark grey) is compensated by filling-in mechanisms that reconstruct the percept close to the original profile for the stimulus illustrated in Figure 3.8 (light grey). (b) Craik–Cornsweet illusion. The physical luminance profile (black line above the stimulus pattern) of this stimulus is characterised by contrast edges of opposite sign without changes of mean luminance – rather different from the luminance steps shown in (a). Filling-in mechanisms, however, generate a reconstructed profile (light grey line below stimulus pattern) that resembles that in (a), which explains the illusory perception of a bright region embedded in a darker background.

is identical in the centre and the peripheral regions, and is changing only in the visible boundary regions. This illusion demonstrates the filling-in mechanism: surfaces between boundaries are apparently filled with uniform brightness. Note that this is an 'inverted' illusion, where the perceived brightness profile is reconstructed from an ambiguous luminance profile, assuming certain properties of the outside world such as uniform coloration. The Craik–Cornsweet illusion demonstrates that if in the attempt to reduce redundancy only changes in intensity are encoded, uniform properties of the physical properties need to be assumed between such changes in higher-level interpretation from sparse data. In consequence, subtle gradients are ignored.

ADVANCED BRIGHTNESS PERCEPTION: DOES THE BRAIN KNOW THE LAWS OF PHYSICS?

The Craik–Cornsweet illusion is a first indication that in perception the relation between physical properties and internal representations can be non-veridical in such a way that the most likely surface property is recovered. When a not perfectly flat sheet of paper that is placed on a black background is illuminated from the side, for instance, the uneven paper surface will show slight variations of luminance – shading. Still it will be interpreted not as a piece of paper with faint grey stains but as perfectly white, the visual system reconstructing the uniform white surface property between the strong luminance boundaries. We encounter capabilities of the visual system like this, which go beyond the most basic effects of visual encoding covered so far, in a range of contexts that are related to recognition of objects and making them available to interaction. Three examples of such phenomena are described briefly to close the chapter with a wider perspective, which will be further expanded in Chapter 13.

Looking through a transparent surface, like tinted glass or wrapping paper, is a not uncommon situation that changes the luminance (or colour) of all objects behind the transparent material. When reading a newspaper while wearing dark sunglasses, however, you don't get the impression that it is printed on grey paper (and just from wearing pink sunglasses you will not get the impression you are reading the *Financial Times*). Somehow, therefore, the brain is able to account for transparency. At the top of Figure 3.10a you see a light grey rectangle that is partially covered by a slightly darker, transparent rectangle. When looking at this image you would not interpret it as three adjacent shapes covered with three different paints, which is however the preferred interpretation as soon as the figure is disintegrated into three separate shapes (bottom of 3.10a). The perception of transparency is a very powerful tool for the visual system that helps us to recognise physical properties of the world surrounding us (Metelli 1974).

In the Checker Shadow Illusion (Figure 3.10b) a diffuse shadow is cast over a regular pattern of dark and bright tiles, which changes the physical luminance of individual elements considerably. In our internal representation, however, the surface is still covered with dark and bright tiles. This leads to the effect that two tiles that are perceived as belonging to the set of bright and dark tiles, respectively, actually have the same physical luminance. Once again, it seems as if the visual system uses good knowledge of the laws of physics, and by realising that a shadow cast over the tiling pattern is able to retrieve the surface properties – in this case the colouring of each tile, independent of illumination condition – of objects for the internal representation of the outside world. It is important to note that it is the intrinsic properties of objects that is important to understand and remember, and that this goes far beyond just taking and storing images (Adelson 2001).

When thinking about the mechanisms for this correction of perceived brightness, a possible candidate could be to detect the shadow and then subtract its contribution to the illumination of the tiles, and thus recover the original luminance of each tile. The Corrugated Plaid

Figure 3.10

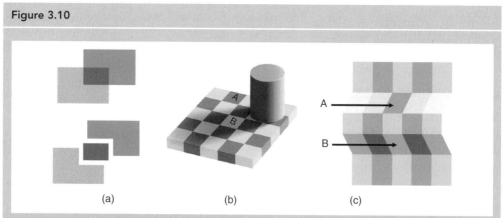

(a)   (b)   (c)

Higher-level aspects of brightness perception. (a) Transparency: When three shapes covered with a particular combination of grey (bottom) are arranged in a special way (top), transparency is perceived. (b) Checker Shadow Illusion: Perceived brightness in regions of a regular tiling pattern that are overcast by a shadow differs from the physical luminance of these regions: tiles A and B have the same luminance but differ in perceived brightness (©1995, Edward H. Adelson) (c) The Corrugated Plaid Illusion demonstrates that a similar difference of brightness for areas of identical luminance (regions A and B) can be perceived in the absence of explicit shadows as well, if they seem to be exposed to different illumination.

Illusion, shown in Figure 3.10c, demonstrates that a similar difference of brightness for rectangles of identical luminance (indicated by black arrows) can be perceived in the absence of explicit shadows as well. Here it seems to be the three-dimensional interpretation of the image as a folded set of squares painted with different greys that is crucial for the illusion, which might be related to an implicit reduction of illumination on the seemingly downward-facing surface region. When the set of squares is perceived as folded horizontally such that the two rectangles appear to sit on the same plane, luminance and brightness are both identical. Whereas one might think that this illusion could suggest that the brain somehow has to reconstruct some rather complex variations of surface orientation and lighting conditions, there are proposals to show how the same behaviour can be modelled with some rather simple and pragmatic computations (Adelson 2000).

Take Home Messages

- visual information is reorganised, compressed and categorised by parallel and hierarchical processing mechanisms to encode information efficiently in the visual stream
- the encoding of levels of grey in static images is one of the most basic tasks performed in the visual stream, determining perceived brightness
- opponent filters encoding by centre–surround receptive fields is a crucial strategy to enhance local contrast and remove redundancy, and crucial for brightness perception
- opponency can account for a number of illusions such as simultaneous contrast, but additional mechanisms (like filling-in) are required to deal with other aspects of perception
- illusions are often explained as high-level mechanisms that construct solutions to puzzles; many illusions are a consequence of basic information processing strategies, while others require higher-level mechanisms that are helpful to reconstruct the most likely properties of physical objects

Discussion Questions

- How many different shades of grey can humans discriminate? How does this compare to technical systems?
- Describe the action of concentric receptive fields, and how they can act as spatial filters.
- What is meant by cortical 'filling-in'?
- Discuss the phenomenon of transparency in the context of brightness representation.

4 | VISION 2: COLOUR

OVERVIEW

Why do humans have colour vision? In other words, what can we see in a colour but not in a black-and-white movie, and what are you missing from everyday experience if you are colour blind? Recognising the value added by colour information to everyday experience is the starting point in studying the physical basis and the neural encoding of colour in the human visual system. Colour space, defined by hue and saturation, is a crucial concept to compare the number of different colours and saturation levels that can be seen, and to assess colour resolution of natural colouration and technical displays that surround us. A brief reflection on colour names highlights how difficult it is to describe colours in everyday language, and the cultural dependence of such descriptive terms. To put these observations into a conceptual perspective, the 'trichromatic' and 'opponent process' theories of colour vision are introduced, which account for properties like colour mixing and colour contrast, and for a long time have been discussed as alternative 'theories' that exclude each other. Science has now accumulated a wide body of evidence recognising the two perspectives as complementing each other, reflecting different stages of neural encoding. Some spatial and temporal aspects of the neural encoding of chromaticity are compared to that of brightness, which prepares us to understand the phenomena of colour contrast and after-effects. Finally, a few higher-level mechanisms in colour vision, such as assimilation and colour constancy are considered, suggesting that context-dependent colour information is represented in rather different ways at different levels of the brain, providing vital cues to navigating the world under a wide range of operating conditions. The reconfiguration of information in the visual system brings us back to the initial questions about the behavioural and evolutionary aspects of colour vision.

PHYSICAL PROPERTIES OF COLOUR

The first and most immediate question we should ask ourselves is: Why do we have colour vision? What can we see in colour, which we can't see in black and white, or, in other words, what is the added value of a colour? Comparing old-fashioned black-and-white movies with contemporary film, or 24 bit digital monitors,, we might simply say it is more realistic and it is more pleasant to the eye. Obviously, it is more convincing and pleasant to see artificial renditions of the world that resemble the real world, as we do in the contemporary movie – however, this doesn't answer the question why we have colour vision, because it only reminds us that we need to find out what is the evolutionary advantage of seeing colours in the real world. So let us look at the example in Colour plate III, Figure 1, which illustrates some interesting aspects of object identification. Imagine you want to point a friend towards your car, which you left in a car park in the midst of many other cars. In order to identify your car, you either would need to describe exactly the location where you left it, or you would need to describe the peculiar make or the properties of your car such as the size or shape, any characteristic damage or fancy engineering work such as extra exhaust pipes. If, however, you have access to colour vision you just could point your friend towards the bright blue car. Colour vision adds a lot of extra information to your retinal images! We make constant use of this extra information. Just think of red and green traffic lights or the use of the colour orange in advertising. Colour also helps us to recognise objects and to keep them in our memory (Gegenfurtner and Rieger 2000). In terms of our evolution, where traffic lights and mobile phone ads didn't feature highly, it is argued that a key function of colour vision is related to tasks like the detection and recognition of predators, prey or fruits that are often distinguished by a strong contrast to the green foliage in which they are embedded (Osorio and Vorobyev 1996).

The second question we should ask, which is perhaps even more fundamental than the first one, is what is colour and how can it be described. For a physicist, who masters the twentieth-century knowledge of electromagnetic waves, this question is easy to answer: each pure or 'monochromatic' light source can be described by its wavelength within the visible range of electromagnetic waves, which is perceived as a particular colour, and its intensity, which is perceived as brightness (Hubel 1988). A natural light source, such as the sun, is rarely monochromatic (i.e. a single wavelength) but usually is the combination of a range of wavelengths that contribute to the light with different intensities – this distribution of wavelengths between 400 nm (violet) and 700 nm (red) is called the 'visible spectrum' of the light source (see Colour plate III, Figure 2a). Although the light source is made up from several monochromatic components, an observer cannot separate these components of its spectrum and perceives it as one single colour: the spectrum of a (white) fluorescent light, for instance, has a number of bright peaks superimposed on a broad wavelength distribution across the entire visible range – which you only can see on their own if you separate them by means of a prism (or by looking at the bands of colour in the reflections from a CD!). It is important to note that wavelength and relative intensity of each wavelength constitute two independent dimensions, which are both needed to describe the light, apart from its overall brightness.

PERCEPTUAL PROPERTIES OF COLOUR

Whereas the physical description of colour is comparatively easy, albeit specific equipment is required to record the spectrum of a particular light source, the perception of colour is immediate, but difficult to describe. The most important relationship between the physics and perception of light has been captured by Isaac Newton (Newton 1704) in his radical statement: 'the rays, to speak properly, are not coloured. In them there is nothing else than a certain power and disposition to stir up a sensation of this or that colour'. In other words, there is no immediate relationship between the physical properties of the light beam, which cannot be seen directly, and the perceived quality of the corresponding area of the visual field, which appears to the observer as one particular colour. However, the perceived colour of objects is what matters in everyday life - professionals like painters, drapers and printers know very well that the choice and persistence of colours is key to their business. In the current day and age it would be considered almost impossible to sell a newspaper or magazine printed purely in black and white rather than being illustrated with colour photographs. Despite its great importance, the perceptual quality of colours is very difficult to describe. We will look now at various possibilities of identifying particular colours and arranging them in a systematic way, and will return in the next section to the question of how the physical properties of light are encoded in the visual system to generate such perceptual properties.

In the first instance, we tend to identify colours by names such as 'yellow', 'red' or 'green'. It is a commonplace that it can sometimes be rather difficult to convince different observers to agree about the name of a chosen colour, and indeed different individuals use the same names for only a small number of colours (Boynton and Olson 1990). However, it is crucial to define perceived colours precisely, for instance when one tries to reproduce colours veridically, or when a colour should be reserved for a particular use, such as particular colours 'owned' by a brand. Just think of the impact of a special red that is used to advertise a certain fizzy drink, and equally is associated with the overcoat of Father Christmas. Colour systems such as the CIE 1931 colour space (Broadbent 2004) were developed to reliably identify colours across inter-individual differences. Systematic experiments to investigate accurately the use of colour names with a general colour system built from colour chips that are easy to use (Munsell 1912; Munsell and Farnum 1941) started in the 1960s. Apart from confirming scientifically a considerable variation between individuals in the use of colour names, an interesting observation was made when comparing colour names in different cultures. The system and number of colour names can vary considerably in different cultures, and additional colour names seem to be introduced in languages in a peculiar order (shown in Colour plate III, Figure 3a), which resembles an evolutionary sequence (Berlin and Kay 1999). Even more intriguingly, the frequency of using colour names in English seems to reflect this hierarchy of colour names, and there is some discussion whether the order of acquisition of colour names follows a similar sequence (Pitchford and Mullen 2005). The biggest limitation of colour naming in describing percepts arises from the fact that there is only a small number of true colour names that require inherently difficult categorisation (Davidoff 2001), whereas there is a huge number of different colours – as a work-around, we often tend to use mixed names or well-known objects to refer to a colour, like 'blue-green' or 'plum'. Still, can you easily agree with your friends exactly what a 'tomato-red' T-shirt is?

Since the different colours seem to be located in a continuum of subtle changes between their appearance, a lot of effort by many thinkers and practitioners has gone into designing systems of similarity that can be used to arrange colours in a systematic way, which is sometimes referred to as a 'colour atlas' (Irtel 2000). The rationale behind various colour schemes led to sometimes heated debates, for instance between the scientist Newton and the poet Goethe, about the value, limitations and flaws of each of these systems (Duck 1988). In the most simple version of a map, colours can be arranged according to similarity on a circle, as illustrated in Colour plate III, Figure 3b based on colour labels used for Munsell chips. Whereas it is clear that this basic 'Munsell colour wheel' covers some very prominent colours, there are many mixed colours missing from the wheel, and it presents only a single level of saturation (how pale or strong a colour is, sometimes also known as 'chroma') and a single level of brightness.

There is now general agreement that the best way of arranging colours is according to their similarity thus allowing for smooth neighbourhood relationships and well-defined distances. This method leads to the colour wheel (cf. Colour plate III, Figure 3b), which follows the sequence of colours in the rainbow: red, orange, yellow, green, blue, indigo and finally violet, which is close again to red and closes the circle. The next step is to add concentric circles of the same sequence of colours, which differ in the strength of the colours from pale white in the centre to very strong colouration in the outer rings. This arrangement of colours creates a two-dimensional colour wheel, reflecting the two independent physical dimensions and corresponding to the two independent perceptual dimensions, which are usually referred to as *hue* and *saturation*. Hue refers to the perceptual quality that is related to discriminating categories of colour, like red, green, blue, and their intermediate stages. The saturation refers to the perceptual quality related to be intensity or richness of colour sensation – it tells us how strong or vivid a colour is as compared a pale grey region. Two patches in a visual scene, which differ in their hue or saturation, or both, but are identical in their brightness, are called isoluminant – they only can be discriminated on the basis of their colour. It is worthy of note that in the colour space contrast can be created in two independent dimensions, through differences in hue or through differences in saturation, while keeping brightness contrast constant (cf. Colour plate III, Figure 2b). If we also consider the intensity (overall energy) of a light source, which will affect its brightness, we have to deal with a set of colour wheels that contain dark (low-intensity) and light (high-intensity) colours, and correspondingly vary from black to white in the centre of each wheel. A more comprehensive system that adds the brightness dimension (called 'HSB' with reference to the three independent components, hue, saturation and brightness) therefore looks more like a cylinder, with the *brightness* axis running up and down through it. Each horizontal slice of the cylinder then looks like a solid colour wheel, in which the *hue* is given by the angular position and the *saturation* by the distance from the centre.

In summary, at constant brightness a two-dimensional system can be understood as a prototype for a reasonable perceptual description and neural representation of arbitrary colour stimuli. In other words, such a colour space could be used to measure perceived colour. The metric of such measurements is based on the fact that every spectral composition of a stimulus, at a given brightness, can be converted into a unique combination of hue and saturation. Such a colour space can then be used to investigate colour perception objectively and systematically, for instance using the standardised set of coloured chips developed by Munsell that covers the complete colour space (Munsell and Farnum 1941). Using these Munsell chips, discrimination thresholds can be measured for similar colours, which are perceptually just about separable, which allows us in turn to estimate the number of different colours we can see: about 5 million! Note that this about 1,000 times more than the number of grey levels, which we are able to discriminate, but only a third of the colours that can be produced by means of a 24-bit computer display (16 million colours). This supports the general statement made at the beginning of this chapter that colour vision increases considerably the amount of information that can be collected by the human visual system.

THEORIES OF COLOUR VISION

The relationship between the physical properties of light and the perceptual quality of colour needs to be addressed by developing a theory of colour vision, which in itself should be related to the physiological properties of the neural system that is responsible for the transformation of this visual stimulus into a percept. In the basic condition an appropriate model is given by the properties of the colour space, with independent encoding of hue and saturation, but on top of this a valid model also needs to explain other perceptual phenomena in the colour domain. A good theory of colour vision needs to consider the physiological basis of colour processing in the visual system, which was briefly mentioned in Chapter 2 in the overview of the visual stream. Additional detail will be filled in where needed, but the colour vision stream is not discussed comprehensively because our focus is on the fundamental design principles of colour vision, and not on the actual implementation in the nervous system. In the following sections, the two central historical theories of colour vision will be reviewed, compared and put into the context of more recent research.

The first theory, which is usually referred to as the *theory of trichromatic colour vision*, is attributed to its most prominent promoters, Thomas Young (Young 1802) and H. v. Helmholtz (von Helmholtz 1852). This theory is based on the fundamental observation of additive colour mixing: superposition of coloured spotlights produces new colours. Most importantly, each coloured spotlight can be generated by superimposing three basic colours, sometimes referred to as 'primaries' (see Colour plate IV, Figure 1a). This phenomenon, for instance, provides the rationale for designing RGB computer and TV screens, which in each pixel mix red, green and blue light to create any visible colour. It should be noted in passing that additive mixing of spotlight colours is quite different from subtractive colour mixing in paints – the pigments that define the perceived colour of a paint remove specific components from the spectrum of the illuminating light in the reflected light (i.e. blue paint removes green and red components from a white illuminant), which leads to radically different mixing properties that resemble tinted filters.

The crucial observation supporting the trichromatic theory of colour vision is that in a controlled experiment any colour can be matched by the additive superposition of three differently coloured lights (see Colour plate IV, Figure 1b) that serve as 'primary' colours. Two such lights that are composed of different spectral components but appear identical to the human observer are called 'metamers'. This could happen in the simple comparison of white sunlight, which covers the full spectrum with the combination of red, green and blue monochromatic lights, as in the basic case shown in Colour plate IV, Figure 1a, or by mixing carefully the same primaries to generate the light blue-green shown in Colour plate IV, Figure 1b. Blue, green and red are a popular choice for the primaries corresponding to the wavelength sensitivity of the three types of photoreceptors that can be found in the retina (Hubel 1988), which by the use of different light-sensitive pigments are tuned to short (S), middle (M) and long (L) wavelengths, respectively. As shown in Colour plate IV, Figure 2a, each receptor type absorbs light over a broad range of wavelengths and peaks at different locations. The relative activation of these three receptors gives rise to the phenomenon of metamers (see Colour plate IV, Figure 1b): each light source will activate the three receptors in a particular proportion that can be matched exactly by another light, for instance an appropriate combination of the RGB primaries, which therefore must lead to the same perceived colour. This characterisation of perceived colour space, however, only holds for the 'normal' visual system. In humans, we can find a variety of genetic alterations that affect the structure and function of retinal photopigments and lead to substantial changes in the range of perceived colours, which are commonly known as 'colour vision deficiencies' or 'colour blindness' (Sharpe et al. 2001).

Note that the design of the sensory system, that is, the spectral sensitivity of the photoreceptors, is limiting the information that can be collected, and thus determines the perceptual properties, as incorporated in the trichromatic theory of colour vision. The physiological colour space directly related to the photoreceptor sensitivity (LMS space) is used to determine specific colours, which allows experimenters to separate photoreceptors in psychophysical experiments. The LMS colour space can be converted into other systems of colour definitions (for instance RGB, CMYK or CIE colour norms) that are used in technical contexts such as monitors, or computer graphics software like Photoshop. Colour plate IV, Figure 2b shows the locations of the photoreceptor optima and of the RGB primaries in the CIE 1931 colour space, indicating schematically how the gamut of all visible colours (i.e. all different values of chromaticity in this diagram) can be generated from a combination of the primaries, and can be picked up through the different activation levels of the three receptor types.

Although the trichromatic theory of colour vision provides a good explanation for additive colour mixing and the existence of perceived colour metamers, there are other aspects of colour perception that are not accounted for by this theory. The fundamental observation that there is no colour that is perceived as 'greenish' red or 'blueish' yellow, and no 'redish' green or 'yellowish' blue, suggests that red and green, as well as blue and yellow, seem to exclude each other in perception. This mutual exclusion of two pairs of basic colours is the starting point for the *opponent process theory of colour vision*, which was developed by E. Hering in the late nineteenth century (Hurvich and Jameson 1960). The central suggestion is that the perceptual space of colour vision is determined by two pairs of opponent colours that exclude each other, constituting a red-green and a blue-yellow axis of colour perception, respectively. Arguably, the opponent process is most visible in the phenomenon of contrast enhancement in the colour domain where, for instance, a light grey line appears pale green in front of a red background and pale red in front of a green background (see Colour plate IV, Figure 3a). Similarly, a homogeneous colour field tends to look more yellow in front of a blue background, and more blue in front of a yellow background (see coloured Koffka ring in Colour plate IV, Figure 3b). Simultaneous colour contrast is skilfully employed by many painters, and features strongly in the aesthetic theory of some artists such as Josef Albers (Albers 1975).

The enhancement of colour differences across space resembles simultaneous brightness contrast that was described in the previous chapter, apart from the fact that it always operates in the blue-yellow or green-red colour direction (see Jameson and Hurvich 1964). This similarity of contrast enhancement in the brightness and colour domain, respectively, suggests that similar opponent processing mechanisms are underlying the perceptual phenomenon. Indeed, neurons have been found in the LGN and primary visual cortex (DeValois and Jacobs 1968; Hubel 1988), which have distinct receptive field regions that are preferentially sensitive to opponent colours. Yet some other neurons, called 'double opponent cells', have concentric receptive fields (similar to those that we encountered in the previous chapter in the brightness domain), which increase their activity when the centre is stimulated by one colour and decrease their activity when the centre is stimulated by the opponent colour, and respond inversely during stimulation of the surround (Livingstone and Hubel 1988; Ts'o and Gilbert 1988). Colour opponency in these neurons needs to be generated through reorganisation of the spectral information captured by the S, M and L photoreceptors for each stimulus location (Chatterjee and Callaway 2003), as has been predicted on the basis of psychophysical results (Hurvich and Jameson 1960). Most importantly, this reorganisation of the encoding of colour in the nervous system between the retinal input count of representation at higher cortical levels allows us to regard the trichromatic theory and the opponent process theory no longer as competitors for a single explanation of colour vision, but instead as complementary explanations that describe different aspects of the visual system by different coding strategies at different levels of neural processing (see Colour plate V, Figure 1). The heated scientific debate about which of the two main theories of colour vision is right was dissolved into peaceful coexistence by assuming two processing stages!

SIMULTANEOUS AND SUCCESSIVE COLOUR CONTRAST

Colour contrast may be experienced not only simultaneously across space, but can also be perceived in time, as after-effect: after staring at images of high contrast for some time, an opposite polarity after-image is perceived when you look at a white or grey surface. For instance, after fixating the black dot in the centre of the left panel of Colour plate V, Figure 2 for a minute and then turning to the black dot in the right panel, you see a pink ring embedded in a pale green region. More generally, prolonged exposure to highly saturated versions of simple coloured patterns leads to the perception of soft patterns of the opponent colour when the stimulus is removed and a uniform surface is shown. Such successive colour contrast, or colour after-effects – opponent processing in time – are another dramatic demonstration of the perceptual organisation of colour space along the two independent dimensions red-green and blue-yellow. How can we explain after-effect, what happens in the neurons encoding colour when such after-images are perceived?

Three aspects of visual encoding are important to understand after-effects (Anstis et al. 1978; Jameson and Hurvich 1964). (1) *Adaptation* is a natural property of sensory neurons, which reduces the response of individual cells during prolonged stimulation. Immediately after the onset of the red-green stimulus, when looking at the central fixation dot, the response of individual neurons sensitive to red or green jumps to a maximum value, depending on their location in the visual field, which determines whether they are stimulated by red or green image regions, and then gradually returns to small levels by reduction of their sensitivity. Note that this 'adaptation' means that only temporal changes are encoded, and the response is reduced when the stimulus is constant. This mechanism removes redundancy in the time domain, similar to the removal of redundancy in space by means of opponent receptive fields, which you read about in the last chapter. Note that it also means that there is some kind of temporal filling-in because colours are not perceived as fading with time. (2) *Opponency* in the colour domain, according to the opponent theory of colour vision, means that stimulus components of opposite quality (red-green, or blue-yellow) are subtracted from each other at each given location in the receptive field. Therefore the perceived colour at any given location is determined by the difference between green and red activation. In the red areas of Colour plate V, Figure 2 the green input is zero, and the subtracted result of the opponent mechanism corresponds to the red input, adapting from a strong initial activity to much-reduced levels after continuing stimulation; the inverse will happen for the green areas, where the red input is zero, and the green input reduces sensitivity through adaptation. (3) The *after-effect* is perceived by looking at the neutral stimulus, the white field, which provides the same stimulus energy to the red, green, blue and yellow colour channels (remember that white light contains all colours and equally stimulates all photoreceptors). At the end of the adaptation period locations previously stimulated by green light are less sensitive to green than to red, and vice versa. After stimulus offset, when looking at the fixation spot in the white field, the white light appears light red where the green light was shown before, because a larger neural signal is generated in the non-adapted red channel than in the adapted green channel, producing a red response after subtraction in opponent cells, and vice versa for regions that previously were exposed to red. This local imbalance between the red and green input to the opponent mechanism means that after stimulus offset weak colours are perceived with opponent hue to that presented before. What we observe, is colour contrast enhancement in the time domain. Colour after-images can also be used to make greylevel photographs appear coloured, after the adaptation: to a coloured version of the same photograph in which the natural colours are inverted (see http://www.johnsadowski.com/big_spanish_castle.php).

The adaptation and after-effect phenomena discussed so far are reflecting mechanisms that change the properties of neurones, and thus of sensory systems, at rather short timescales of

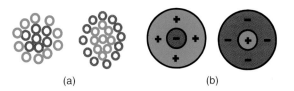

(a)   (b)

Colour plate I, Figure 1 Two-dimensional receptive fields as seen in top view on the retinal projection of the visual field. (a) Plotting the receptive fields of retinal ganglion cells with a spotlight reveals their structure (Kuffler 1953); regions on the stimulus screen which activate (green circles) and deactivate (red circles) the neurons distinguish ON-centre and OFF-centre cells. (b) Schematic sketch of concentric receptive fields as found in ganglion cells or LGN neurons; regions of the visual field that excite (green) and inhibit (red) a sensory neuron, respectively, are illustrating the opponency for the centre and surround.

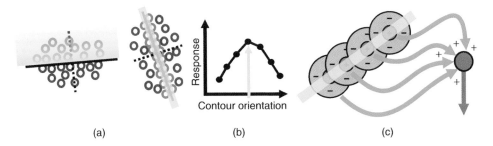

(a)   (b)   (c)

Colour plate I, Figure 2 Orientation sensitive receptive fields. (a) Plotting the receptive fields of simple cells in the visual cortex with a spotlight reveals their structure (Hubel 1963); regions on the stimulus screen which activate (green circles) and deactivate (red circles) these neurons; note that the best stimulus for these field structures, leading to maximum spike rates in the neuron, are a luminance edge (shown here as yellow edge) or a bright line (yellow bar). (b) Such a receptive field structure leads to orientation tuning – the preferred stimulus generates maximum activity at a particular orientation (indicated by yellow arrow). (c) Schematic sketch (after Hubel 1988) of how a set of concentric receptive fields as found in ganglion cells (green spots with pale red surrounds) regions can be integrated (green arrows) to design a simple cell (blue) that preferentially responds to an oriented line (yellow bar).

Colour plate I, Figure 3 Simultaneous contrast illusions explained. The small grey square looks brighter when embedded in a dark large square (centre left panel) than when embedded in a bright square (centre right panel), although it has the same shade of grey. A centre-surround receptive field (sketched as in Colour plate I, Figure 1b) receives less inhibition by the dark surround (pale red in left panel) than by the bright surround (saturated red in right panel), whereas the excitation from the centre (saturated green) is identical in both conditions. As a result, the final activity level that determines perceived brightness is higher with the dark background than with the bright background.

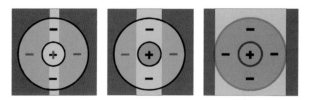

Colour plate I, Figure 4 Centre-surround receptive fields are tuned to stimulus size (here: a bright stripe of variable width in front of dark background) or spatial detail. A narrow stimulus stripe (left panel) leads to small excitation and small inhibition, and therefore to a small filter response; a medium-sized stimulus stripe (centre panel) leads to large excitation and little inhibition, and therefore to a large filter response; a wide stimulus stripe (right panel) leads to a large excitation and a large inhibition, and therefore to a small filter response.

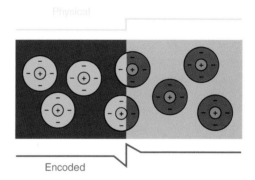

Colour plate I, Figure 5 Centre-surround receptive fields increase contrast (the relative difference of brightness) at a luminance border and suppress redundant signal components (signals which do not contain information) in regions without luminance change. The luminance levels across the border of the dark-bright stimulus field ('physical') are indicated by the yellow step function above the stimulus sketch in arbitrary units. Inside the dark field, the ON-centre receptive fields (sketched as in Colour plate I, Figure 1) generate very little excitation and no inhibition (pale red and green), so the final filter response is close to zero; inside the bright field, strong excitation is balanced by strong inhibition (saturated colours), so the final filter response is close to zero again; on the left side of the border, the inhibition is stronger than the excitation, so the final filter response is negative; on the right side of the border, the excitation is stronger than the inhibition, so the final filter response is positive. The strength of the filter responses is indicated by the red profile ('encoded') below the stimulus sketch in arbitrary units.

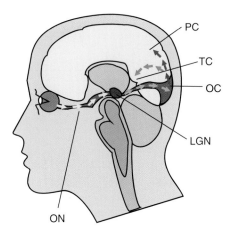

Colour plate II, Figure 1 Processing in the visual stream. The visual scene is captured by the left and the right eye and transmitted through the optic nerve (ON) and the Lateral Geniculate Nucleus (LGN) into the occipital cortex (OC), from where it is distributed into various parts of the parietal (PC) and temporal (TC) regions of the cortex. In this network of serial and parallel processing, different components of the incoming information (features) are dealt with separately, to be later recombined (in a process called 'feature binding' by psychologists or 'data fusion' by engineers) to form unitary perceptions for a range of high-level processes, such as recognition, decision making or motor planning and control.

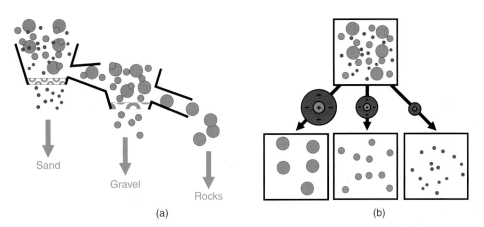

Colour plate II, Figure 2 Filtering. (a) Think of the brain as a gravel pit: when the sorting engine is fed with a mix of rocks (blue disks), pebbles (green), sand (red), different grains are separated by a set of sieves which act as a filter – and different grains can be collected in different containers. (b) In the same way, think of the visual stream in the brain as a set of filters (spatial frequency channels, indicated by concentric receptive fields) that separate features of different spatial scale (or size) – and image representations with coarse (blue discs) to fine spatial grain (red dots) are generated in the brain.

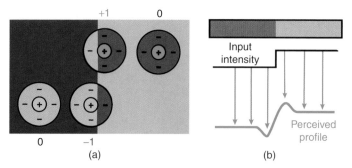

Colour plate II, Figure 3 Contrast enhancement (similar to Colour plate I, Figure 5). (a) Opponent ON-centre receptive fields – shown as simplified opponency model (cf. Figure 2.9) with a central excitatory (light and saturated green) and a surrounding inhibitory (red, pink) sub-region – at a different spatial position of a pattern with a prominent luminance step; reduced response (0) in coherently dark and bright areas: excitation and inhibition cancel each other; negative response (−1 in arbitrary units) at dark side of boundary: more inhibition than excitation; positive response (+1) at bright side of boundary: more excitation than inhibition. (b) schematic sketch of the encoding of a luminance step function (intensity function, black line) is encoded through such opponency operators into a profile encoded in a activity profile which corresponds to the perceived contrast enhancement.

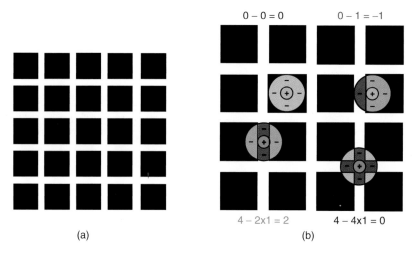

Colour plate II, Figure 4 (a) Can you see grey spots in the white intersections of lines of this 'Hermann Grid'? (b) Opponent receptive fields – shown schematically as in Colour plate II, Figure 3 – at different spatial positions of the Hermann grid would generate no response within the black squares (top left: no stimulation of excitatory and inhibitory regions) and a smaller response in the intersections of the edges (bottom right: full excitation and inhibition) than in the edges themselves (bottom left: full excitation, some inhibition). However, for the same reason the squares should be darker in regions close to the white edges (top right: some inhibition, no excitation).

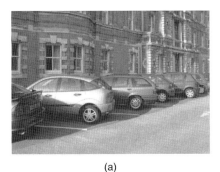 

(a)   (b)

Colour plate III, Figure 1 When trying to identify one particular object within a group, such as an individual car in a car park (see black and white picture in (a)), you could describe the exact location, or use of a set of properties such as shape, size or any engineering peculiarities. If you are able to perceive colour you just need to know how it is painted (see the blue car in the picture colour picture (b)).

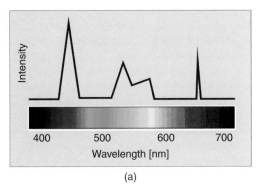 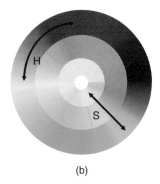

(a)   (b)

Colour plate III, Figure 2 The physics of colour. (a) The physical description of the light source is defined by the combination of wavelength and relative intensity between 400 nm and 700 nm, its 'visible spectrum'. (b) The perceptual description of colour reflects these two independent dimensions because we need to identify a position along the colour wheel (e.g., blue, green, yellow, red, indicated by arrow H) – the *hue* of the patch of image we are looking at – and *the saturation* of the perceived colour in the patch (indicated by arrow S). These two dimensions are independent of overall amount of light captured by the eye, which corresponds to *brightness*.

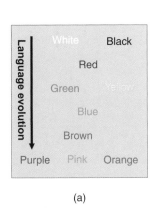 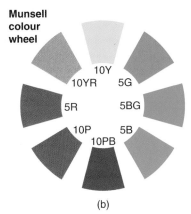

(a)   (b)

Colour plate III, Figure 3 Identifying colours. (a) Colour names are notoriously variable in their use and appear in a particular order in different languages, suggesting some kind of evolution. (b) In this simple Munsell colour wheel the different hues (at fixed saturation and brightness) are arranged in a circular fashion such that neighbouring colours resemble each other.

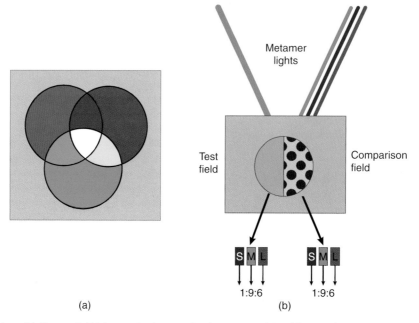

(a)   (b)

Colour plate IV, Figure 1 Trichromatic theory of colour vision. (a) Additive colour mixing in spotlights: red and green superimpose to yellow; green and blue superimpose to turquoise; blue and red superimpose to purple; and all three lights superimpose to white. (b) The key experiment to support the trichromatic theory demonstrates that any arbitrary colour projected into a test field can be matched by the superposition of three primary colours superimposed onto a comparison field, such that the two fields cannot be separated from each other by a human observer.

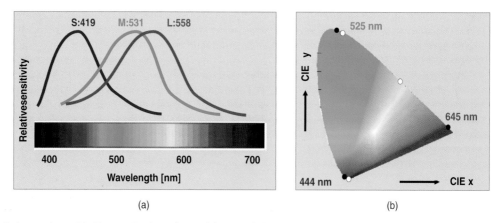

(a)   (b)

Colour plate IV, Figure 2 Physiological basis of the trichromatic processes of colour vision. (a) Absorption spectra for the three types of cones in the retina that preferentially respond to short (S: blue line), medium (M: green line) and long (L: red line) wavelengths of monochromatic stimuli. (b) This photoreceptor colour sensitivity is located in key locations in the CIE 1931 colour space (white dots indicate optimum sensitivity for S, M, L), indicating that from the combined activation of these receptors the full gamut of all visible colours can be encoded. The diagram also shows the locations of the RGB primaries (black dots, plus characteristic wavelengths) – all visible colours can be generated by a combination of these three primaries.

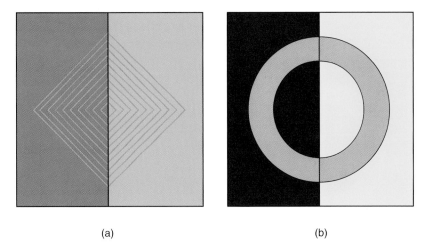

(a)   (b)

Colour plate IV, Figure 3 Simultaneous colour contrast illusions. (a) The diagonal lines generating the diamond shape pattern appear slightly tinted greenish in front of the red background, and pink in front of the green background, although they are printed in identical grey. (b) Partitioned 'Koffka Ring' in the colour domain – the left half of the ring (blue background) appears more yellow and the right (yellow background) half appears more blue.

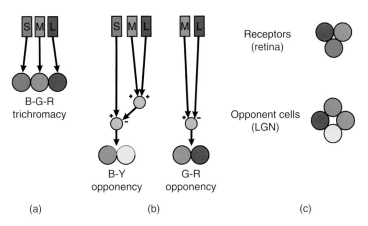

(a)   (b)   (c)

Colour plate V, Figure 1 Connectivity of retinal photoreceptors in colour vision. (a) In the retina the three types of photoreceptors tuned to different light wavelengths (S, L, M) separate three colour channels that are the basis for trichromatic encoding with primaries such as red, green and blue. (b) In the LGN and cortical areas the S, L and M inputs are reorganised to generate colour-opponent properties along the Blue-Yellow and Red-Green colour axes. (c) The coexistence of these two processing stages means that at different levels of the visual system different properties of colour vision can be found: trichromatic colour mixing at retinal level and colour opponency at LGN and cortical levels.

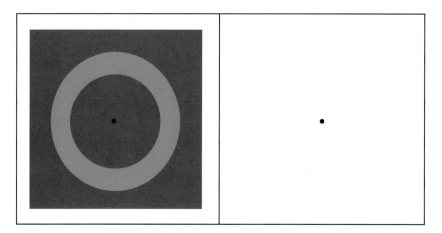

Colour plate V, Figure 2 Fixate the black dot in the centre of the panel for about 60 seconds and then look at the black dot on the right! What you will see, is a pink ring embedded within a light green region – an opponent colour after-effect.

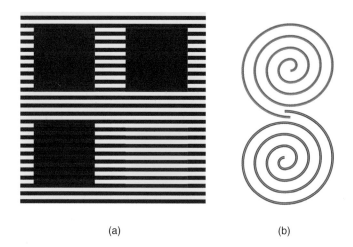

(a)   (b)

Colour plate V, Figure 3 Colour assimilation. (a) Superposition of yellow or blue strips (bottom) on red squares (top) makes the red change its appearance dramatically – this Munker-White Illusion is a case of colour assimilation, where object boundaries override simple colour contrast effects. (b) In the Watercolour Illusion the coloured lines enclosing white image regions are spreading their chromatic properties into these regions as 'neon colours'.

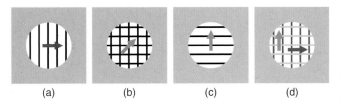

(a)   (b)   (c)   (d)

Colour plate VI, Figure 1 Motion plaids. Compound patterns, created by vertical gratings moving horizontally (a) and horizontal gratings moving vertically (c) appear to move diagonally if the components are similar (b), but are perceived as transparently sliding across each other if the components differ in colour or other properties (d).

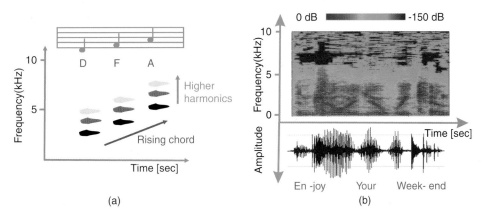

(a)   (b)

Colour plate VI, Figure 2 Spectrograms. (a) The representation of a simple rising chord; the composition of different frequencies and amplitudes is indicated by different greylevel patches as function of time, with a set of higher harmonics for each of the three tones, D, F and A. (b) Spectrogram of a male voice speaking the phrase 'enjoy your weekend' (intensities of individual frequency components are now shown in colour code); the spectrum contains a wide spread of frequencies with characteristic rising and falling tones; at the bottom the corresponding waveform envelope is shown (measured as picked up by a microphone), mainly showing the dynamics in the volume of the voice.

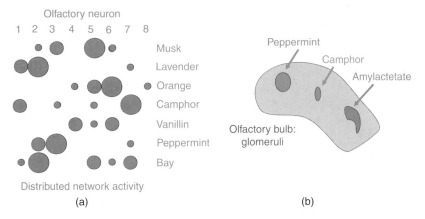

(a)   (b)

Colour plate VI, Figure 3 Neural code of olfaction. (a) At receptor level each sensory neuron (columns) responds to a range of stimuli (rows) and each stimulus activates a range of sensory neurons (columns), constituting a population code. (b) At the level of the olfactory bulb, the activation of individual glomeruli reflects particular stimuli, that is, different stimuli can be mapped to different locations.

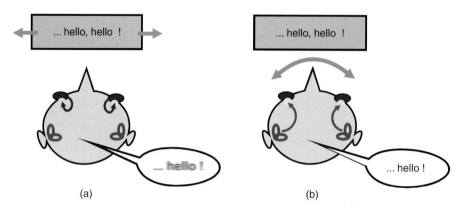

Colour plate VII, Figure 1 Vestibulo-ocular reflex (VOR). (a) When you move a page with text (green rectangle) from side to side (green arrows) in front of you eyes (blue) at a high speed, the text becomes blurred (thought bubble at the back of the head), because the eyes (driven by the retinal motion signals, blue arrows) cannot follow the movement fast enough. (b) When you shake the head at the same speed (green arrow), the text is not blurred, because the vestibular signals (red arrows) can drive compensatory eye movements at higher speeds.

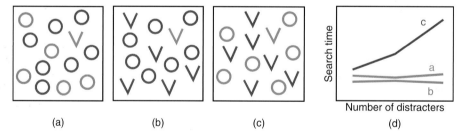

Colour plate VII, Figure 2 In an 'odd item out' task, which requires the participant to find a singleton in a group of distracters, some elements pop out immediately, such as the single V among different O's (a), or the single blue symbol among different red symbols (b). (c) In contrast, the search for a singleton defined by conjunctional features, such as the blue V amongst blue O's and red V's, requires effort and attention that guides a serial search through all items.

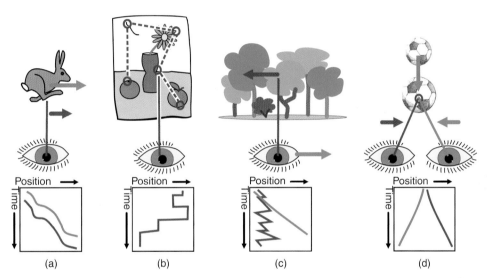

Colour plate VII, Figure 3 Sketches of how the eye moves in the environment for four different types of eye movements. Direction of gaze is indicated by red/green line connecting the left/right eye to the location fixated (red circle) and movement of observer or objects are symbolised by blue arrows. The space–time diagrams (cf. Chapter 6) show the position of the object (blue line) and eye (red and green line) as function of time. (a) Smooth pursuit. (b) Saccadic scanning. (c) Optokinetic nystagmus. (d) Vergence.

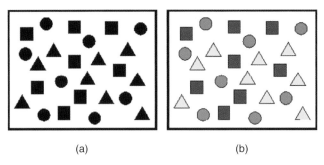

(a)   (b)

Colour plate VIII, Figure 1 Synaesthesia. The random set of three types of simple black shapes (a) can be experienced by synaesthetes as associated with three basic colours, red squares, blue circles and yellow triangles.

(a)

(b)

Colour plate VIII, Figure 2 The appearance of two species of Damsel fish living together in the Great Barrier Reef, Pomacentrus amboinensis (a) and Pomacentrus moluccensis (b), look pretty much identical to the colour system of humans (left). In UV light that is outside of the visible range of most animals but not of Damsel fish (right), however, there are distinct facial patterns that can be recognised by these animals. (Courtesy of U. Siebeck, UoQ, Australia.)

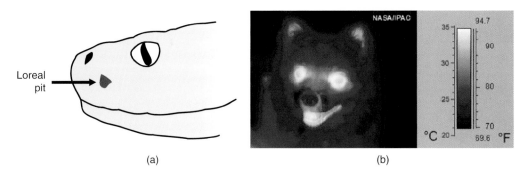

(a)   (b)

Colour plate VIII, Figure 3 Infrared vision. (a) The loreal pit organ is used by rattlesnakes for imaging heat patterns and allows them to hunt in the night. (b) Thermal image of a dog (from Wikimedia Commons, http://en.wikipedia.org/wiki/File: Infrared dog.jpg, accessed on August 8, 2009); the temperature colour scale shows that most of the body heat is lost through the eyes, mouth and ears.

seconds to minutes. Such plasticity is very important for living beings to respond in the best possible way to a changing environment, and technically speaking to move a system into a state where its operating range captures and processes the information available most efficiently. On a much longer timescale, we can interpret learning as plasticity with a similar function: as a child you have to learn that you pick and eat strawberries when they are red, but let them grow when they are still green, and have to learn how to use a knife to cut the strawberry into pieces. Apart from such elements of cognitive or motor learning, our sensory systems can be changed on a long timescale of days or weeks, by repetitive exposure to the same stimuli, and performance for perceptual tasks can improve substantially in what is called 'perceptual learning' (Fahle 2002). In colour vision a very peculiar case of plasticity was described on an intermediate timescale, the so-called McCullough effect: After a long exposure to patterns composed, for instance, from regions with red-black vertical gratings and others with green-black horizontal gratings, black and white gratings will appear pale green if oriented vertically and pale red if oriented horizontally (McCollough 1965). This contingent after-effect (it is called contingent because it relies on a combination of colour and orientation, and not on retinal location) works on an extended timescale – you not only need to look at the coloured induction pattern in the order of several minutes, but the after-effect most weirdly can stay with you for days! Recent work (Vladusich and Broerse 2002) suggests that this effect can be interpreted as result of a correction mechanism for colour-related imperfections of the eye (known as 'chromatic aberration'). All this evidence seems to suggest that slow and long-lasting adaptation processes in the visual system enable humans to adjust to changes of their typical environmental conditions.

In summary, simultaneous and successive contrast illusions demonstrate that image properties are not perceived in absolute terms, but relative to their immediate environment in space and time. We therefore can conclude that opponency, leading to contrast enhancement and redundancy reduction, is a fundamental process in the visual system, which is operating in the spatial and temporal domains. What does this mean in terms of understanding the function of sensory systems? We have as a starting point to develop a more general *theory of vision*, such as the general role of opponent filter mechanisms, which can be implemented as adaptation mechanisms and centre–surround receptive fields, and is perceived as the increase/decrease in the apparent brightness of a line in front of a darker/brighter background (see previous chapter), the same perceptual changes for colour, or for other features such as orientation (Harris and Calvert 1989) or even faces (Hurlbert 2001; Zhao and Chubb 2001).

CAN WE SEE TRUE COLOURS?

The phenomena described so far, such as trichromatic metamers, spatial colour contrast and colour after-effects, demonstrate very clearly that there is no one-to-one relationship between the physical nature of the world surrounding us and its neural representation as available to perception – we are far away from perceiving 'true colour'. Furthermore, there are substantial individual differences in describing colours, which may have perceptual or cognitive origins (Davidoff et al. 1999), and there are some indications that there are cultural and possibly even gender differences in perceiving colour (Hurlbert and Ling 2007). It might be necessary to dig deeper and ask what we mean by true colours, and what we are really interested in when collecting information about our environment. At closer inspection, the spectral composition of a light source in itself might be fairly irrelevant, and it is object properties that are important for an animal or a person operating in a complex environment. The surface colour of a fruit, for instance, is an indicator of its state – we like it ripe and sweet – so we can ignore the actual spectral composition of the light reflected from such a surface, which can vary considerably depending on illumination (Osorio and Vorobyev 1996). The spectral composition of daylight changes dramatically during the day (Wyszecki and Stiles 1982), and the light reflected from a white sheet of paper contains more short wavelengths at noon (in particular when looking at the north sky) but is dominated by long wavelengths at sunset. Nevertheless, the white paper does not appear to the human eye as tinted blue or red, but is always perceived as white. The veridical representation of surface properties, independent of illumination, is known as 'colour constancy', which is attributed to adaptation and contrast normalisation mechanisms (Land 1977; Webster and Mollon 1995). The same mechanisms are responsible for perceiving surface colours correctly in bright sunlight, in the shade, or when looking through coloured filters, such as tinted sunglasses.

The importance of objects for visual perception may be key to understanding a variety of other illusions that are related to biasing perception towards uniform colours within enclosed regions, which is related to the transparency perceived for completed shapes (Anderson 1997). The Munker–White effect (White 1979) shown in Colour plate V, Figure 3a in a colour version (Schober and Munker 1967) demonstrates the assimilation of surface properties, which induces a change of perceived colour in some areas to make them appear more similar to their immediate neighbourhood. Note that this effect shifts perception in the opposite direction of simultaneous contrast. In the example of Colour plate V, Figure 3a the coloured strips are perceived as more yellow when crossed by yellow gratings, and more blue when crossed by blue gratings, whereas the two red squares behind the gratings have exactly the same colour (see top panels). Such assimilation, being the opposite effect of simultaneous contrast, typically is related to the use of periodic occluders (gratings) and clearly outlined simple objects. In Colour plate V, Figure 3b another assimilation effect is shown, the 'watercolour illusion' (Pinna et al. 2003). The coloured boundaries of the spirals spread as 'neon colours' into the physically white regions between the spiral lines. The images shown in Colour plate V, Figure 3 should remind us how much perceived colour can differ from the actual physical stimulus, and that in order to understand such perceptual distortions we need to know which perceptual tasks had been driving the evolution of neural encoding.

Take Home Messages

- colour vision adds value to visual processing by making chromatic information available that can be used for object recognition
- the basic properties of coloured light – spectra of light with different wavelengths – is the basis of designing systems to describe colour space (colour atlas)
- the trichromatic theory and the opponent process theory are the two major attempts to understand colour vision, which explain different aspects of perception, and can be related to different neural mechanisms
- the encoding of contrast in space and time reflects general principles of neural information processing and explain simultaneous and successive contrast illusions (after-effects)
- higher-level colour mechanisms, such as colour assimilation and colour constancy, emphasise the importance of recovering the properties of surface properties, and highlight the ecological function of colour vision

Discussion Questions

- Discuss the importance of colour vision in everyday life.
- What is meant by 'colour wheel'?
- Compare and evaluate the two most important theories of colour vision.
- How can we explain colour after-effects?

5 VISION 3: FROM IMAGES TO SPACE

OVERVIEW

We are living in a world with three spatial dimensions and an additional temporal dimension – but the eyes provide us with flat (2D) images. A single, static image, like a painting or photograph, contains a plethora of information, and humans have highly developed processing mechanisms to extract such information. Brightness and colour perception, shape perception and object recognition can operate to a large extent on the basis of static 2D representations. Adding depth information, however, has vital relevance for organising behaviour, because we operate in a dangerous 3D environment, and any predecessor in our evolution misjudging the distance of a branch in the canopy of the jungle, or being unaware of the abyss at a cliff, would have little chance to let us inherit genes that would determine such fallible depth perception. Our survey of visual depth information starts with pictorial cues: perspective, texture, contrast, size, occlusion; then moves on to binocular cues: signals generated by the movement of the eyes (vergence, accommodation) and by the different viewpoints of the two eyes (stereopsis); and finally describes dynamical cues (motion parallax), which is similar in its geometry to stereo, but very powerful at long distance. The range of possible depth cues and the range of processing mechanisms that are available to the human observer is discussed in relation to operating constraints (such as critical range), deficiencies (e.g. stereo-blindness) and applications (magic eye, 3D, IMAX®). A number of depth and size illusions, and their possible explanations, concludes this chapter: constancy scaling, Ponzo illusion, Ames room, hollow face illusion.

THE THIRD DIMENSION OF THE WORLD – DEPTH PERCEPTION

The world around us has four dimensions, three in space, and one in time. As illustrated in Figure 5.1, a real object can extend in one dimension, x, thus forming a line, or in two dimensions, x and y, thus forming a plane, or in three dimensions, x and y and z, thus forming a three-dimensional body in space. Such a body, in addition, can move or change its shape – such changes make use of the fourth dimension of our world, time. On the other hand, visual perception starts with retinal images as input information, which by their very nature are two-dimensional at any given moment. So how does the brain and reconstruct a third dimension from flat retinal images? Some initial hints about how to answer this question can come from the study of the art of painting. In the artistic representation, the eye, and the brain, is tricked by a painter who is producing no more than a flat image as a representation of the three-dimensional world which then serves as a stimulus for the eye. In many cases, with regard to depth perception, looking at painting would be very similar to looking at a photograph of the world, which usually would give a convincing impression of three dimensions. Because the eye itself represents the outside world, presenting an artificial representation of the world (a photograph or painting) to the eye

Figure 5.1

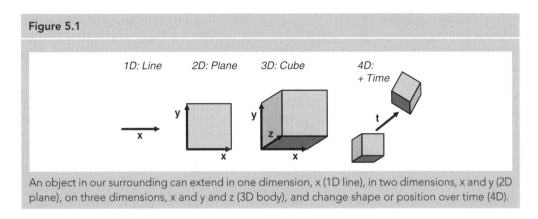

An object in our surrounding can extend in one dimension, x (1D line), in two dimensions, x and y (2D plane), on three dimensions, x and y and z (3D body), and change shape or position over time (4D).

can resemble perceptually looking at the real world, if the artificial representation contains all relevant cues that the brain needs to extract depth from flat retinal images. This is the reason why paintings, and later photographic images, have proven themselves to be such successful tokens of reality. Over the centuries of art history, painters have developed a very powerful tool box that helps them to create the illusion of depth on a flat canvas (Gombrich 1982) – Titian's painting *Bacchus and Ariadne* (1520, national Gallery London), for instance, is a vivid illustration of this point. Titian is using perspective, occlusion, shading and relative size to recreate the third spatial dimension, and telling the viewer the tragic story of Ariadne in dramatic detail – her body language expresses a mixture of curiosity and fear when she encounters Bacchus' raving party. If you look closely at the painting, you can also see how Titian gets hold of the fourth dimension, by creating a convincing impression of movement when Bacchus leaps from his chariot, and by symbolically expanding the narrative into the past (look at the ship in the background, which abandoned poor Ariadne on the island), and the future (look at the stars in the sky, which predict the transfiguration of Ariadne into a stellar constellation).

Apart from scientific curiosity about how the processing problem of depth can be resolved, what is the origin of the interest in, or fascination for, depth perception? Depth perception gives us access to the three-dimensional structure of the world, to the spatial relationships between objects and their shape, and tells us about distance. Grasping a piece of sugar on the breakfast table is a rather different control problem from moving a mouse cursor across the computer screen, and requires a completely different representation of task space. Having a clear view of the three-dimensional structure of the branches in the canopy of the rainforest was absolutely essential for the survival of our evolutionary ancestors, who simply would have crashed if they had made a mistake in trying to catch a branch while swinging from tree to tree. It is immediately obvious that during evolution an animal equipped with highly developed depth perception has an advantage over an animal that would navigate the canopy by trial and error. Equally, there are immediate evolutionary benefits arising from a highly developed visual system that allows for accurate estimation of distance – it helps us to assess the distance we would need to walk to a water source, for instance, or the distance from which a predator is watching us, or, in the modern world, the distance of a car on collision course. These random examples demonstrate how essential depth perception is for survival – we therefore can hardly be surprised to see that the visual system has a number of highly specialised modules dedicated to this purpose. This may also explain that some aspects of depth perception are well developed in the human infant from early on, possibly related to the onset of exploratory behaviour such as crawling in the first year of life (Gibson and Walk 1960).

And yet again, perception can leave us with fascinating puzzles about the relationship between physical reality and perceptual presentation. Flat images, like the line in Figure 5.2a, provide convincing representations of three-dimensional objects, although there is no doubt that they are nothing else than lines on a piece of paper. In this particular drawing of an 'impossible object' we easily interpret the left and right part of the figure as different 3D-objects, despite the fact there is no single object that can correspond to this combination of lines. Note that the impossibility of such an object, however, does not mean that you cannot build a real object that creates the very same illusion when seen from a particular angle (one such demonstration can be found in Gregory 1968). Interestingly, such relations between pictorial representation and reality appear to be closely connected to cultural practice (Deregowski 1972). Line drawings of three-dimensional objects can be substantially different from those that we are used to from West European representations. In some indigenous African cultures, we find drawings of elephants in which several views are combined in a single representation – the leg, ears and trunk of the elephant stick out from the torso in a bird's eye view, as if a giant had flattened the beast with the huge iron! Perspective drawing, which is perceived as 'naturalistic' and which determines the conventions of three-dimensional representation in Western Europe today, was championed during the Renaissance in the fifteenth and sixteenth centuries (Johnson 2005), replacing earlier painting practices, such as the characteristic side views and story lines in Egyptian paintings, or the ceremonial line-up of plane figures in Byzantine icons, which were characterised by a flat world and the symbolic representation of spatial relationships. The desire to create realistic representations of the natural world was reborn in the Renaissance, leading to a wide use of 'trompe-l'œil' (French: 'trick the eye') paintings in the Baroque, and is surrounded by a number of almost mythical anecdotes about the power of such illusionistic paintings, such as Cardinal handing a pen to the Pope asking for a signature, only to realise that this pope was nothing else than a painting of the Pope by Raffael. With the ascent of photography, such realism has lost its power, and obviously the intentions of modern painters are anything else than trying to create one-to-one representations of the outside world (Gombrich 1977). Art history, however, is providing plenty of evidence of

Figure 5.2

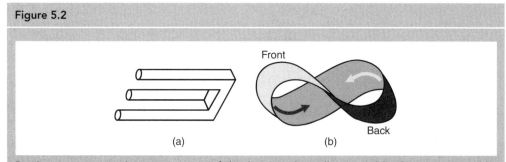

Front

Back

(a)   (b)

Puzzling questions in the interpretation of depth. (a) A physically impossible object generated by the projection of three-dimensional objects into two-dimensional line drawings – what looks like a Trident on the left turns out to be a U-shaped frame on the right. (b) In this physically possible but paradoxical structure, the so-called Mobius Belt, the two opposite surfaces of the belt in fact are a single surface as you can convince yourself when you follow the bright 'front' surface in the foreground to the medium grey surface in the background (bright arrow) and the bright 'back' surface in the foreground along its path to the medium grey surface in the background (dark arrow). For a nice artistic illustration of this paradox, see 'Mobius Belt II' by M. C. Escher (Escher 1971).

how easily the human visual system generates depth information from flat images, which it constantly needs to do, because nothing else than flat images is projected through the lenses on the retinal image plane of the eyes. Quite astonishingly, when looking from a shallow angle at a photograph or a painting that portrays an architectural space in linear perspective, it still gives the impression of a three-dimensional space, although all the geometric rules of perspective, which are the basis of such depth perception, are clearly violated under these conditions (Hagen 1980). Again, the relation between pictorial representation and reality can be very loose without irritating our perceptual system, or mental representation.

This reconstruction of the third dimension from the flat images captured by the eyes relies on a multitude of cues that can be derived from the real world. Painters concentrate on 'pictorial cues', which are visible in the static image of a single eye, such as relative size, perspective, occlusion, texture, contrast or shading. Two eyes are needed to capture 'binocular' depth information, which in many ways is more reliable. For instance, differences in the images from the two eyes (stereo), eye movement (oculomotor) signals such as movements that change the angle between the two eyes' gaze directions (vergence), and changes of the depth of focus of the lenses (accommodation) can only be used in the real, three-dimensional, world (Gibson 1950), and therefore often compete with pictorial cues (and mostly loose in the case of competition: see Hagen 1980). Finally, a powerful cue about distance arises from motion parallax, the relative shift of the retinal image when the observer moves through the world. These different cues will be described in the following sections.

PICTORIAL DEPTH CUES

Using a wide range of pictorial cues, depth information can be directly extracted from a static monocular image, both in image representations, which even may be simple sketches, and in natural scenes (Gibson 1950).

Arguably the most fundamental pictorial cue to depth is *linear perspective*, which is based on the simple geometrical fact that parallel lines in space, when projected on an image plane such as the retina, will converge on a single point – the so-called vanishing point. This effect is most obvious in architectural environments (see Figure 5.3a), which in the western world are made up almost exclusively of parallel and orthogonal lines. We are so much used to living in a rectangular environment that we easily misinterpret situations in which these conditions are violated (Figure 5.11). Linear perspective had been used in Roman paintings, but was later abandoned in western visual arts, only to be rediscovered during the Renaissance. Artists like Vasari developed a comprehensive theory of linear perspective, which from then onwards was used as a recipe to create the impression of highly naturalistic environments (Johnson 2005). The fact that linear perspective has only been used in certain periods of art history, and in certain cultures, raises the question whether the linear perspective is a perceptual universal based on the biological substrate of the human visual system or a historical and cultural construct (Deregowski 1972). It also seems clear that children need several years to develop the skill of perspective drawing (Chen and Cook 1984), and it has been debated whether this is the mere result of specific training. One might even ask whether to follow this 'convention' should be systematically encouraged in the educational curriculum, or whether it restrains the creative development of children. It is clear, however, that violations of the rules of perspective in pieces of art are highly visible, and usually employed consciously by artists and architects in many cultures who focus on other messages than just the realistic representation of the physical world.

For objects of known physical size, the *angular size* in the retinal image provides direct information about the distance from the observer (see sheep in Figure 5.3d). This is a simple consequence of projection geometry, which prescribes that angular size is inversely proportional to the distance. Using the inverse of this relationship is a most useful way of estimating the distance of dangerous objects, like predators whose body size should be well known to prey animals. In the modern world, for instance, from the angular size of the image of a car we (usually) can get a reliable feel about whether this car is far enough for us not to bother, or so close that we had better make a run. Indeed, we intuitively interpret angular size in many contexts as a token of distance, and it is generally believed that our knowledge about approaching objects is often based on changes in angular size (Lee 1976). Furthermore, there is evidence that this kind of information processing is available to infants at a very early age (Yonas et al. 1982), suggesting that angular size is an ecologically valid cue that can be trusted in many situations. It must not be forgotten, however, that this information can

Figure 5.3

(a)   (b)

(c)   (d)

Pictorial depth cues provide direct information about distance in a static, monocular image. (a) Linear perspective, which is most visible in architecture: parallel (white) lines in physical space converge in the image plane to the vanishing point on the horizon (St. Michel, Scriptorium). (b) Contrast and colour saturation: At large viewing distances the contrast in the retinal image is reduced, leading to 'aerial perspective' (Namadgi NP). (c) Texture: The retinal image of the surface structure, or visual texture, changes with viewing distance (Siena, Campo). (d) Size and height: The angular size of an object of constant physical size, here a sheep, decreases with distance from the observer (two sheep of similar physical size marked by white ellipses), and the height at which it is seen in the visual field increases with distance (Seven Sisters, Sussex).

only be used reliably if the assumptions about physical size are correct, and misjudgements by car drivers about the size of pedestrians can lead to casualties (Stewart et al. 1993)! Equally, and for the same geometrical reasons, for all objects that are attached to a flat ground plane we can work out from the *elevation* of this object in the visual field how far it is from us in the outside world (Bertamini et al. 1998). In simple creatures living on the surface of a level environment, such as crabs inhabiting mud flats, the height cue is so reliable that all objects that appear higher than the horizon line are interpreted as larger than the animal, and therefore as potential danger triggering an escape response, whereas moving objects below the horizon are accepted as part of the social communication system (Zeil and Hemmi 2006).

The retinal image of the surface structure, or visual *texture*, changes dramatically with viewing distance (such effects on tiling with two materials are shown in Figure 5.3c). This is partially due to the limited spatial resolution of visual system, which has been discussed in Chapter 3, which removes fine special detail from the retinal images of the surface texture. In addition, atmospheric disturbances such as haze, fog or rain reduce visibility with increasing distance. The change of surface texture is a very powerful cue for depth, raising a rather challenging problem for computer graphics, when rendering meshwork models of digitally produced objects with surface textures (Bülthoff and Mallot 1990) – without appropriate depth adjustments of such surface textures, watching digitally enhanced movies or playing video games would be rather disappointing for customers, and therefore much less successful, because the impression of depth and space would not be naturalistic.

For similar reasons, but at a much larger scale of distances, the apparent *contrast and colour saturation* in the retinal image is reduced at large viewing distances. This can be best seen in natural environments, where atmospheric factors such as haze, or in the extreme case fog, affect visibility. In Figure 5.3b a mountainous landscape is shown, where the clear image in the foreground fades into a faint mountain skyline close to the horizon, whereas the somewhat pale hills in the midrange still allow us to get a rough idea about their vegetation. This powerful, but often overlooked, phenomenon is usually referred to as 'aerial perspective', and has been developed to perfection by painters such as Leonardo da Vinci who used it very effectively in his background landscapes.

Closer objects occlude more distant objects. This very simple and – apart from partial coverage by transparent objects – reliable fact makes *occlusion* an unambiguous and perceptually powerful cue for depth order. On the left side of Figure 5.4a, three spheres of decreasing angular size are arranged such that the largest one occludes the medium-sized sphere, which occludes the smallest, and a clear depth order is established by occlusion that is in agreement with such angular sizes created by spheres of identical physical size: the farther away an object is, the smaller it looks; the closer object occludes the more distant one. On the right side of Figure 5.4a, the sphere with medium angular size occludes the smaller and larger spheres, suggesting that it is closest to the observer. Because its angular size is the same as on the left side, but it must be closer, it occludes the other spheres and its physical size must be smaller (and conversely, the sphere with the largest angular size has been pushed back on the right side, and therefore must be physically larger). This is exactly what you perceive when you compare the left and right side of Figure 5.4a.

Equally strong cues for three-dimensional structures are provided by *shading and cast shadows*, which arise from the illumination of a natural scene. The flat disc shown on the left of Figure 5.4b is perceptually transformed into a sphere by adding shading to the pictorial representation (middle), and attaching a grey diffuse spot (right), which signifies the shadow cast on the supporting surface, or texture (far right) further enhances the impression of three-dimensional

Figure 5.4

(a)

(b)

(c)

More pictorial depth cues. (a) Occlusion: Spheres which are closer to the observer occlude spheres which are further away. (b) Shading: Adding a luminance gradient to a circular region in the image suggests to the observer that the depicted object is not a flat disc but a three-dimensional sphere. This is further enhanced by adding texture cues as in the picture of a football. (c) Cast shadows: Attaching a cast shadow to an object in a 2D image further enhances the convincing impression of a 3D object, and also can disambiguate the position of such an object in space.

shape. The geometry of reflecting light from curved surfaces is a property that again has been used comprehensively by artists since the Renaissance, and, in reverse, is an aspect of sensory information processing that seems to be firmly embedded in the human visual system (Blake and Bülthoff 1990). Even more strikingly, the visual system seems to have an intuitive understanding of how shadows are cast from solid objects. The separation of the cast shadow from the object is only possible if an object no longer rests on the support plane. Indeed, the sequence of positions of spheres and cast shadows shown in Figure 5.4c physically corresponds to a sphere that is sitting on the ground on the left, and hovering at increasing levels above the ground in the middle and on the right, but staying at the same distance from the observer. If the cast shadows would have been attached to all three of these spheres, they would be interpreted by the human visual system as rolling on the ground on a diagonal path, increasing the distance from the observer, and hence being of different physical size (Kersten et al. 1997).

BINOCULAR AND DYNAMIC DEPTH CUES

Why do we have two eyes? There may be a number of different possible answers to this question, but in terms of perception there are two dominating aspects. Firstly, by having two eyes, we can extend our visual field. When closing the left and the right eye in alternation, you can immediately experience that the images from the two eyes overlap in some regions, but also cover exclusively some other areas of the visual field. Therefore, as illustrated in Figure 5.5 the combination of the two retinal images generates a larger visual representation of the outside world than each eye would provide in isolation (Gibson, 1979). This sketch also indicates that the relative position of particular objects, such as the feet of the observer, differs in the images from the two eyes. You can easily confirm this by focusing on your

Figure 5.5

| Left eye view | Right eye view |

The left eye and the right eye pick up different images of the environment (here the office of the author, as seen from the desk); these two images can be combined to retrieve stereo and oculomotor signals as depth cues (cf. Gibson 1979)

extended thumb and closing one of the two eyes in alternation. In addition to extending the visual field, the combination of such positional information from the different viewpoints of the two eyes is extremely valuable, because it allows for the precise depth measurements through *stereopsis*.

One way of using the separate images from the two eyes to estimate distance would be to fixate a particular object of interest, which will end up projected in each eye onto the fovea, the region of highest resolution on the retina. For a close object, one would need to turn both the eyes inward, which is called 'convergence'. For a distant object, the convergence of the viewing directions of the two eyes will be decreased, and they will be more or less parallel when looking at the distant horizon (see left panel of Figure 5.6). You can elicit these 'vergence' eye movements yourself, by looking firmly at your thumb while extending your arm and bringing it closer to your nose and back. If you observe the eye gaze of someone else making these fixation movements under your instructions, you will see that the eyes go through alternations of convergence and divergence movements, when the thumb is getting closer and farther from the eyes, respectively. With a little training you can even observe your own vergence eye movements in front of a mirror. From this systematic change of the difference of viewing angle between the two eyes the brain can estimate by means of simple trigonometry the distance of the object in focus, as long as the distance between the eyes is known. Similarly, the position of focus in depth, which is determined by the ciliary muscles controlling the eye's lens curvature, and thus eye accommodation, can be used by the brain as another physiological depth signal (Howard and Rogers 2008).

Stereopsis, on the other hand, is a visual mechanism of estimating the distance of objects that are not focused on, but instead is derived based on small shifts of corresponding projections in the two retinal images (Julesz 1971). Consider an observer fixating the horizon (close to infinity), thus aligning the optical axes of the left and right eyes (i.e. the viewing angle in respect to the fovea) such that they end up in a more or less parallel direction (see Figure 5.6a). An object that is located along the line of sight in the

Figure 5.6

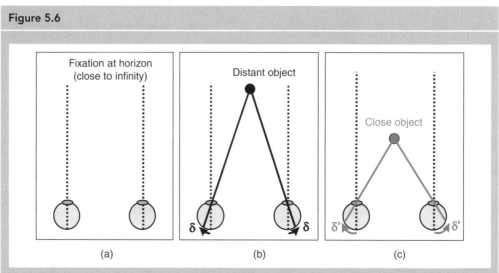

When the two eyes focus on the distant horizon their gaze direction is almost parallel (a), and an object located at a large distance is projected on opposite sides close to the fovea (b) whereas an object located close to the eye is projected further away from the fovea (c). The disparity δ (δ'), the angular distance of the projection of an object from the centre of the fovea, is inversely related to the distance of the object from the eye fixation, and therefore can be used as crucial distance measure for stereoscopic depth perception.

far distance will be projected on the retina at a small distance, or disparity δ, from the centre of the fovea (Figure 5.6b). A closer object, on the other hand will be projected on the retina at a much larger disparity, δ', from the centre of the fovea (Figure 5.6c). You can easily see from this sketch that the distance of an object from the observer is systematically related to the disparity, δ, at which the object is projected in the two images relative to the fovea.

The basic geometry shown in Figure 5.6 served as the starting point for a comprehensive theory of stereoscopic depth perception (Marr and Poggio 1979). Obviously, we so far have only considered the simple condition of directing the eyes straight ahead at infinity distance. A general model needs to consider fixating targets at arbitrary distances and estimating the distance of objects that may be located closer to or more distant from this point and in a range of directions, which complicates the geometry but does not prevent a solution to the distance estimation. The most important extension of the simple configuration for the more general case is schematically sketched in Figure 5.7. Again, the fixated object is projected on the centre of the fovea on both eyes. Objects that are located at similar distance to the right or left of the fixation point, on a virtual circle called 'Horopter', are projected to corresponding locations of the two retinae to the left or right of the fovea in both eyes. On the other hand, for other distances projections are no longer at corresponding locations on the two retinae, and more distant objects are projected with 'uncrossed' disparity on 'nasal' regions of the retina (i.e. closer to the nose), whereas nearer objects are projected with 'crossed' disparity on 'temporal' regions of the retina (i.e. in the outside regions). There still are a few simplifications in this portrait of stereovision (for a comprehensive view, see Howard and Rogers 2008), but the computational details as well the physiological aspects of implementing these mechanisms in cortical neurons are

Figure 5.7

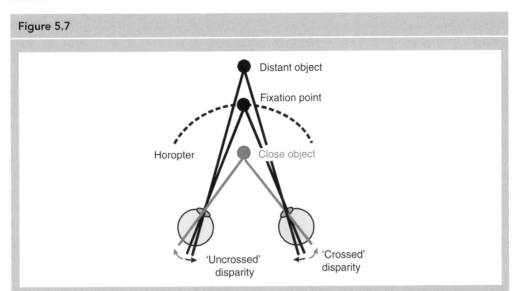

When the two eyes fixate an object at midrange distance, the distance of other objects can be recovered by simple triangulation. Objects that are projected to corresponding locations on both retinae are located on a virtual 'horopter' circle (black broken line) that passes through the fixation point. Objects that are further away than the fixation point are projected with 'uncrossed' disparity on 'nasal' regions of the retina (dark grey lines). Nearer objects are projected with 'crossed' disparity on 'temporal' regions of the retina (light grey lines).

outside of the scope of this introductory textbook. The most important point to remember about stereovision is that from the two independent views provided by the two eyes, the visual system can estimate the distance of individual objects relative to the fixation plane by a simple geometric method, 'triangulation'. Many authors consider stereopsis as the most reliable and most important depth cue, because there is an exact relationship between the information contained in the two monocular images and the distance of the projected object, which can be used to reconstruct exact 3D information. On the other hand, owing to the spatial resolution limits of the visual system the optimal operating range for stereopsis is restricted to regions comparatively close to the body, and many individuals, for instance, when suffering from amblyopia, have rather poor stereo vision (Hess et al. 1990).

Similar geometric relationships are the basis of dynamic depth perception. Instead of sampling the environment with two eyes and reconstructing depth from these two images, in dynamic depth perception images taken in sequence from different viewpoints with the same eye are compared with each other in order to reconstruct distance. The basic phenomenon of 'motion parallax' is very well known to all of us (illustrated in Figure 5.8a) and can be perceived in monocular vision (i.e. with one eye): when you look out of the window of a moving car or a train, you see close objects moving very fast (e.g. bushes next to the road or track) whereas distant objects are passing very slow (mountains close to the horizon), or even appear to be stationary (such as the moon or sun, which even can lead a clever child to ask 'why is the moon following us?').

The underlying geometry for this phenomenon is sketched in Figure 5.8b, which again is based on the basic fact that the angular shift of an object in two images taken from two

Figure 5.8

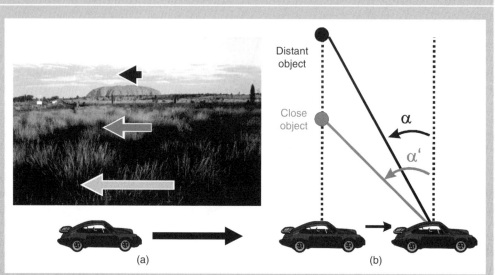

Motion parallax. (a) When passing static objects at constant speed, the angular speed of an object that is projected onto retina depends on the distance of the object to the observer. (b) The inverse relationship between an object's angular speed in the projected image (indicated by the angular displacement, α, of the object for a given time interval) and the distance of the projected object (dark and light grey disks and lines), the 'motion parallax', is used for distance estimation by human observers and other biological systems.

different viewpoints depends on the viewing distance of the observer. In the present case, for a given displacement (or speed) of the observer, be it by movement of the car or the train, the angular shift of the position of an object in the retinal images will depend on the distance of this observer. The inverse relation between the angular speed in the retinal position and the distance of the projected object is called 'motion parallax' (Rogers and Graham 1984), and is used comprehensively by many biological systems to retrieve visual information about the three-dimensional structure of the environment (Collett 1978).

DEPTH AND SIZE ILLUSIONS

As we have seen in previous sections of this chapter, a wide range of pictorial binocular and dynamic depth cues is available to the brain. Each of these depth cues has its own scope and limitations, so it is likely that discrepancies between the different pieces of information will be possible, and the brain has to decide which of the depth cues is more reliable than others in a particular situation. The inability to resolve conflicting information under certain circumstances is nicely demonstrated by depth and size illusions. When the visual system has to judge the size of an object in the three-dimensional environment, it can use independent information about its distance to retrieve from the retinal (angular) size of this object its physical size. The disregarding of angular size in order to make a judgement of perceived object size, independent of viewing distance, is called 'size constancy' (see Gregory 1998). This is illustrated in Figure 5.9: A football has been placed in the bottom left corner of the photograph of the Campo in Siena, and in this place looks like a reasonably

Figure 5.9

The two footballs on the left side of the image have dramatically different angular size, but are perceived as having similar physical size. The ball on the right (short arrow) has the same angular size as the one indicated by the long arrow, but is perceived as smaller because it appears to be much closer. The correction of angular size with perceived distance is called 'constancy scaling'.

sized football. It also seems to be of the same size as the second football, which can be seen in the same image slightly higher up, (indicated by long arrow), and appears farther away from the viewer along the boundary between the two tiling patterns. The physical sizes of these two footballs are perceived as identical, although the angular size of the second one is about a third of the first one. On the other hand, the third football, placed on the lower right side of the image (indicated by short arrow), is perceived as ridiculously small, closer to a tennis ball, although it has the identical angular size to the second football, which can be explained by the fact that it appears to be placed at the same distance as the first football, which has an angular size about three times as large. Size constancy means that angular size is related to perceived distance before to inform judgements about perceived object size. In reverse, the size will be perceived incorrectly for an object whose distance is misperceived owing to ambiguous or misleading distance cues or context, and as a result size illusions would be experienced.

As the 'misplaced' football on the right side of Figure 5.9 suggests, objects of constant angular size when presented at two different perceived distances may be interpreted as dramatic differences in object size: whereas in Figure 5.10 the kangaroo jumping on to the road from the left side looks like a reasonably sized specimen, the second kangaroo, crossing the road from the right and further up in the image, appears like a giant creature, which was supposed to have become extinct long before mankind sent cars on the road. This phenomenon is called a 'size constancy illusion' – a misjudgement of perceived object size on the basis of contextual depth information. Note that there is a solution for this picture to be interpreted

Figure 5.10

Size constancy illusion: The perceived physical size of each kangaroo is judged in its spatial context – since the left one is believed to be close to the observer it looks smaller than the right one, which is believed to be far away and with the same angular size would be a giant.

without getting startled about giant kangaroos, if the second kangaroo, coming from the right, is actually jumping with a very high leap on the road, in the same depth plane as its sibling coming from the left. In this case, distance, angular size and physical object size would be identical to both animals, but the right one would need to elevate itself high above the road surface. Note also that shadows cast from the animals onto the road surface would be one way of disambiguating this situation, because the separation between animal and shadow would indicate its height over ground.

The size constancy illusion is sometimes regarded as the basis of the Ponzo illusion (Leibowitz et al. 1969), that is, the perceived size difference of two identical horizontal lines enclosed by two oppositely tilted lines (see Figure 5.11a). This phenomenon can be interpreted as an effect of size constancy, because the two converging lines suggest a perspective context. The illustration in Figure 5.11b demonstrates how two white bars differ significantly in their perceived size – although their angular size is identical, you can use a ruler to confirm that they are identical – when put at two locations (perceived distances) of a rail track, which generates in real life the same basic geometric conditions as the simple line drawing on the left side of the figure (after Gregory 1968). Similar size constancy effects are debated as a possible cause for other size illusions, such as the moon illusion (Kaufman and Rock 1962), which refers to the observation that a full moon looks larger when it is close to the horizon and close to trees and houses, than when it is high up in the sky, apparently far out in space.

A stunning size constancy illusion in real space can be experienced in the Ames room (Behrens 1987; Dorward and Day 1997), where the size even of a familiar object, such as a person, can be perceived largely distorted, because the misleading geometry of the surrounding space generates an incorrect frame of reference. Figure 5.12a shows a photograph of two Fimbles sitting in a small-scale Ames room, and it appears that the right character,

Figure 5.11

(a)   (b)

Ponzo illusion (left) and possible size constancy explanation (right). The converging lines suggest a perspective which puts the two horizontal lines at different apparent distance – in a natural environment the lower (close) bar between the converging rails looks much smaller than the upper (distant) bar.

Figure 5.12

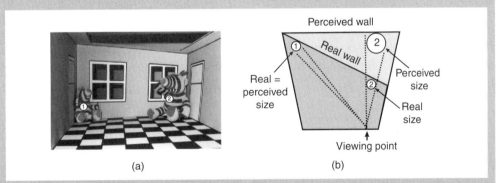

(a)   (b)

Photograph of an Ames room with two toy characters (Fimbles) of equal physical size, as seen by the observer (a) In the top view of the room's geometry (b) the real (dark grey trapezium) and illusory (light grey trapezium) shape of the room becomes apparent, which illustrates how the two characters, '1' and '2', that are sitting at different physical distance are perceived to be located in the same viewing distance, and hence are attributed with a different size.

wearing a badge with the label '2', is much larger than the left one (label '1'). In reality, as can be seen when the room is inspected from the top, both Fimbles were produced for toy shops in exactly the same size. They just sit at different distances from the observer, who is unaware of the special design of the room, which is not rectangular but distorted in such a way that the back wall is actually linked to the left side wall at a much larger distance than to the right side wall. In a bird's eye view of the room, sketched in Figure 5.12b, it becomes apparent that the right wall of the room is much shorter than the left one, therefore the character '2' is sitting closer than character '1', and appears as larger in the projection on the eye, or the camera in Figure 5.12a. The awkward shape of the room remains hidden to the observer looking from the viewing point in the front wall, because all geometrical shapes, like windows and floor tiles, are adjusted such that the room appears regular and the side walls and back wall appear to be at right angles to each other – as a result the observer believes the two Fimbles are sitting at the same distance, and perceptually rescales their relative size.

The size illusion in the Ames room is a case in point for *constructivist theories of perception*: the knowledge of the rules of perspective and the assumption of rectangular architecture force the visual system to construct the apparent size difference. This way of drawing conclusions about what is seen in the retinal images is called 'unconscious inference' (see Gregory 1997). However, one could ask why, applying the same theoretical framework one could not also argue the other way round: Why are we not using our knowledge (assumption or expectation) about identical physical body sizes to reconstruct a veridical, non-rectangular geometry of the room?

A similarly stunning case of misperceived depth is the 'hollow face illusion' (Hill and Bruce 1993). When you look at the inside of a face mask (often demonstrated with a face mask of Charlie Chaplin), and you close one eye and don't move your head (to exclude stereoscopic and motion parallax information), the surface looks no longer concave but convex, that is, protruding from the background, and therefore a perfectly normal 3D shape of the face appears. This phenomenon is usually interpreted along the same lines as constructivist theories (Gregory 1998). It seems that an assumption made by the visual system that we cannot see inside a head, and therefore the only 'reasonable' solution, or at least the preferred one to an ambiguous visual stimulus, is to perceive a convex 3D shape under a different illumination. Similar assumptions seem to be built into the visual system about the direction of natural illumination (Ramachandran 1988), so that ambiguous shapes from shading are usually seen as if the light comes from above (see Figure 5.13).

Figure 5.13

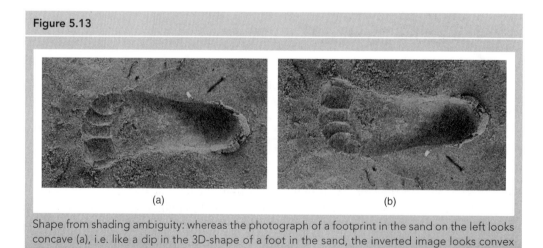

(a)   (b)

Shape from shading ambiguity: whereas the photograph of a footprint in the sand on the left looks concave (a), i.e. like a dip in the 3D-shape of a foot in the sand, the inverted image looks convex (b), i.e. like the same shape protruding from the background.

APPLICATIONS

A large number of cues leading to depth perception have been discussed in this chapter, and a number of misperceptions, distortions and illusions that are closely related to the inverse mapping problem: from flat images provided by the eyes only under a restricted range of conditions unambiguous depth information can be retrieved. This problem can motivate low-level computational (Marr and Poggio 1979), as well as high-level cognitive theories (Gregory 1997) of perception, which are based on bottom-up information processing or top-down application of knowledge about the outside world, respectively. Irrespective of such theoretical approaches, it is clear that the visual system is highly evolved to solving the task of depth perception by maximising the information available (for instance, using two eyes) and optimising the processing mechanisms (for instance, extracting motion parallax information).

Human cultural and technological history, in turn, has witnessed a long series of highly sophisticated techniques to create the (illusory) experience of depth in the absence of real space. This development includes the mastering of pictorial depth cues, in particular linear perspective and the effects of lighting and reflections, in the Renaissance (Gombrich 1982), as well as early technical gadgets to use stereopsis to produce depth impressions, such as dual-image viewers or the Wheatstone stereoscope (Wheatstone 1838). In the twentieth century, technology went on to produce red-green anaglyphs (Julesz 1971), lenticular rasters on fancy postcards and stereotests, or even single-image stereograms (Julesz and Miller 1962; Tyler and Clarke 1990), which were commercialised by Tom Baccei and Cheri Smith in 1991 as 'Magic Eye' (MagicEyeInc 1993). The big challenge is to create 3D movies, and after some clumsy initial attempts to employ red-green anaglyphs in the 1970s, the currently most advanced technology is used in a small number of IMAX® Cinemas, based on polarised filters. To this end two synchronised films are shot at eye separation, usually by means of a double lens camera. These two films are then projected simultaneously through inverse optics and polarisers, to keep the two views separate in their light polarisation, and observers see the two images with the two eyes separately through polarising goggles. Additionally, large, close to panoramic screens help to exploit the 3D depth information contained in optic flow (large scale motion parallax). As a result, a very convincing experience of space is created that leaves the audience stunned!

Take Home Messages

- the world is three-dimensional (3D), but the eyes provide two-dimensional, flat (2D) images; as a consequence depth perception is the reconstruction of the third dimension from flat images
- the brain constructs depth information from 2D images, using a bag of tricks that rely on pictorial, binocular and dynamic cues
- the mechanisms evolved in human vision for the perception of depth give rise to illusions; conflicting depth and size information can lead to perceptual ambiguities, which are often resolved by assuming size constancy, or in relation to known properties of the geometrical configuration and lighting conditions in our environment
- the mechanisms of depth perception are the basis of various applications, exploiting the full range of depth cues, from the art of illusionist paintings to the use of modern technologies like double projections in combination with polarising filters

Discussion Questions

- Discuss the main pictorial depth cues.
- What is meant by size constancy? Illustrate your answer with some examples.
- How is the distance of objects recovered from two-dimensional images by stereopsis?
- Can you explain the size illusion experienced in the Ames room?

6 VISION 4: TIME AND MOTION

OVERVIEW

What is the role of temporal information? Observers can exploit changes in their environment at different scales, ranging from high-frequency flicker to slow changes or memories of past events, which eventually form our society's history. After a short discussion of possible mechanisms to detect temporal change (flicker detectors), and their relevance in a behavioural context, this chapter will focus on the combined change in time and space –motion. Some physical properties of basic motion phenomena will be illustrated with space–time diagrams, and a simple motion detector will be developed on the basis of such a representation. This basic motion detector will be introduced as a tool to study brain function – questions such as apparent and real motion, motion correspondence, structure from motion, or perceptual organisation, a core theme of Gestalt Psychology, will be discussed in the context of motion processing mechanisms. It will be asked what solutions are required to deal with the most significant and the most challenging motion vision problems. Neural and perceptual mechanisms are then related to technical systems and applications, and illustrated again by the powerful data compression methods related to motion encoding. Understanding motion encoding mechanisms, and their limitations, will be directly related to explanations of stunning motion illusions, such as motion after-effects, the aperture problem, motion plaids and the Barber's Pole illusion.

MOTION: CONNECTING SPACE AND TIME

To understand the relationship between space, time and motion we need a bit of very basic physics background, which can be easily explained by a simple example: Consider an astronomer who is watching the night sky to find stars. Each star is seen from the earth's surface at one particular position and at a particular time. If our astronomer is watching two stars at the same time, they will appear to her at a spatial distance (related to the dimension x, see Figure 6.1a). If these two stars are very close to each other, that is, the distance is decreasing, she finally might no longer be able to separate them, reaching the limits of spatial resolution, which we discussed in Chapter 3. Equally, under certain atmospheric conditions the astronomer might see a star appearing, disappearing and reappearing. In this case, the star is visible in temporal intervals (related to the dimension t, see Figure 6.1b), and she is perceiving flicker, if the star appears and disappears at regular intervals. Similar to periodic special patterns, or gratings, which we encountered in Chapter 3 as the basis for assessing the spatial resolution of the visual system, the periodic temporal change that we see in this example is theoretically interesting, because such flicker allows

Figure 6.1

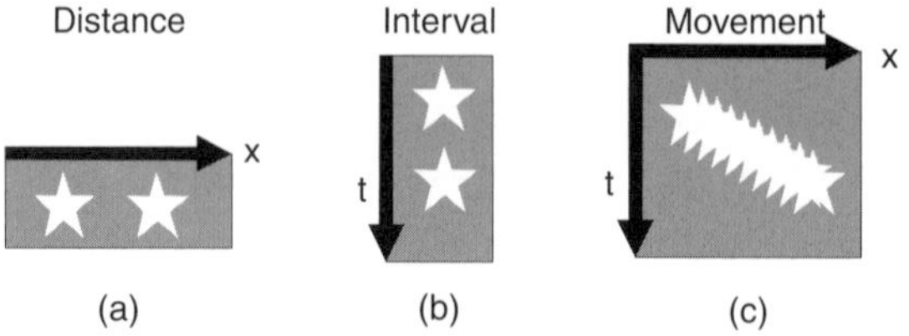

Stars appear in the night sky in particular locations, and at particular times. (a) Two stars seen at the same time at two locations (space dimension x) need to be separated by a minimum distance in order to be discriminated from each other. (b) A single star can disappear and reappear in the same location at certain intervals (time dimension t). (c) A star can move across space and time; in the x–t diagram the location of the star is plotted along the horizontal axis (x) as function of time along the vertical axis (t).

us to describe systematically the temporal properties and limitations of the visual system. Most importantly, when flicker gets faster and faster, or is increasing temporal frequency, at some point it cannot be discriminated any more from continuous light – this point is called the flicker–fusion frequency, and it indicates the maximum temporal resolution of the visual system (Kelly 1972; Zanker and Harris 2002). The temporal resolution can vary considerably between individuals, with lighting conditions and with the location in the visual field (Kelly 1962). You can easily observe this when you look at the continuous light that you see being emitted from a neon-lit advert (or some other fluorescent light source), and then compare it with the flickering brightness that you see when you see the same advert or light source in the periphery of your eye. It is interesting to note that the spatial resolution is highest in the central visual system, the fovea, whereas the temporal resolution is highest in the periphery (Snowden and Hess 1992). This is often interpreted as a functional specialisation of the fovea for scrutinising detail, whereas the peripheral visual system is important as alarm system, alerting an animal to rapidly appearing objects.

Finally, our astronomer might detect a star moving across the sky – in this case the star is changing from one location in space at one instant in time to another location in space at another instant in time. This movement can be very fast, such as for a shooting star, which is not really a star, or it can be slow, in which case it usually would turn out to be the light of an airplane passing by and not that of a star. Note that by definition a star has a fixed position, in a first approximation, whereas planets move around the stars – therefore the movement of the star as seen from the earth's surface is only a result of terrestrial motion and thus much too slow to be perceived by the human visual system (some animals, however, are able to pick up such slow motion, see Horridge 1966). Whatever the speed of such a movement, it is important to understand that motion is the simultaneous change of position in space and time, and therefore can be best illustrated as a space–time diagram (x–t-diagram, see Figure 6.1c, plotting the location x of the star along a function of time t). This method of illustrating motion reflects the essential link between space and time through motion; and it is very important, because it gives us a means of describing stimulus conditions for the visual system in a purely static medium, such as the page of book, and it will be used comprehensively in the following sections.

Because we are living in a space–time continuum and things are happening to living beings in space and time, movement could be regarded as one characteristic feature of life itself, at least for animals. In consequence, motion perception is absolutely crucial for the survival of an organism, be it the movement of prey to be caught, the movement of predator to avoid, or the movement of branches in the wind, or waves on the surface of the sea. If a young child did not have a superb sensory system specialising on motion perception, it would not survive the dangers of modern traffic for a single day. Conversely, a well-investigated patient with brain damage to their occipital lobe in the cortex, who is suffering from severe impairments of motion perception, is experiencing substantial difficulties in mastering real-life situations that are absolutely trivial to everyone else, and has developed a number of 'work-arounds' to get on with their everyday life (Hess et al. 1989). Motion perception, therefore, not surprisingly, is a prime example for the study of brain function, where a combination of neuroscientific methods has led over recent decades to vast growth of our knowledge about how the brain solves complex processing tasks, and responds to diverse environmental challenges (Smith and Snowden 1994; Zanker and Zeil 2001): substantial progress has been made to understand how the physiological substrate of motion vision, and psychophysical experimentation, together with computational modelling, contribute to a comprehensive understanding of the fundamental processing mechanisms. Some of these aspects will be covered in the following sections.

REPRESENTING MOTION

In order to develop a model for the visual detection of motion, or in other words in order to understand how motion is detected in the visual system, we need to start with the physical characteristics of motion resulting from the link between space and time. On one hand, the spatial component of displacement – the distance between two locations in one, two or three spatial dimensions – determines the *direction* of motion. On the other hand, the temporal component of displacement – how much time is needed to cover a certain distance – determines the *speed* of motion. Each movement can be completely characterised by its direction and speed, or its 'motion vector'. How can these two aspects of motion be illustrated in static images?

Artists, in their attempt to express a meaning or to represent the world in a very naturalistic way, have developed various techniques of representing motion in static pictures (Gombrich 1982). These techniques range from depicting animals or humans in postures that are clearly related to movement, as found an early art forms and developed to perfection during the Renaissance, to the use of speed lines or motion streaks in cartoons (Burr 2000), and multiple phase images in Futurism and Cubism (Braddick, in Gregory et al. 1995). If you were to describe the traffic situation after a car accident on a piece of paper, you would presumably draw a little sketch similar to the one shown in Figure 6.2a, with a picture of a car and an arrow indicating its movement. The direction and speed of the car's movement would be indicated by the direction in which the arrow is pointing and its length, respectively. In an attempt to provide precise and complete information, a physicist would use a space–time diagram (Adelson and Bergen 1985), similar to that shown in Figure 6.2b. Here, the direction and speed up of the car is exactly reflected by the orientation of the arrow in x–t space (cf. Figure 5.1c), with leftward or rightward motion being indicated by an arrow pointing to the left or right, respectively, and smaller inclinations of the arrow to the horizontal indicating faster speeds.

Figure 6.2

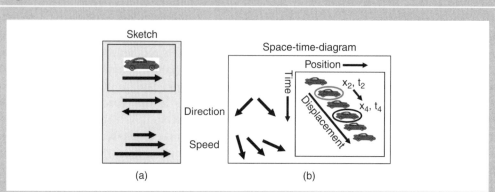

Pictorial representation of a moving car. (a) Simple sketch of a moving car with an arrow indicating the direction (forwards, backwards) by the direction it is pointing in, and speed by its length (from slow to fast). (b) In the x–t-diagram the location of the car is plotted in steps along the horizontal axis as function of time along the vertical axis; the orientation of the car's displacement in x–t represents directly and exactly the direction and speed of this movement (for instance, from the coordinates x_2, t_2 to x_4, t_4); fast (slow) movement generate small (large) angle between the horizontal and the displacement arrow.

A MOTION DETECTION MODEL

Based on the physics of motion, it is clear that the task of motion detection is to assess the position shift of an object or feature in the image as function of time – think of a motion detector as space–time mechanism that captures the displacement steps in an x–t-diagram as shown in Figure 6.2b. Technically, detecting the coupled relationship of changes in space and time is known as 'spatio-temporal correlation' (Borst and Egelhaaf 1989; Reichardt 1961). Looking at the x–t diagram can be very instructive to answer the question about the minimum requirements for a computational model of motion detection. The task of such an elementary motion detector (EMD) is to detect an object at one position and instant of time (e.g. x_2, t_2), and then to detect the same object at another position and instant of time (e.g. x_4, t_4). In order to do so, the visual system needs to sample at least two positions in space, and two positions in time, and make a logical connection between two space–time points: only if the object was at (x_2, t_2) AND (x_4, t_4) has it moved between these two points. The circuitry and functionality of such an EMD, as initially proposed by Werner Reichardt and colleagues and therefore often called *Reichardt detectors* (Borst and Egelhaaf 1989), is illustrated in Figure 6.3 for a light spot moving from left to right (inverse results are generated by motion in the opposite direction). The model critically requires the following components:

- two spatially inputs, separated by $\Delta\varphi$, to measure changes across space, $x_i - x_{i-1}$
- two temporal filters, in the simplest case a delay operator with the time constant τ that is slowing the signal down, to measure changes across time, $t_i - t_{i-1}$
- a logical comparator (which is an essential 'non-linear' operator) to evaluate the coincidence of spatial and temporal changes, in this form of the model a multiplier π (which only will generate a non-zero output if both input signals are different from zero)

- a subtraction unit (Δ) to remove signal components that are unrelated to motion, and thus increase directional selectivity

With these processing elements incorporated in the EMD, the original signal from one point in space is compared with a delayed signal from a neighbouring point in space, returning a positive output if an object moved from the first to the second point and a negative output if the object moved in the opposite direction: this is called directional selectivity. There are alternative models to this particular implementation and to this overall design, such as energy models (e.g. Adelson and Bergen 1985), or gradient models (e.g. Johnston et al. 1999). All of these computational models have their particular advantages and difficulties, but in essence each of them is designed to return a signal that reflects the direction and speed of visual motion, and perform this task well within certain limits, and with varying robustness to noise (Borst 2007).

Figure 6.3

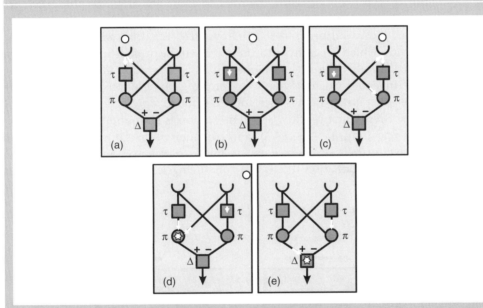

Five phases of an EMD model responding to a light spot (white disc at the top of each panel) moving from left to right. (a) The light spot is stimulating the left input element (half circle), sending a signal into two transmission lines (white arrows); (b) signals have travelled along the two lines, entering the left delay filter (τ) where it slows down; (c) the two initial signals continue to travel down the lines, the left one still held back in the delay filter, the right one reaching the right multiplier (π) where it is deleted because there is no coincident signal in the other input line of the multiplier (1*0=0); the light spot in the meantime reaches the right input element, sending signals into the two other transmission lines; (d) the signals from the right input line has reached the right delay filter, where it is slowed down, and has been travelling at full speed to the left multiplier where it coincides with the signal from the left input element and therefore generates a signal in the multiplier (1*1=1, white star); (e) the signal from the left multiplier has been travelling towards the subtraction unit where it generates a positive EMD output (1−0=1), and the remaining signal from the right input element reaches the right multiplier, where it is deleted because there is no coincident signal arriving from the left input element (0*1=0).

REAL AND APPARENT MOTION

An important feature of the EMD is that it not only responds to real motion, which is the continuous and smooth displacement of an object or feature in the visual field (see Figure 6.4a), but also responds to the step-like displacement of image features, 'apparent motion', as illustrated in Figure 6.4b as a space–time diagram. Apparent motion, sometimes also called 'Phi motion' (Anstis 1970), is a result of discrete displacements (Anstis 1980) such as the dot jumping to the right in Figure 6.4b, which is perceptually equivalent to a real, continuous displacement. Please note that the orientation in space–time, which is the characteristic feature of motion and the aspect of the visual stimulus to be detected by the motion detector, is identical for the two types of stimuli (indicated by red arrows in Figure 6.4). So it is not surprising that the EMD, extracting spatiotemporal correlation – or orientation and space–time – generates corresponding results for real and apparent motion (Zanker, 1994).

The effect of apparent motion has been known for a long time, and the sequential presentation of images showing different phases of a motion sequence was used as props in the parlours of the chattering classes and at country fairs, and is sometimes used by students to animate their textbooks with 'thumb movies' by drawing little phase sketches on the margins and then flipping through these very rapidly. For instance, the Victorian 'zoetrope', invented by W. G. Horner in 1834 (Croy 1918), is a drum with slits and phase pictures on the inside, which generate a little movie when the drum is spun and the image sequence is viewed through the slits. A pioneer in this area was Eadweard Muybridge who in one sense invented cinematography by printing phase photographs of moving animals and people on a disk, which is then rotated through a projection device (Herbert et al. 2004). In the twenty-first century, apparent motion is surrounding us everywhere, being the basis of television, movies, DVDs and computer animations – engineers have been highly creative in their efforts to generate highly compressed movie formats that contain the minimum information to create a convincing sensation of motion, such as

Figure 6.4

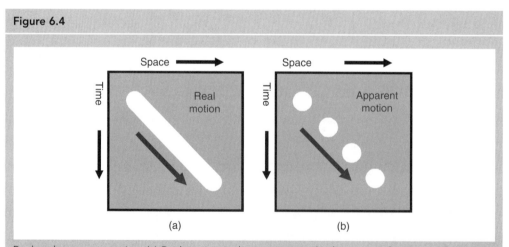

(a)   (b)

Real and apparent motion. (a) Real motion is the continuous displacement of an image features in space and time. (b) Apparent motion is a displacement of image features in discrete steps in space and time – for instance, a movie that you watch in the cinema is a rapid sequence of static images in which individual objects such as animals, cars, footballs, dancers, etc., are changing shape and are displaced by variable amounts between these images.

MPEG, MP4 or AVI files, which enable you to send and receive animated clips through your mobile phones.

Apparent motion was 'discovered' experimentally by Sigmund Exner (1876), who demonstrated that motion is an independent sensation in space and time. His ingenious experimental set-up involved brief light sparks that were presented sequentially with high temporal precision at defined locations in the visual field, which were controlled by the use of a screen with a small aperture (see Figure 6.5). Fast on–off switching of the light at a constant location will eventually reach 'flicker fusion frequency' at which single events are no longer visible (top panel in Figure 6.5d), and a continuous light demonstrates that the temporal limit of vision has been reached. Accordingly, spatial fusion is determined by presenting light sparks next to each other at smaller and smaller distance (middle panel in Figure 6.5d): when they get in very close proximity, below the limits of spatial resolution, single locations are no longer visible, and a single merged blob is perceived, which demonstrates that the spatial limit of vision has been reached. Using the same temporal and spatial parameters, light sparks are then presented at fusion frequency in alternating locations below spatial resolution distance (bottom panel in Figure 6.5d): a new perceptual quality emerges, the light source now being perceived as moving back and forth. This apparent motion phenomenon was recognised by Exner as proof that motion vision, by combining stimulation in space and time, is a unique sensory quality that is independent of spatial and temporal vision in isolation. By alternating the projection of the two sparks between the two eyes he was also able to demonstrate that apparent motion is extracted in the cortex, rather than in the retina (see Figure 6.5a–c).

Figure 6.5

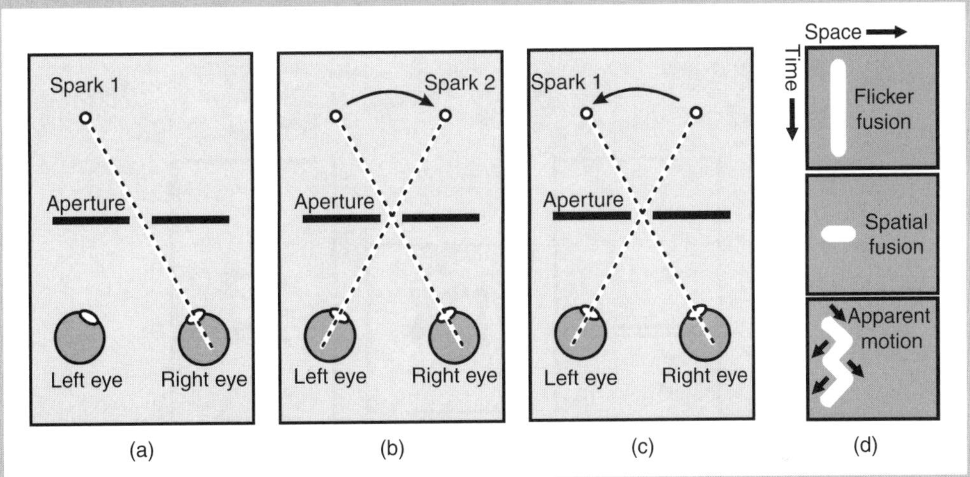

Schematic sketch of Sigmund Exner's experiment to demonstrate that motion vision is an independent sensation that goes beyond the spatial and temporal resolution limits of the human visual system. Brief electric sparks (small white dots) are presented in alternation at two separate locations (a, b, c, b, c, ...), creating the sensation of apparent motion between the left and right location. Presenting the two sparks to different eyes by use of an aperture demonstrates that the apparent motion percept is not generated in the eye but in the brain. Apparent motion is still perceived when the spatial and temporal parameters are chosen such that pure temporal change (going beyond flicker fusion) and pure spatial separation (going beyond spatial resolution) is no longer visible (schematically shown in (d) as x–t diagrams).

MOTION CORRESPONDENCE

In the early twentieth century apparent motion was interpreted as a case in point for the 'laws of Gestalt' (see Chapter 13), demonstrating the principles of proximity and common fate that were believed to guide perception into interpretations of the input that lead to simple and regular configurations (Wertheimer 1912). A crucial aspect of apparent motion is that correspondence in space and time needs to be established between an object (or feature) in consecutive presentations. This is simple in the case of isolated objects, as used in the previous sections. Under such conditions apparent motion is detected by an EMD as good as in the continuous displacement of real motion, and no high-level processing strategies such as Gestalt laws are required (for an example of such an equivalence, see Gregory and Harris 1984). However, ambiguous motion stimuli involving several identical objects can be constructed that are believed to identify such high-level motion processing mechanisms as the basis of matching across space and time, which is required for motion perception (Ramachandran and Anstis 1986). A typical phenomenon to support this claim is the rapid alternation between two frames with dots in opposite corners of a virtual square (see Figure 6.6a) that can be perceived as two dots jumping up and down, or as two dots jumping left and right (see Figure 6.6b). In such a situation human observers can see one or the other percept, and switch between the two 'solutions' in irregular intervals, which is called 'bistable' perception. If an array of several ambiguously alternating dot pairs is presented, they are perceived as moving synchronously, either all horizontally or all vertically, and they all switch between these two solutions in synchrony. When the separation of the dots in the two frames is reduced either horizontally or vertically, the percept becomes biased towards motion in the direction of the shorter distance (see Figure 6.6c). Vertical or horizontal neighbourhood can resolve the ambiguity, establishing correspondence

Figure 6.6

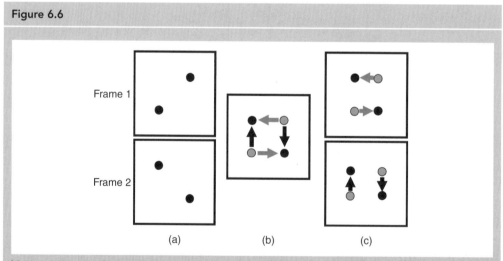

Motion correspondence. Alternating the two frames shown in (a) leads to a bistable percept as sketched in (b): the two dots can be perceived as jumping back and forth horizontally (light grey arrows) or vertically (dark grey arrows), because each of the two percepts are equivalent 'solutions' to the ambiguous stimulus. (c) If the horizontal (top) or vertical distance (bottom) between the two possible dot locations is reduced, a unique solution is enforced to perceive horizontal (light grey arrows) or vertical motion (dark grey arrows) – this is in agreement with the Gestalt law of 'proximity'.

between closer objects in the presence of other identical, but more distant objects. This observation is interpreted as evidence for the Gestalt laws of 'proximity' – close objects are grouped together by such high-level perceptual processes. Please note that EMDs with appropriate spatial tuning ($\Delta\varphi$ matching the shorter distance, see above) will produce the same effect.

As we have seen in the dot-pair stimulus, the discontinuity in apparent motion stimuli can lead to ambiguity because objects need to be identified in successive frames of a motion sequence, thus solving the 'correspondence problem'. If objects are identical, correspondence may be established through proximity to disambiguate the motion percept, as shown in the example illustrated in Figure 6.6, but the reverse can happen as well, when coherent motion is used as a cue to group a subset of dots into a common structure. The situation for this to happen is illustrated in Figure 6.7. In a static display containing a set of identical dots, the viewer would not recognise that a subset of these dots is actually placed on an invisible circle (shown in the sketch of Figure 6.7 as a grey circle, but not present in the stimulus display). When this subset of dots is moving, all in the same direction, the circular structure immediately becomes visible – it 'pops out'. Motion correspondence in this case establishes a group of dots that belong together and form a common object, an effect that is attributed in Gestalt Psychology to the 'law of common fate' (Wertheimer 1912). This effect can go much further and extend to the recognition of the three-dimensional structure of an object, such as a sphere or cylinder, by means of the differential motions of dots covering its surface, in the absence of any other cue to define its 3D-shape. In any static frame of such a stimulus sequence, you only would see a bunch of random dots, but when the full movie sequence is displayed you see 'structure from motion' (Bradley et al. 1998; Ullman 1979).

Starting from the problem of how to solve the 'correspondence problem' in apparent motion stimuli, we have seen in this section how traditional high-level explanations originating from Gestalt Psychology can be used to account for striking perceptual effects, which are based on principles to organise the information picked up by the sensory system as sparse, noisy and ambiguous data sets. The problem with these high-level explanations is that they make use of general principles that can account for such effects, but that these principles are closer to a description than to a mechanism that would offer a functional basis of how the information is processed. On the other hand, we have good computational models, such as the EMD, that are biologically plausible and very powerful in explaining basic aspects of

Figure 6.7

Structure from motion. In a group of randomly distributed dots you would not notice that a subset of dots form a circle (indicated in this sketch by the grey circle, which would be absent in the real stimulus), but when they are moving together they immediately pop out as a circle of dots, attributed to the Gestalt law of 'common fate'.

motion detection. So the obvious question is: would such low-level processes be a good basis to account for effects related to motion correspondence in apparent motion? Indeed, it has been argued that low-level motion models can account for apparent motion (because they detect orientation in space–time, see Figure 6.4) and implicitly 'solve' the correspondence problem (Zanker 1994). Furthermore, by incorporating such models in extended networks and applying segmentation algorithms, more complex problems, like structure from motion, can be resolved as well (Nowlan and Sejnowski 1994). This approach offers advantages over invoking abstract Gestalt laws, because it not only provides a computational mechanism, but also refers to the neural substrate of sensory information processing, and therefore relates to the evolutionary pressures and behavioural relevance that shaped these aspects of motion processing: motion information is crucial to detect objects in our environment and to recognise their 3D-shape.

MOTION BEHIND APERTURES

Another phenomenon that has attracted the attention of students of perception for a long time is the perceived direction of contours moving behind apertures (Wallach 1935). The most prominent example of misperceiving the direction of motion is the Barber's Pole illusion (see Figure 6.10): A vertical cylinder covered with a diagonal spiral stripe pattern is spinning around a vertical axis, and therefore generating purely horizontal motion – nevertheless the pattern appears to move vertically! To understand how this happens, we need to look at a simplified stimulus configuration. Imagine a single diagonal line moving vertically or horizontally (indicated in Figure 6.8a by grey arrows). If only the centre of this line is visible through a circular window, or aperture (circles in Figure 6.8a), in both cases they would seem to be moving diagonally (black arrows) because the ends of the lines that can tell the true direction of motion is occluded. The 'aperture problem' refers to the fact that locally, within an aperture, the displacement of a straight contour cannot be determined unambiguously (Hildreth and Koch 1987). In the circular aperture in Figure 6.8b a set of arrows shows some of the many different directions in which the line could have been displaced behind the aperture to reach the dotted line position; the direction of motion is 'under-determined', generating an ambiguous stimulus. The perceived

Figure 6.8

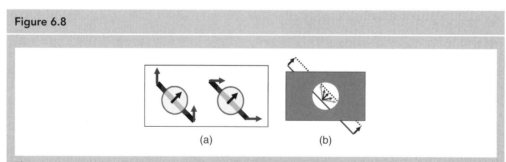

(a)   (b)

The aperture problem. (a) Seen through an aperture (transparent grey circles), a diagonal line moving vertically (left, grey arrows) or horizontally (right, grey arrows) appears to move perpendicular to the contour orientation, i.e. diagonally (black arrows). (b) Inside the circular aperture, the diagonal displacement of the line could have moved in many different directions (set of arrows in different shades of grey) – this ambiguity is resolved by the visual system as moving perpendicular to line orientation (black arrow).

direction inside the aperture is perpendicular to the line orientation, as indicated by the black arrow, which in this example corresponds to the true direction (see black arrows at the end of the lines).

A further instance of the aperture problem is the cause of the rotating spiral illusion (see Figure 6.9). When a spiral pattern is rotating (indicated by white arrows), human observers perceive an expansion, which does not reflect the physical movement. This illusion is generated by the function of local motion detectors: because their receptive fields act as physiological apertures, they pick up the motion components perpendicular to the local contour orientation (black arrows), which generates a pattern of expansion.

Based on this analysis of the perceived motion direction of a single line moving behind an aperture, it is easy to understand that periodic lines, or gratings, presented behind an aperture usually lead to an unambiguous perceived motion direction, perpendicular to the orientation of the grating. But what will happen if two such components, one vertical grating moving rightwards and one horizontal moving upwards (Colour plate VI, Figure 1a and c, red and green arrow, respectively), are superimposed to a compound pattern, as a so-called motion plaid (Colour plate VI, Figure 1b)? Do you expect to see one direction at a time and switch between the two possible directions of this ambiguous stimulus as a bistable percept? Would you see both directions simultaneously? Or might you see a mixture? Under most conditions, a rigid rectangular grid is perceived moving diagonally (blue arrow in Colour plate VI, Figure 1b), but if the two gratings differ in spatial frequency, contrast or colour (see Colour plate VI, Figure 1d), both directions can be perceived simultaneously and the gratings appear transparent, sliding across each other (Adelson and Movshon 1982). Interestingly, at different stages of the visual stream in the primate cortex neurons have been found that either respond to the component gratings or to the compound pattern (Movshon et al. 1985). This finding reflects the hierarchical encoding strategy of the brain, which is believed to be crucial to the solution of the aperture problem in motion plaids.

Figure 6.9

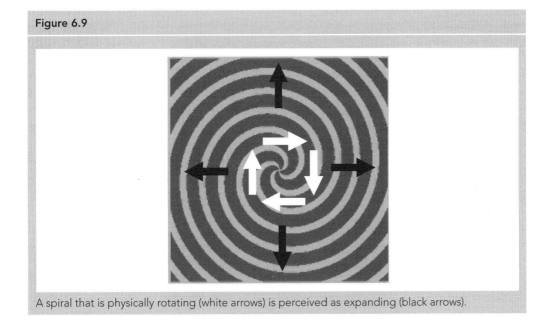

A spiral that is physically rotating (white arrows) is perceived as expanding (black arrows).

Figure 6.10

Barber's Pole illusion in the real life (Old Woking, Surrey): a vertical cylinder painted with a diagonal red and white spiral pattern is rotating around the vertical axis – despite the horizontal physical movement of the pattern, human observers perceive vertical motion of the red and white stripes.

A different stimulus, which also demonstrates how ambiguous local motion information can be integrated into a coherent motion percept, can be constructed on the basis of the Barber's Pole illusion (see Figure 6.10). Artificial versions of the Barber's Pole can be generated in computer animations by having a diagonal grating moving behind apertures of variable shape (Fisher & Zanker, 2001), where the perceived motion direction is determined by the dominant orientation of the aperture (indicated by arrows of different shades of grey in Figure 6.11a). If we construct a grid of thin horizontal and vertical slits and move the diagonal grating behind this grid, horizontal motion is perceived in the horizontal slits, and vertical motion is perceived in the vertical slits (indicated by black and white arrows in Figure 6.11b). The question arises of which direction is perceived at the intersections between horizontal and vertical slits (see transparent disc in Figure 6.11b). It turns out that the directional ambiguity at these intersections leads to a bistable percept, switching between horizontal and vertical at irregular intervals, which can be biased into one direction by changing the geometry of the slits, thus changing the integration conditions of local motion signals (Castet and Zanker 1999).

FINALLY, THE WATERFALL ILLUSION

Let us briefly return to the rotating spiral shown in Figure 6.7c. If you look for some time at the centre of the rotating spiral, it appears to expand, and then turn your gaze to a static object, it seems to contract. What you experience is a motion after-effect, which has

Figure 6.11

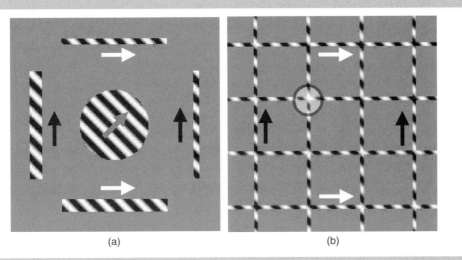

(a)   (b)

Barber's Pole illusion. (a) In artificial Barber's Pole stimuli, a diagonal grating is moving behind vertically and horizontally oriented apertures, and vertical (black arrows) or horizontal (white arrows) motion is perceived; in a circular aperture diagonal motion (grey arrow) is perceived. (b) If the diagonal grating is moved behind a grid of vertical and horizontal slits, vertical (black arrows) or horizontal (white arrows) motion is perceived at the same time; the perceived direction at the intersection points (transparent disc) can be bistable, depending on the geometry of the slits.

been studied for a long time and is often referred to as 'Waterfall illusion', because it has been best known as the illusory motion of static objects like rocks or trees after looking for extended periods at the flow of a waterfall (Wade 1994). The important aspect of this well-known observation is the explanation of the after-effect, which resembles that of successive brightness and colour contrast that were discussed in Chapters 3 and 4 (Mather and Harris 1998). Extended motion in one direction will adapt motion detectors that operate in opponency with other motion detectors that are tuned to the opposite direction – when a static stimulus is presented, the balance between the activities of these two opponent detectors is changed such that there is more activity in the detectors tuned to the previously unstimulated direction than in the detectors tuned to the previously stimulated direction, and illusory motion in the direction opposite to that of the adaptation stimulus is perceived. This adaptation and after-effect can be in a homogeneous direction for large areas of the visual field, such as in the waterfall, or arranged in specific patterns, such as the adapting expansion from the rotating spiral, which leads to contraction of static patterns as after-effect. It is also retino-topic, that is, it is locally restricted to previously adapted regions of the visual field (Wade et al. 1996). The similarity of the phenomenology of adaptation and after-effects in such different stimulus modalities as brightness, colour, motion, or even in face perception (Zhao and Chubb 2001), supports the claim that adaptation and opponency are fundamental mechanisms of efficient encoding in neural systems, which should be found across all sensory domains because they contribute to encoding strategies that make best use of the limited processing capacity of neural systems.

Take Home Messages

- motion is the change of position across time: the crucial stimulus feature is spatio-temporal correlation
- a simple motion detector (EMD) accounts for the perception of real and apparent motion, which is widely used in technical systems (e.g. movies, computer animations)
- motion perception is used as a tool to study the basic principles of brain function, such as adaptation and opponency, which are very well investigated in simple and highly evolved animals, including humans
- a wide range of motion illusions that are perceived by human observers can be explained by these low-level mechanisms of motion detection, including motion correspondence problems that have traditionally been interpreted in terms of perceptual organisation
- direction ambiguities are the basis for fascinating illusions (relating to the basic 'aperture problem'), which help us to understand mechanisms of local and global motion processing

Discussion Questions

- What is the difference between real and apparent motion?
- How can the effects of motion correspondence be experimentally investigated, and what can we conclude from this phenomenon about the function of the visual system?
- What are the fundamental processing elements for a simple motion detecting mechanism?
- Describe the motion after-effect, discuss its underlying mechanisms, and compare it to corresponding illusions in other stimulus domains.

HEARING 1: SOUND AND NOISE

OVERVIEW

Why is hearing so important for humans? What were the evolutionary pressures, and what makes the auditory sensory system so powerful? The acoustic channel gives us access to vital information, it is essential as an alarm system, helps us in orienting through our environment, and is the basis of communication by using simple signals and language. To understand the design of the auditory system, and to appreciate what we able to hear and what we cannot hear, we have to begin with the physical nature of sound, and its transduction into neural signals as the starting point of the auditory stream into the auditory cortex. The extraordinary sensitivity and adaptability of the acoustic sense is made possible through an intricate mechanical design of the middle ear, and a sophisticated encoding of sound waves into electric signals in the inner ear, which includes neural sharpening of tuning through lateral inhibition and active processes to set the operating range. Auditory information is encoded in terms of frequency (tonotopically organised frequency channels) and amplitude (response rates of individual neurons that may be combined in a population code), corresponding to the perception of pitch and loudness. Hearing performance can be described accordingly by systematic measurements of auditory sensitivity as a function of frequency, which is represented by 'equal-loudness contours'. The concept of receptive fields and tuning will be revisited in the acoustic domain, and frequency masking will be presented as an experimental paradigm to demonstrate the existence of frequency channels, and their relevance for the operation of the auditory system in natural environments. The exact measure of sound pressure (in dB) will finally put into relation with the perception of loudness in its ecological context of typical environments experienced by humans, and some practical consequences in the context of occupational and environmental health are discussed.

WHY DO YOU NEED EARS, WHY SHOULD YOU LISTEN?

The first question about auditory perception needs to be why hearing is important for us as human beings. Sounds signal events, and because we are interested in events that happen in our environment, hearing opens a powerful channel to collect a range of information from the outside world. The sound of an approaching train or braking car, a mouse rustling in the leaves, the impact of the snowball on a window, or raindrops tapping on a tin roof, are some random examples of how we use our ears to orient ourselves in a cluttered environment, and relate to other objects and creatures. Most importantly, important alarm signals are transmitted through the auditory channel, and many animals have developed highly specialised hearing mechanisms to pick up the sound of approaching predators, or trace animals of prey. But there is more to hearing, because we not only hear sound passively generated by other animate or inanimate objects, but we also generate sound to be heard by others. Just like the songs of birds, the courtship signals of insects, or alarm calls of higher mammals, humans communicate by producing acoustic signals. Acoustic communication in humans has developed into a highly sophisticated system, language, which requires a fine auditory system to receive and extract all the information contained in acoustic signals, sometimes hidden in very fine nuances. Because hearing is so essential for communication, and communication is crucial for social interaction, the auditory system has a particular importance for humans, and in consequence is a highly developed part of the human sensory system. Some psychologists would even argue that as a sensory modality hearing is even more important than vision. This view is not only supported by the fact that a core aspect of the human condition is the ability to communicate through spoken language, but also by the observation that our emotional balance is strongly affected by sound – just think about how distressed you can become by loud noise, and how relaxing it is to listen to music.

So let us think for a moment what are the most interesting problems related to auditory perception, and what are the most challenging questions for the psychologist who is studying sensory systems. Once the basic mechanisms of encoding and decoding of acoustic signals have been understood, there are a lot of exciting questions about more advanced stages of auditory perception, such as: How does the brain enable us to recognise spoken words and the voices of individual speakers? What are the mechanisms of separating independent signal sources in a mix of voices coming from a group of people or different melody lines coming from a symphony orchestra? What is the influence of experience and knowledge on auditory perception? What is the perceptual basis of harmony, and why are some sounds always perceived as nice and others as terribly unpleasant? Whereas some of the more challenging questions will be addressed in the next chapter, we first turn to basic mechanisms of encoding sound signals in the human sensory system, and will start this by discussing the physical nature of sound.

THE NATURE OF SOUND

Any sound source, be it an exploding balloon or the plucked string of a guitar, is emitting spherical pressure waves that expand from the sound source and travel through the air in all directions. Regular shells of air compression and rarification emerge from the origin of a sound (schematically illustrated in Figure 7.1a), similar to the concentrically expanding ripples on a pond when a stone is dropped into the still water surface (Figure 7.1b). For the case of a pure tone the simple physical event of creating a regular pattern of increasing and decreasing air pressure – both in space and time – can be exactly and simply described by a travelling sinewave (Barlow and Mollon 1982). The sinewave is characterised by two parameters, its amplitude and frequency. The amplitude (see Figure 7.1c) is the distance between the maximum (peak) air pressure and the minimum (trough) air pressure; the amplitude determines how loud a tone is perceived. The frequency of a pure tone (see Figure 7.1c) is the number of pressure changes per unit of time, which is measured in cycles per second, or Hertz (Hz), or the inverse of the duration of the full cycle of a complete wave, the period from the highest pressure through the lowest pressure back to the highest pressure; the frequency determines whether a tone is perceived as high or low, which commonly is referred to as pitch (Plack 2005).

This simple description of pure tones allows us to arrange them in a coherent system in a physical parameter space, which directly corresponds to their perceptual quality. The system is very well known because it is nothing else than the musical scale, which is to be learnt when one wants to master a musical instrument (Pierce 1992). Imagine, for instance, the arrangement

Figure 7.1

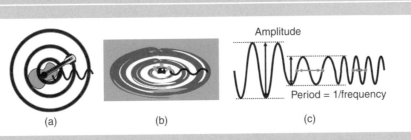

Sounds emitted from a musical instrument or other sound sources are spherical pressure waves in the air (a), similar to the radiating ripples on the water surface, when a pebble is tossed into a still pond (b). A pure tone is represented by a sinewave (c) travelling through space (air pressure as function of space or time), which is characterised by its amplitude and frequency (inverse of period).

Figure 7.2

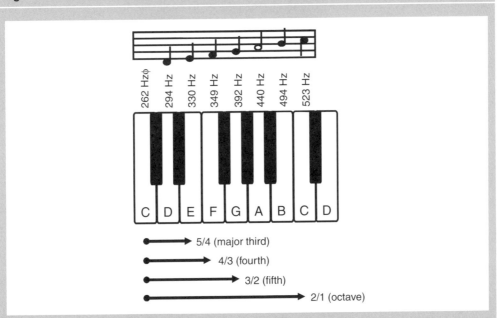

Musical tones as arranged on a keyboard (middle) correspond to notes on the musical score (top), and characteristic frequencies of the sound waves are generated by pressing this key. In the diatonic scale shown here (C-major), tones are related to each other by characteristic frequency ratios, or 'harmonic intervals' (bottom). The tone 'A', corresponding to 440 Hz, is often used as absolute reference for tuning an instrument.

of tones on the keyboard, which directly correspond to the notes on the score sheet for the piece of music that you want to play. Figure 7.2 illustrates how seven keys arranged on the keyboard could generate a C-major diatonic scale. The rise in frequency of the musical tone generated by pressing the keys corresponds to the increasing pitch perceived by the listener. Obviously, this musical scale does not require a keyboard, but it can be produced on any musical instrument, as well as by the human voice. For singers, 'solfeggio' is often used to transcribe tones of the scale into syllables – just think of the famous song 'Do-Re-Mi' that Fraulein Maria uses to teach the musical scale to the von Trapp children in *The Sound of Music*. As you can see in Figure 7.2, only very few of the tones are characterised by simple-to-remember integer frequencies, such as the 'A' at 440 Hz. Also the relationships between the frequencies of consecutive tones are not linear (the differences tend to grow with increasing frequency). The reason for this is that the steps of the musical scale are not defined by constant differences in frequency, but by multiples, that is, constant frequency ratios. An octave interval, the seven full tone steps that lead to the next tone with the same name, for instance, corresponds to the doubling of the frequency. Similarly, a frequency ratio of 3/2 relates to a harmonic interval called a 'fifth' that spans five full tones, and 4/3 to a 'fourth', etc. (Pierce 1992).

If the tone is unambiguously characterised by its frequency and amplitude, which correspond to perceived pitch and loudness, why is it that the same tone sounds so different when generated by different instruments? Indeed, there is more to a tone than just a simple sinewave (Evans 1982b). The crucial point is that musical instruments cannot generate pure tones but produce complex waveforms that are composed of several sinewaves (illustrated in Figure 7.3 for the superposition of two sinewaves). In order to generate a simple sinewave, or pure tone, you would need an electronic synthesiser as introduced to music production in the 1960s, and later developed into very powerful and now widely used tools to create electronic music that can sound truly natural (Russ 2004). Produced by a natural instrument, or indeed by the human voice, a tone with exactly the same pitch can sound so differently, because the sinewave that defines the pitch – the so-called fundamental, f_0 in Figure 7.3 – is superimposed by a number of additional sinewaves with higher frequencies, which are integer multiples of the fundamental – the so-called 'harmonics'; a single harmonic with $f_1 = 2 * f_0$ is shown in Figure 7.3. The number, frequency ratios and relative amplitudes of the harmonics determine the exact waveform of the tone generated by a particular instrument, the so-called frequency spectrum, which is perceived as 'timbre', independent of the perceived fundamental frequency, its pitch. The outstanding capability of the human auditory system is the reason why to the trained ear it is immediately clear whether a tone A, for instance, was played on the piano, harpsichord, guitar or xylophone. Now imagine the complexity of the auditory recognition task when more complex sounds are generated by adding further fundamental frequencies when playing a chord, or when a large-scale orchestra is working on a single bar of a symphony!

Figure 7.3

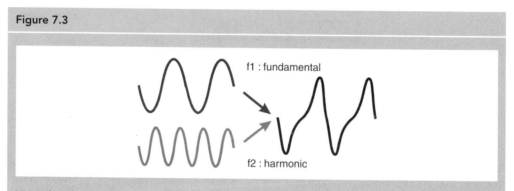

Natural tones generated by musical instruments are composed of the fundamental frequency f_1 (also called 'first harmonic'), perceived as pitch, and a set of harmonics (only the second harmonic $f_2 = 2 * f_1$ is shown here) which generate a complex waveform that is characteristic for the sound source and is perceived as timbre.

Finally, what happens when you superimpose random tones, or in other words produce a large number of pressure waves with independent properties at the same time? When a pure tone can be compared with throwing a pebble into a still pond, this is a situation that resembles tossing a handful of pebbles into the pond, or raindrops falling on the water surface. At some point individual waveforms can no longer be distinguished and disappear into an irregular pattern of surface movement. The interference between the initial waveforms generating such random patterns in the sound space makes it difficult to separate the individual contributions, or tones. The superposition of many tones with random amplitude and frequency sounds like irregular noise (Evans 1982b). This expression has a special meaning for information theory: the absence of any regularity in a signal means that it does not contain any information, which is called 'white noise', no matter whether it is an acoustic signal, a visual or any other signal. What you hear and see when your television is detuned, that is, as generating random auditory and visual signals, is white noise!

THE EAR: A HIGHLY SOPHISTICATED SENSORY ORGAN FOR ACOUSTIC SIGNALS

The sensory organ to pick up auditory information is the ear (see Figure 7.4), which works as a transducer, converting sound waves into neural signals. This biological system is characterised by an amazing functionality, which is not matched by any artificial system engineered by humans. For instance, the ear is operating with outstanding sensitivity (Gulick et al. 1989): the absolute threshold of hearing corresponds to sound levels that generate eardrum vibrations as small as 0.01 Nm (less than the diameter of a hydrogen atom; the diameter of a human hair is a million times larger!). The only visible part of the ear, the earlobe, or 'pinna' (sometimes also called 'auricle') arguably is the least relevant part of the ear, which mainly operates like a funnel to conduct the air pressure wave into the ear canal, leading to the eardrum,

Figure 7.4

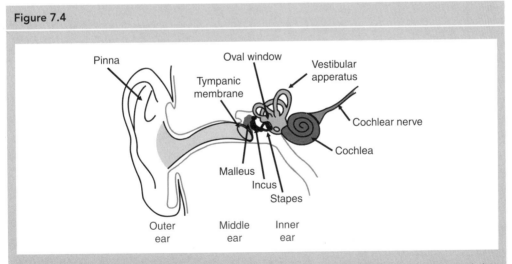

The ear is a sophisticatedly engineered sensory organ to pick up sound down to impressively low physical limits. The sound is conducted by the pinna into the ear canal leading to the eardrum (tympanic membrane), where it transformed by the three ossicles (malleus, incus and stapes) into movements of the fluid in the cochlea, behind the oval window. The mechanosensors in the cochlea transform movement into neural signals that are sent through the cochlear nerve (or 'auditory' nerve) into the brain.

or 'tympanic membrane', which starts vibrating in the frequency of the air wave. Whereas the pinna and ear canal are referred to as 'outer ear', the section from eardrum to oval window is the 'middle ear', which is a fine mechanical structure known to many of us because it can fall victim to rather painful middle ear infections. The eardrum vibration is amplified in the middle ear, adapting it from the gas medium in the outer ear to the liquid medium in the inner ear, by means of three tiny bones known as the ossicles: the hammer, or 'malleus', the anvil, or 'incus', and the stirrup, or 'stapes' (Evans 1982a). This conversion process from low-power movement in air to high-power movement in fluid is called 'impedance matching'.

The transformation of auditory information from mechanical oscillation into the neural code happens in the inner ear, which is the bony labyrinth containing a system of small cavities, or tubes that are filled with a viscous fluid. The two main functional parts of this system are (i) the vestibular apparatus, the organ of balance that consists of three semicircular canals and the vestibule, and (ii) the cochlea, the organ responsible for hearing, which contains the sensory surface that encodes sound. The mechanical stimulation is transmitted from the eardrum through ossicles on to the oval window, a membrane at the front end of the cochlea (Evans 1982a), where the oscillations are converted to pressure waves in the cochlea, which generates a travelling wave of the basilar membrane in the 'organ of Corti' (Plack 2005). The peculiar mechanical properties and their possible role for hearing were studied ingeniously by G. v. Békésy, who used microsurgery to observe the motion of tiny silver particles introduced into the cochlea (von Békésy 1961). He was awarded the Nobel Prize for his discoveries.

The cochlea is an extended canal system filled with viscous liquid that is coiled into a helical shape (see Figure 7.5a), hence the name cochlea, which is Latin for 'snail'. The essential part of this structure is the flexible basilar membrane separating two canal sections, which

Figure 7.5

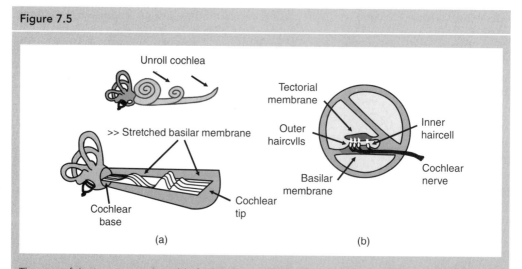

The part of the inner ear responsible for hearing is a helical structure, the cochlea, which can be seen in (a) as schematically uncoiled into an elongated tubular system. This segmented tube contains an extended 'basilar' membrane that is set into vibration (a travelling wave, similar to shaking a sheet, shown schematically in white region) by the sound transmitted by the ossicles through the oval window into the viscous fluid of the cochlea. Small haircells on the basilar membrane, shown in a cross-section across the cochlear tube in (b), are shifted relative to the tectorial membrane, and the bending of the cilia (hairs) leads to electrical activation. As a result, the travelling wave is transformed into neural signals that are sent through the cochlear nerve to the brain.

is covered with small hair cells that convert mechanical deformation, enhanced through a cover sheet, the 'tectorial membrane', into electric signals (see Figure 7.5b) – the transduction process that is crucial for all neural encoding in sensory systems. The full stretch of basilar membrane, together with its associated mechanosensor array of small hair cells, constitutes the 'organ of Corti' inside the cochlea, which is responsible for hearing (Gopen et al. 1997). One of its peculiar features of this design is that the vibrations of the basilar membrane are picked up by the hair cells and converted into a space-specific representation of tones. The sound transmitted through the oval window into the cochlea fluid generates a travelling wave, an oscillation that moves along the length of the basilar membrane. Given the mechanical properties of the membrane the wave is reaching a maximum amplitude at a location that is determined by the frequency of the stimulus. For small frequencies (low pitch tones) the largest oscillation is found at the apex of the cochlea, far away from the oval window, whereas large frequencies (high pitch tones) lead to the largest oscillation amplitude at the front end of the cochlea, close to the oval window (see Figure 7.6a, top to bottom). Because the location of the strongest mechanical, and therefore strongest electrical signal, depends systematically on the frequency of the stimulus, the organ of Corti generates a map of decreasing pitch along the extension of the basilar membrane, from the oval window to the apex of the cochlea. In other words, a spatial code for stimulus frequency is generated (Evans 1982a). The nerve fibres transmit the electrical signals from the hair cells through the auditory or 'cochlear' nerve to the Cochlear Nucleus and other regions in the brainstem, and from there to the auditory cortex. These neurons carry information about sound intensity by the level of their activation, and sound frequency by means of their location being related at each stage to the region of origin on the basilar membrane. In the auditory cortex, neighbourhood relationships of hair cells are conserved such that neurons are

Figure 7.6

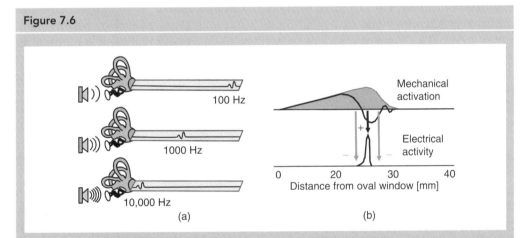

(a)   (b)

(a) Pure tones lead to oscillations in regions of the basilar membrane at locations that are determined by the tone's frequency (from top to bottom: 100 Hz, 1000 Hz, 10,000 Hz). (b) The region of mechanical activation (sketched as black deformation for one moment in time and grey envelope as time average, shown schematically as function of distance on basilar membrane from the oval window) for a given tone is broader than the activation in the neurons (sketched schematically as dark grey profile) in the cochlear nerve transmitting these signals to the auditory cortex, which corresponds to the frequency tuning of the individual neuron. This sharpening of the tuning function is achieved through lateral inhibition, the activation from the surround (grey arrows, "–") is subtracted from the activation from the centre (black arrow, "+").

arranged systematically in order of increasing stimulus frequency (Formisano et al. 2003), which leads to a 'tonotopic map' (from Greek *tonos* = pitch, and *topos* = location) similar to retinotopic maps in the visual system.

Early in the study of hearing function it was noticed that the region of the basilar membrane that is oscillating when any pure tone is stimulating the ear is much more extended than the electrical activity of the hair cells, which determines the range of frequencies that activate any particular nerve fibre in the cochlear nerve (von Békésy 1967b). This means that the frequency tuning of the mechanical system in the inner ear is broader than the frequency tuning in the neurons. So the information has been processed between the mechanical and the neural encoding, in a mechanism that some researchers refer to as 'two-tone suppression' (Moore 2003). The activity of a neuron in the cochlear nerve coding for a particular frequency is determined by the hair cell activation from the centre of the mechanical oscillation, from which the hair cell activation from the surround – the neighbouring regions further up and down the basilar membrane – is subtracted (see Figure 7.6b). Note that the fundamental mechanism in this sharpening of frequency tuning (von Békésy 1967a) shows properties that resemble the lateral inhibition that was discussed in the context of the visual system as basis of contrast enhancement and redundancy reduction through opponency (Chapters 3 and 4).

The brief description of the cochlear function given here is no more than a coarse sketch, if not caricature, of what really happens in the ear (for a more detailed picture, see Plack, 2005) when we are picking up sound – which we do for 24 hours a day, every day of our life. The actual electromechanical events in the ear, including some amazing mechanisms for amplification, selection and protection, are much more complex than could be described here and they are still a matter of landmark research (Mellado Lagarde et al. 2008). Furthermore, we have neglected to discuss aspects of hearing that are not mediated by airborne sound signals but conducted through bone tissue (von Békésy 1949), which is crucial for some hearing aids (Westerkull 2002). For our purpose it is sufficient to conclude that the encoding of acoustic signals requires several 'engineering tasks', which are accomplished by a biological system that has been driven by evolution to astonishing perfection. The outer ear serves as directional collector of pressure waves and conduit into the middle ear, which performs impedance matching, and protects against mechanical overload to the highly sensitive mechanical structures. The inner ear contains a sophisticated electromechanical transducer that includes the first steps of frequency analysis. On its way from the outside world into the cortex, auditory information is processed by the same fundamental mechanisms that we find in other sensory modalities, which we have been discussing in some detail for the visual system. These mechanisms include (i) tuning, the preferential response of a sensor to a dedicated stimulus range (here tone frequency, or pitch); (ii) filtering mechanisms based on lateral inhibition, which sharpens frequency tuning to pitch in the peripheral auditory system; and (iii) sensory maps, the peripheral and cortical representation in which frequency information is ordered in its position in neural networks (tonotopy).

PITCH PERCEPTION: FREQUENCY CHANNELS REVEALED BY MASKING

So far we have looked at the anatomical and physiological aspects of hearing. But how can we study auditory perception, for instance the sensation associated with the frequency of tones, which is experienced as pitch? The most fundamental experimental method is

Figure 7.7

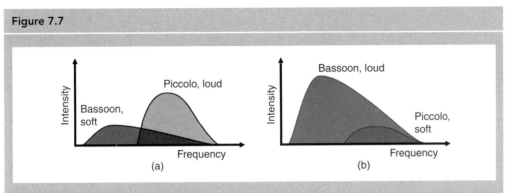

Masking is the perceptual disappearance of one stimulus (sound of the piccolo flute) in the sensory response generated by another, a different, stimulus (sound of the bassoon); the sound intensity of both instruments are plotted as a function of tone frequency. (a) You only hear the piccolo if the bassoon is played very softly. (b) If the bassoon is played at full strength, all its frequency components have a larger amplitude than those of the piccolo, and therefore completely conceal the piccolo's frequencies, which no longer can be heard.

called 'masking', which is a general technique used in many other areas of sensory or cognitive psychology. The phenomenon of auditory masking is schematically illustrated in Figure 7.7 with an example from music – the phenomenon that you can only hear two separate instruments in an orchestra if they differ sufficiently in their frequency spectrum, and are adjusted in their volume such that the frequencies produced by one instruments (piccolo flute, in this example) are not completely eclipsed (or 'masked') by the frequencies produced by the other instrument (bassoon, in this case).

Based on this simple observation, a straightforward and powerful auditory masking experiment can be designed. Participants, or listeners in this case, are asked to detect a target tone (for instance, a pure sine of 1000 Hz) in presence of a mask, which can be another tone with different frequency (Wegel and Lane 1924), or narrow-band noise, which is a small range of different frequencies with a particular centre frequency (Scharf 1971). The intensity of the masking sound is increased until the target tone can be no longer detected and decreased until the target tone is audible again, in order to determine the detection threshold for this target–mask combination. The mask intensity at detection threshold is inversely proportional to the sensitivity of the detection mechanism for this mask frequency, that is, the signal intensity in the subset of neurons that is responsible for detecting the target tone. By repeating the same estimation procedure for a range of mask frequencies the sensitivity profile to stimulus frequency can be described, which is the 'frequency tuning' of the underlying neural mechanism. There are a number of variations of the target–mask conditions that can be used to measure different aspects of the encoding of tones in the auditory system, including the frequency interval that represents equal distances on the basilar membrane (cf. Figure 7.6a), the 'critical band' (Greenwood 1961).

By means of systematic variation of the mask frequency a set of detection thresholds is determined for a given target frequency to determine the psychophysical tuning curve for the neural filter mechanism responsible for this target frequency (Evans 1982a): when the mask amplitude at detection threshold is plotted as function of mask frequency (see Figure 7.8a), low thresholds for masks close to the target frequency indicate high sensitivity of the filter tuned to these mask frequencies, and high thresholds for masks distant from the target frequency

Figure 7.8

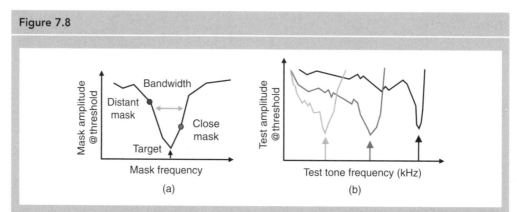

Frequency tuning. (a) Psychophysical measurements are used to determine the amplitudes of a masking sound at variable mask frequencies, which define the threshold for the detection of a simultaneously presented target tone. A mask close in frequency (light grey dot) requires a smaller amplitude than a distant mask (dark grey dot), in order to suppress the detection of the target (black arrow), leading to a U-shaped tuning curve (sketched schematically) that is responsible for frequency selectivity, with a characteristic location on the frequency axis and a particular band-width (grey arrow). (b) In electrophysiological recordings (for instance, from the cochlear nerve) the threshold intensity of a test tone that is needed for eliciting a neural response can be used directly to describe frequency tuning of an auditory neuron (schematically sketched here for three hypothetical neurons with different tuning frequencies, indicated by different shades of grey).

indicate low sensitivity. The minimum threshold (i.e. maximum sensitivity) of the U-shaped threshold curve points to the centre frequency of the filter in question (which is the target frequency in the masking experiment), and the frequency distance between the two points at half-height on the two slopes of the tuning curve is called the 'bandwidth' of the filter. The bandwidth is a measure for the sharpness of tuning – a small bandwidth means that only a narrow range of frequencies is processed by this filter (narrowband), whereas a large band-width indicates much less selectivity for stimulus frequency (broadband). Although this tech-nical language initially may sound surprising in the context of biological systems and human perception, it reflects a practical and theoretical understanding of how pitch is encoded in the human auditory system: an array of neurons (i.e. set of filters) that respond preferentially to a set of different characteristic tones (i.e. are tuned to frequencies) represent pitch in the human auditory system, and are responsible for the detection and discrimination of different sounds (see Figure 7.8b). We should also keep in mind that the terminology used to describe hearing is by no means a stranger to us – it is the same as you will find in the manual of your CD-player, stereo system or digital TV, and the word 'broadband' arguably is the most popular word to use when it comes to your Internet connection.

The physiological basis of pitch perception can be directly observed by means of electrophysi-ological recordings from individual fibres in the cochlear nerve (which is the analogue to the optic nerve in the visual system) – the axons of individual sensory neurons that transmit auditory information from the sensory organ to the auditory cortex. The sound intensity that is needed to generate activity in the nerve fibre is shown schematically in Figure 7.8b as a function of tone frequency for three units that are tuned to different frequencies (for real data, see Evans 1982a). It is immediately clear that each threshold U-shaped response profile can be directly compared to the frequency tuning measured psychophysically (Figure 7.8a) with one target tone. A common

Figure 7.9

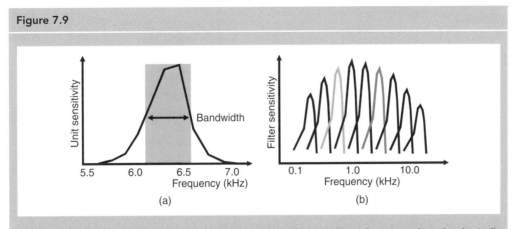

Frequency channels. (a) The tuning function of an individual filter, or channel, measured psychophysically or electro-physiologically, can be represented by a sensitivity profile as function of stimulus frequency with two critical parameters, centre frequency and bandwidth. (b) A set of several frequency channels characterises hearing performance and can be used as a basis to explain the detection of sound and frequency selectivity which is crucial for the discrimination of pitch.

way to represent the masking experiment results and the tuning properties of the neurons that mirror this behaviour is shown schematically in Figure 7.9a as sensitivity profiles (the inverse of thresholds). In this form the curves are inverted from a U-shape to a Bell-shape, where the two more familiar curve parameters, midpoint and dispersion, may be helpful to interpret the meaning of the tuning parameters, centre frequency and bandwidth. Individual neurons tuned to different centre frequencies operate like an extended set of frequency-tuned filters that cover the full range of frequencies (sketched in Figure 7.9b) as the basis for the frequency discrimination involved in auditory perception. Note that this similar strategy of frequency encoding is similar to the encoding called the 'Fourier analyser' in the visual system (see Chapter 3), and the same encoding specialising on noise reduction can be found in digital audio systems!

THE PERCEPTION OF LOUDNESS: MEASURING SENSITIVITY TO SOUND INTENSITY

After having discussed the first aspect of hearing a tone, perceived pitch that is related to frequency, we now turn to the second parameter, the magnitude of auditory sensation, which is determined by the pressure of airwaves and is related to perceived as loudness. Physically, sound intensity is defined by sound pressure level (Pierce 1992), SPL, and measured in decibels, dB, defined as the logarithm of the ratio of the sample sound pressure, I, relative to the pressure of the normal hearing threshold at 1000 Hz (I_0 = 20 micropascals): SPL = 20 * log (I/I_0). This means that when sound pressure grows by a multiple of 10, the SPL value increases by 20 dB (see Table 7.1). Whereas it may initially appear simple to measure loudness, the subjectivity of such perceptual judgements is a substantial problem for such experiments. Nevertheless in several studies an astonishing level of consistency was found (Stevens 1956) when the intensity of tone is decreased or increased relative to a reference tone, and participants are asked to rate the relative magnitude (as multiples of the reference tone): subjective ratings of loudness change proportionally to SPL (see Figure 7.10), suggesting a power law for this subjective estimate (Stevens 1957). Stevens proposed to use 'sones' as units of perceived sound intensity, or loudness (Stevens 1936).

Figure 7.10

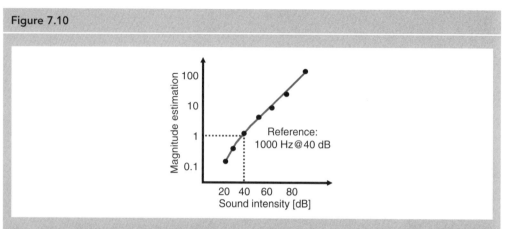

Perceived loudness. Participants are asked to estimate the magnitude of a test tone (for which sound pressure level, SPL, was varied) as multiples of a reference tone (in this example a 1000 Hz tone at 40 dB) – the relationship is approximately linear in this logarithmic scaling.

Table 7.1 The ecology of sound pressure

	0 dB	threshold of hearing (at 1000 Hz)	
	10 dB	normal breathing	
10 ×	20 dB	standing in a forest: leaves rustling in a breeze	
	30 dB	empty lecture theatre	
100 ×	40 dB	College campus at night (without planes)	
	50 dB	quiet restaurant	
1000 ×	60 dB	two-person conversation	
	70 dB	standing at the roadside in Trafalgar Square	
10,000 ×	80 dB	operating a vacuum cleaner	discomfort
	90 dB	getting close to a huge waterfall (Niagara)	danger level
100,000 ×	100 dB	underground train passing the platform	danger level
1,000,000 ×	120 dB	getting close to a propeller plane at takeoff	hearing loss
10,000,000 ×	140 dB	Heathrow: standing near a jet plane at takeoff	pain level

Note: Examples of acoustic environments (third column) that expose a person to a range sound intensity (SPL), as measured in decibels (dB, second column) as logarithmic multiples of the hearing threshold at 1000 Hz; to help with this measure, the factors of sound pressure relative to threshold are given for 20 dB changes in the first column. The last column indicates the risk of the sound levels in a given environment damaging the auditory system.

A method to measure perceived loudness quantitatively, which is not based on subjective ratings and therefore is less dependent on the participant's internal criteria and reliability, involves the comparison of two pure tones that are successively presented in a forced choice paradigm, by asking them to decide which one sounded louder. When one of the stimuli, the reference tone, is kept at constant frequency and SPL, and the SPL of the other stimulus,

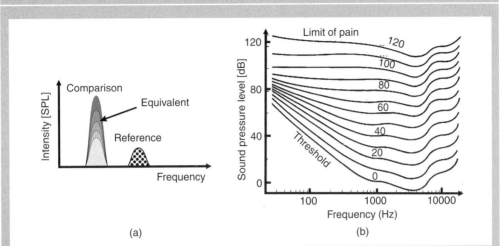

(a)   (b)

Measuring audibility and perceived loudness of tones at a range of frequencies. (a) The basic experimental design involves the evaluation of a reference tone of fixed frequency and SPL (textured Bell shape) and a comparison tone with variable SPL (Bell shapes with variable shades of grey) to establish at which SPL they are perceived as being equally loud. (b) By testing a wide range of frequencies for the comparison tone in this matching paradigm, equal-loudness contours are generated for different intensities of the reference tone, between the threshold of hearing and high SPLs that approach the limit of pain.

the comparison tone, is varied it can be determined when their loudness is perceived as equivalent (see sketch in Figure 7.11a). It is common to use a 1000 Hz tone as reference, which is close to threshold at 0 dB SPL. When the SPL that are perceived as having the same loudness as the reference tone are determined for the full range of audible frequencies, contours of equal loudness can be generated (Berrien 1946). A set of such curves for several intensities of the reference tone leads to a family of equal-loudness contours (see Figure 7.11b), including the absolute threshold contour, which is the basis for the audibility function, or 'audiogram', which describes the limits of hearing performance for an individual as a function of frequency, and therefore is widely used in clinical practice to assess hearing impairments (Moore 2003).

Knowing that audible sound can vary in intensity by a factor of 10,000,000, or 140 dB, it is interesting to ask in which ecological contexts which sound intensities are experienced. As indicated by the set of examples listed in Table 7.1, the sound pressures we are exposed to in natural environments are moderate (unless we are subjected to very dangerous situations, like an volcanic eruption), and high SPLs induce pain, which would trigger escape reflexes. In man-made environments, however, we can be exposed to very high sound pressures that can damage the inner ear, leading to temporary (for instance, when enjoying techno music at close range, if you are lucky) or permanent hearing loss (explosions). Certain work places, such as airports, can present considerable occupational health hazards (May 2000), and protective gear is compulsory. A particular interesting, and highly debated, issue is how to measure and to assess the impact of chronic ambient noise on the population living in the neighbourhood of busy airports (Haines et al. 2001) or on workers in noisy factories. Interestingly, the ear itself, being a biological system, has some protective and repair mechanisms to limit the impact of high pressure exposure (Robinson 2009), and intensive research is carried out to study the regeneration of cochlear hair cells (Corwin and Oberholtzer 1997) that commonly were believed not to recover from damage in mammals.

Take Home Messages

- the auditory 'channel' is an important source of crucial sensory information that opens another window to the world
- the physical nature of sound is based on waves of air pressure, which can be delivered as pure tones, composites, complex patterns or noise
- the ear is a highly sensitive and intelligent device to pick up and convert sound pressure waves into electric signals; the essential transduction is based on the cochlear function in the inner ear
- frequency filtering, which originates from the electro-mechanical properties of the inner ear and is further enhanced by neural processing, is the basis of perceiving pitch; it can be studied electrophysiologically or psychophysically in masking experiments
- sound intensity is the second characteristic property of sound, with high ecological significance, which is perceived as loudness
- hearing shares basic mechanisms with other sensory system, such as peripheral filtering, efficient neural encoding and sensory maps in cortical representation

Discussion Questions

- Explain the physical nature of sound, with reference to the perception of pitch and loudness.
- How is tone frequency encoded in the auditory system?
- What is measured in the unit of 'dB', and what does it mean?
- Describe the impact of sound volume (loudness) with some examples from the real world.

8 HEARING 2: COMPLEX AUDITORY INFORMATION

OVERVIEW

To understand the perception of sound for situations that go beyond simple isolated tones, we need to consider the structure of sound patterns, and systematically describe the performance of hearing in a behavioural and ecological context. Complex sounds are described, and analysed, by means of 'spectrograms', which represent the sound energy in different frequency bands as function of time. This technique provides us with a tool to study the advanced processing of complex acoustic information, such as human speech, laughter or musical harmony. Spectrograms can be related to the equal-loudness contours that describe the range and perceived loudness of audible tones, in order to assess the human auditory experience – this is of particular importance when we compare the limits of hearing to the range of frequencies and loudness that are used for acoustic communication. The spectral composition of human speech is thus discussed in the context of technical communication systems, such as telephones, and of impairments, such as partial hearing loss, and their consequences for organising behaviour. A second area of intense interest for many years has been the perception of music, offering some challenges to the scientific mind – many of these questions have prompted new research efforts connected to the development of modern neuroscientific techniques in the last few years. Finally, we look into the question of how three-dimensional space can be explored with hearing, and how acoustic space is represented in the cortex. A particular challenge is the separation of sound sources in cluttered acoustic spaces with multiple complex sources, and the cocktail party effect is a stunning demonstration of how efficiently the human sensory system deals with this problem. The chapter ends with a short comment on auditory illusions, using the example of Shepard's eternally raising tone, which correspond to similar deceptions of the processing mechanisms in the human visual system.

UNDERSTANDING SPEECH

Hearing has not evolved to pick up simple sounds, or pure tones – these were only introduced in the previous chapter to illustrate the physical properties of sound and the fundamental principles of its encoding. In the real world, more often than not, acoustic events are rather complex combinations of such simple sounds, and the perception of complex sound is the topic of this chapter. Mathematically, according to the so-called Fourier Theory (see Chapter 3), each and every complex sound event can be composed by superposition of a set of pure tones (which are sinewave functions) with varying frequency, phase and amplitude (we saw a simple superposition in the last chapter in Figure 7.3). So any acoustic event can be fully described by such a set of frequency components – in reverse, this means that it can be analysed in frequency channels like the neurons in the cochlear nerve tuned to particular frequencies (and the encoding filter banks in digital recorders). It also means that any acoustic stimulus can be generated by a sufficiently sophisticated set of frequency-specific resonators, as can be found in musical synthesisers. Unfortunately for the puzzled scientist, and fortunately for everyone of us as listener, the auditory system is not that simple, and individual tones are not just superimposed, but they interact in perception: this is called a non-linear system, which is much more interesting but also more substantially difficult to understand, and full of surprises. Nevertheless, the best way of describing sound is to show how it is made up from a combination of frequencies. The 'spectrum' of a tone, or sound, or noise, or any auditory event can be a simple or a complicated pattern of frequencies and intensities. This spectrum is usually modulated from one moment to the next, and therefore such a frequency composition is best described as a function of time, which is called a 'spectrogram' (Moore 2003). The simple case of the three musical tones that are forming a chord can be seen in the schematic spectrogram sketched in Colour plate VI, Figure 2a. You can see a succession of three different clusters with rising fundamental and harmonic frequency (greylevel corresponding to decreasing intensity of higher harmonics), which correspond to the three tones D, F, A (cf. Figure 7.2).

Whereas the structure of such a simple chord is clear and well-ordered, we now need to become aware of the complexity of most common natural tones like spoken words, which is illustrated in Colour plate VI, Figure 2b. Each syllable generates a complex pattern (spectrum) of frequency and intensity (colour-coded in this figure), which is modulated as a function of time – the so-called dynamics. At the bottom of Colour plate VI, Figure 2b you can read the phrase that led to this particular spectrogram and the waveform (for more detail, see Plack 2005), which is the sound pressure track as it would be picked up with a microphone – perhaps you realise how much richer the information is that is given by the full spectrogram (frequency and amplitude composition, i.e. pitch and loudness), as compared to the waveform envelope (sound pressure maxima and minima only, without frequency information). This spectrogram represents the information from which your auditory system extracts the phrase 'enjoy your weekend', triggering a hopefully positive mood, and possibly giving you a signal to pack your bag and escape from the lecture hall! Now imagine how difficult it is to recognise the same word generated by different speakers, at different pitch and timbre, with different accents, or to detect the voice of a particular speaker from different phrases. If you ever worked with a voice recognition system, you may be able to appreciate the complexities inherent in this task, which your brain usually masters without any effort. The secret of speech perception lies in breaking down these complex patterns into simple spectrographic elements. The spectral envelopes of peak intensity at multiple frequencies are the 'formants' resulting from the characteristic resonance patterns of the human vocal system where the voice is generated. Formants with rising, or falling transitions can be mapped to 'phonemes', which are the smallest elements into which spoken language can be segmented. Phonemes then need to be recognised by the auditory system in spite of variability in average pitch, overall duration or intensity (Moore 2003). This closes the loop between speech production, related to the physics of the vocal tract generating elementary sounds with characteristic spectral and temporal envelopes, and speech perception based on neural mechanisms that decompose the resulting sound patterns into meaningful components. It will be interesting to investigate in more detail whether cortical pattern recognition mechanisms underlying such auditory processing resemble higher-level encoding strategies that are well studied in the visual system (King and Nelken 2009).

As can be seen in Colour plate VI, Figure 2, the spectrum of human speech covers a certain range of the audible spectrum, and varies in volume to span several equal-loudness contours (cf. Figure 7.11b), but is restricted to the centre of the full operating range of the

Figure 8.1

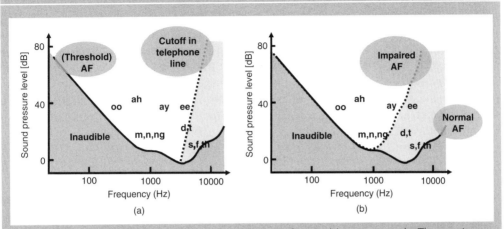

Frequency and intensity (sound pressure level) range of normal human speech. The continuous black line shows the audibility function, which indicates detection threshold for pure tones (AF, cf. Figure 7.11); the approximate location for vowels and consonants is shown by the letters. (a) Cutting off higher frequencies (broken line) by bandwidth-limited technical devices, such as telephones, usually does not impair speech comprehension substantially. (b) Impairments of audibility, such as age-related loss of higher frequencies (broken line), can seriously affect communication.

human auditory system (see Figure 8.1). Normal speech only covers a region of the auditory response range approximately between 300 and 5000 Hz and between 40 and 70 dB, slightly different for males and females. It can be argued that the restriction to the centre of the audible range makes speech recognition less sensitive to noise and supports top-down mechanisms of perceiving speech in noise (Nahum et al. 2008). How constrained this active range is in humans can be appreciated when we compare it to other biological systems, generating and picking up sounds that we cannot hear at all. Whales and elephants, for instance, are using infrasound – frequencies below 20 Hz – to communicate over large distances (e.g. Payne et al. 1986). At the other end of the frequency range, bats, among other animals, are using ultrasound – frequencies above 20 KHz – for navigation and foraging (e.g. Neuweiler 1984). Within the limited range used by humans, vowel sounds are mainly found in the lower frequency region, whereas consonants cover almost the entire range (see Figure 8.1). The specific location of sounds in the frequency-intensity space can vary for individual speakers, and its significance the for speech recognition is a matter of debate, because there is evidence that the temporal envelope of a sound on its own can be very important for understanding spoken language (Shannon et al. 1995).

Arguably of the most serious consequence of hearing impairments is the disruption of the ability to communicate effectively. Interestingly enough, some technical systems such as telephones restrict the range of frequencies to be communicated, and cut off the upper part of the spectrum that is crucial for detecting some consonants, such as 's', 'f', or 'th' (see Figure 8.1a), and do so with minimal effects on speech recognition. Note that for a non-native English speaker, the notoriously difficult pronunciation of 'th' does not seem to matter when talking on the phone. The absence of disruptive effects in this context demonstrates the redundancy of speech communication. Obviously, this redundancy can be used by engineers to minimise the information transmitted by such technical systems while retaining the message of the sound that is produced to the receiver, which actually is the reason for limiting the frequency band transmitted through phone lines. Similar to the image compression techniques that were discussed in Chapter 2, in modern systems the auditory information is compressed by digital technologies, such as mpeg encoding. This redundancy reduction helps to make better use of communication channels – for instance, moments of silence do not need to be transmitted to your mobile phone – and helps to save money, to the customer or the service provider. Equally, it is used to save memory space on audio devices by means of intelligent encoding of sound tracks, allowing you to store many more tracks on your iPod or any other media player. Other technical systems, such as top-end audio equipment, are designed to capture the full range of human audibility without any loss of information, and represent sound with high fidelity ('HiFi').

A natural context in which auditory information is partially lost, without control of whether this information is redundant or essential, is hearing loss. There are many different types of auditory impairments, apart from complete deafness, some of which have profound impact on communication ability and therefore seriously affect the lifestyle and well-being of sufferers. Excessive noise exposure can lead to temporary threshold shifts (auditory fatigue) or permanent (and possibly partial) deafness, as discussed in Chapter 7. The most common hearing impairment is presbycusis, the selective loss of high-frequency sensitivity with age (Patterson et al. 1982). A typical pattern of presbycusis is shown in Figure 8.1b, indicating how the sensitivity for many consonants and some vowels is lost, which reduces speech recognition substantially. Careful evaluation by the audiologist is required to identify the special needs of such a patient and to develop an intervention plan to minimise the impact of such a condition – sadly, presbycusis is not reversible because it is related to mechanical ageing of the inner ear. Because younger people are more sensitive to high frequencies, targeted sounds can be used that are inaudible for older folk, including special ring-tones for mobile phones that owing to their high frequency open an exclusive communication channel for students that is kept private from their teachers, or rather questionable attempts to utilise acoustic repellants against young ASBOs. A particularly annoying and mysterious hearing impairment is tinnitus: sufferers perceive continuous or intermittent humming or ringing in their ear, usually only in one, which cannot be stopped or suppressed. Only after long exposure can some patients learn to ignore the tone, and at some point start losing any sensitivity in the affected frequency range, because they develop selective deafness for this tone. This sound is not just imagination; in some cases it can be picked up by a sensitive microphone placed in the ear canal, which suggests that in this condition the inner ear begins to oscillate autonomously and transmit sound into the outer ear (oto-emissions), but we are far from understanding the condition or developing a remedy or cure (Jastreboff and Hazell 1993). Given the consequences of any of these conditions for communication and social life, lot of research is targeted at the development of hearing aids. The diagram in Figure 8.1 also makes clear that it is not sufficient just to increase the volume (as was done in early hearing aids), because for wide regions the threshold has been raised to unattainable values. More annoyingly, general amplification will intensify the noise as much as the tones that should be heard. What is needed is an intelligent device that amplifies and suppresses selectively, according to the needs of the individual patient – but it seems to be difficult to match the sophistication of the human ear. For some forms of hearing impairments related to inner ear malfunction, cochlear implants – which basically replace the sensory transduction process by an electronic acoustic sensor that is connected to the auditor nerve – have been one of the more successful techniques to partially restore hearing function (Moore and Shannon 2009).

YOU MAY LIKE IT – OR NOT: MUSIC!

There are few sensory events that affect us so strongly and comprehensively as music. Why are these complex acoustic stimuli perceived so immediately, and why are they so closely connected to emotional responses (see Figure 8.2)? More basically, what makes a sound pleasant? And what makes a sound unpleasant, or even aversive? Pleasant and aversive sounds are decoded effortlessly and quickly, so do humans from all educational and cultural backgrounds have the same emotional responses to different categories of sound? At least within Western society, there seem to be some acoustical events that we all agree sound horrible: just think of fingernails scraping blackboards, or the squeaking of grinding disks (or the drill of your dentist)! The universality and the biological function of rapid, reliable categorising aversive sounds (Czigler et al. 2007), often consistently between individuals, is still a matter of scientific debate (Cox 2008). On the other hand, the positive emotions are usually associated with experiencing music, which can sometimes elevate into near-mythical quality. The astronomer Johannes Kepler (1571–1630), when studying the movement of the planets in the nocturnal sky, was searching for the musical harmony of the spheres (Gingras 2003). Music is often believed to exert magical power, and a common thread of narrative reaches out from antiquity (just think of the story of Orpheus who could bring rocks to life with the sound of his lyre) to modernity about the healing power of music. We may smile when we hear of the 'letter from the Reverend Dr Doddridge at Northampton, ... of one, who had no Ear to Music naturally, singing several Tunes when in a Delirium', but being reported in the *Proceedings of the Royal Society* (Doddridge 1753) it was certainly regarded as solid empirical evidence about the very special nature of music. And we should never forget how popular the so-called Mozart effect was for many years, and similar ideas continue to be commercially exploited: There were various claims that listening to music by Mozart would have surprising effects on various aspects of learning and development of humans (for the scientific end of this hype, see Rauscher et al. 1993), which could raise IQ, and there are urban (or rural) myths that the milk yield can be boosted by playing Mozart to cows. Later research has shown that there are little if any consistent effects of Mozart on cognitive performance, although there is evidence that listening to music in general can have some beneficial effects on patients with epilepsy (Jenkins 2001).

Figure 8.2

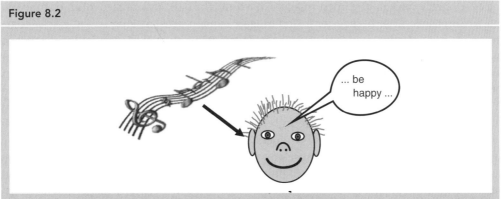

Music can have an immediate and substantial effect on our emotional well-being. Understanding the 'magic power' of such acoustic events in terms of information processing mechanisms is arguably one of the greatest challenges for researchers studying auditory perception.

Perhaps we should step back from the excitement of such glowing promises and ask more modest questions, which can be addressed with robust scientific methodology. Our knowledge of the basic function of the auditory system should provide us with some tools to help us study advanced levels of processing acoustic information, such as the perception of music. When it comes, however, to the scientific study of music, things get immediately complicated again – and we are confronted with a number of problems, such as the wide range of different methods to look at different aspects of music perception and production, the wide range of different music styles and demands, and the different levels of involvement in music, which need to be a investigated in their own right. First of all, music starts with music production, and music production requires a sophisticated coordination between sensory and motor activities, which involves the precise timing of actions in relation to percepts, and complex feedback mechanisms to control the musical output that require thorough knowledge of the instrument. It has been suggested that the perceptual features of music are integrated in the premotor cortex with appropriately timed and coordinated actions (Zatorre et al. 2007). Therefore, when investigating the performance of the musician, it is very difficult to separate perceptual from motor control aspects. To complicate things even further, completely different approaches to music production become apparent when the reproduction of extensively rehearsed musical sequences in an orchestra is compared with the free improvisation in jazz. During improvisation a dissociated pattern of activity is observed in the prefrontal cortex, and the deactivation of some areas and activation of others is interpreted as reflecting internally motivated processes that are not determined directly by the stimulus – patterns that you would expect for spontaneous improvisation. This incoherent activity pattern is accompanied by coherent activity in the sensorimotor area of the neocortex, related to planning and execution of finely controlled motor patterns, and a deactivation of limbic structures that are believed to drive motivation and emotion (Limb and Braun 2008).

One of the key aspects of music perception is related to the easiness and reliability with which we can recognise rhythms and melodies, musical motifs, individual singer's voices, instrumentations, the style of individual composers or interpreters, musical genres and historical periods (Longuet-Higgins 1979). Although no performance or recording of a piece of music is exactly the same as any other, we immediately recognise Vivaldi's 'Seasons' even if it is enslaved as a ring tone, or identify Paul McCartney's 'Yesterday' even if it is weeping from the ageing elevator speaker in a noisy shopping mall. Although some amazing expertise can be developed to pick up the finest nuances in a tune, the basic task of recognising a tune can be accomplished even by Reverend Doddridge's acquaintance, as long as she is in a coma (see above). To classify and identify such a wide range of acoustic objects, the brain needs to combine representations of advanced musical features such as rhythm or tonality into 'conceptual structures' (Longuet-Higgins 1979). An attempt to break down the many processes involved in music perception into subunits that can be studied on their own can be found in Figure 8.3. This 'neurocognitive model' of music perception (Koelsch and Siebel 2005) joins together neuroanatomical knowledge and electrophysiological responses to stimulation with music to develop a flow diagram of the processing steps that can account for low-level feature and pattern recognition, being interpreted as syntax (structure), such as rhythmic grouping, melody and harmony, and link it to high-level mechanisms to extract semantics (meaning) and emotional content that affects the autonomic nervous system. Although the arrangement of processing steps in this model is informed by the anatomical structure of the brain and by the timing of neural activity, the lines between the various boxes shown in Figure 8.3, that is, the connectivity of processing units, may appear a little strenuous and unspecific,

Figure 8.3

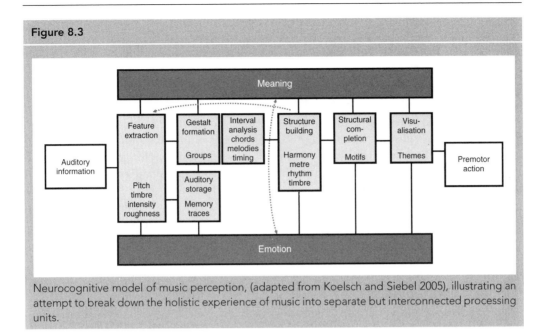

Neurocognitive model of music perception, (adapted from Koelsch and Siebel 2005), illustrating an attempt to break down the holistic experience of music into separate but interconnected processing units.

as if each box is connected almost to each other, suggesting that the logic of sequential steps in a processing chain is not always clearly defined.

Looking into the functionality of any of the processing boxes shown in Figure 8.3 we find some answers to the challenging questions about detailed mechanisms, but also many more fascinating, and unresolved, problems. Just as an example, what makes combinations of tones sound dissonant or consonant, what is the basis of harmony? There is a long history (and there are substantial intercultural differences) of considering the frequency relationships between tone intervals that sound harmonic (see Chapter 7), such as the idea that temporal patterns of activations show certain similarities for tones that are perceived as consonant (e.g. Boomsliter and Creel 1961). Indeed, there can be temporal synchrony between auditory neurons that encode frequencies generated by tone pairs that are in harmonic or octave relationships, but such phase locking should also happen for simple frequency ratios that are not classified as harmonic intervals. An alternative idea is based on the frequency ratios of higher harmonics in naturally produced sounds such as speech, for instance 2:1, 3:2, 4:3, etc., are learnt from early childhood to support pitch detection, and that the familiarity with such frequency ratios determines what is perceived as similar or consonant (Terhardt 1974).

Looking at earlier steps of the music processing stream, it is known that there are comparatively simple grouping mechanisms related to the onset of brief acoustic stimuli, when signals that are repeatedly synchronised are grouped together (Darwin 1997). For the most early processing steps, which include the perception of pitch, we should briefly discuss a phenomenon that has a particular importance for musicians, the perception of absolute pitch. Whereas everyone is very well able to distinguish the pitch of two tones, and reasonably adept in telling which is the higher one of the two, there are only a few individuals who can perceive the pitch of an isolated tone without any reference. That is the reason why musicians use a resonating instrument with constant pitch, such as a tuning fork, to anchor the tuning of their instrument, or set the initial pitch of their voice. Absolute pitch, however, is the ability to identify a tone by naming or singing it without referring to such an external standard. It is generally believed that this ability is inborn, and there are attempts to unravel the genetic basis of pitch recognition (Drayna et al. 2001). On the other hand, there is evidence that there is a substantial involvement of long-term memory with particular importance of early infancy (Levitin and Rogers 2005), and that accuracy of pitch judgement can be improved by practice (Cuddy 1968).

Neuroscience has started to make a valuable contribution to our understanding of how music is perceived and produced. For instance, brain imaging techniques can be used to identify the neural substrate and some processing aspects of music. Alternatively, by studying the impact of brain damage on the abilities of musicians, such as Maurice Ravel (Sergent 1993), the neuroanatomy of musical function can be traced and related to perceptual and cognitive networks. The interaction of syntactical structures and semantic content in the processing of music (Koelsch and Siebel 2005) links music closely to language, and in tonal languages, such as Mandarin or Cantonese, pitch is not only used to alter the emotional vein of spoken words, but their meaning. Based on these observations, one could speculate about its evolutionary relationship – is music a form of communication that has evolved from speech, has language developed from basic musical utterances, or can we regard music and language as independent developments that share some parts of the cortical hardware and some modules of information processing? The close link of music to the emotional content of vocal expressions, and the functional interactions between music and speech are indirectly demonstrated by the observation that the perception of emotional content in speech is facilitated in practising musicians (Strait et al. 2009). With a growing level of expertise, musicians show stronger and stronger responses in subcortical structures that are involved in the communication of emotional states, in line with behavioural observations that musical training facilitates the processing of the emotional content of acoustic signals. Many aspects of music production and perception have been studied in their relation to cortical function with a range of imaging methods, such as the homogeneity of the spatial distribution of EEG activity during listening to music (Bhattacharya and Petsche 2001), the overlap and separation of music and language in cortical processing (Steinbeis and Koelsch 2008), or the relationship between musical imagery and expertise (Herholz et al. 2008). But it is perhaps the contribution of subcortical structures to music processing that is most surprising. Wong et al. (2007) studied the encoding of pitch in the brainstem and found that this is more robust for musicians than for controls, which could be interpreted as top-down effects on the early neural representation shared by music and speech, from the cortex to the brainstem, which in turn could explain why musicians appear to be so good at learning languages!

AUDITORY SPACE

To complicate things further for the brain that has to make sense of complex acoustic patterns, sounds are not coming out of nowhere, but are generated and localised in the world around us – we need to consider acoustic space. Just as visual stimuli arise from a three-dimensional space, and objects can be placed at (almost) any location in this space, sound can originate from arbitrary locations in the very same three-dimensional space. In contrast to the visual system, which starts with two-dimensional images from which three-dimensional space is reconstructed (see Chapter 5), the auditory system has to build a spatial representation from much poorer information: each ear samples sound at a single point in space and therefore essentially is a one-dimensional sensor handling an information stream that does not contain any spatial information. The most important – but not the only – feature of hearing that allows us to explore

Figure 8.4

Auditory space. When you close your eyes and listen to your environment you can pick up many sounds as illustrated schematically in this sketch, the engine of a scooter, the rustling of leaves in the wind, the chopping of a helicopter, the tapping of a youngster bouncing a ball, the song of birds, and so forth. How does the brain recognise these sounds and localise them in space? As suggested by this image, and the instruction to close your eyes, interaction with other sensory systems such as vision supports auditory perception, and we will return to this issue in Chapter 11.

auditory space is the use of two ears, which sample sounds from two separate positions in space (Plack 2005; Schnupp and Carr 2009). Comparing the sound sequences entering the two ears can be used to determine the location of a single sound source, and consequently to separate several simultaneous sound sources at different locations in the environment (see Figure 8.4). In technical systems, such as recordings of concerts or sound tracks for movies, multiple microphones are positioned at various locations to recreate spatial sound effects. Additionally, there is a fundamental difference in the use of temporal information. Sound is a phenomenon that essentially requires time to be detected, because the most elementary information, the tone, is carried by waves, which are temporal modulations of air pressure, and the dynamics of these waveforms are crucial for the separation, grouping and recognition of acoustic objects such as phonemes in speech. In contrast, temporal change is not a prerequisite for visual perception: we have no difficulty in seeing static images that are flashed very briefly.

This cursory overview of the information processing issues related to auditory space raises a number of questions, such as: Can we hear in two, or three dimensions? How well can the auditory system localise objects? What are the limits of hearing several objects at the same time? Sound localisation is based on spatial cues generated by the way in which sounds interact with the ears and the head, depending on the direction of the source (Moore 2003). Combining the information from both ears by 'binaural processing' is the most important mechanism in finding the horizontal position, or azimuth, of a sound source (Middlebrooks and Green 1991), which can make use of two different cues. (i) The head creates an acoustic shadow for sound waves, which leads to higher sound intensity in one ear than in the other (see Figure 8.5a). At high frequencies, this difference in sound pressure can reach levels

Figure 8.5

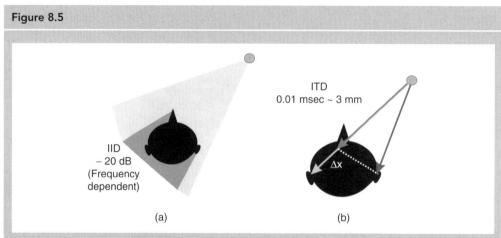

Binaural direction cues that can be used for localisation of sound in a horizontal plane. (a) Depending on the location of a sound source, the intensity reaching the two ears can differ considerably, generating an interaural intensity difference (IID). (b) The location of a sound source determines the distance from the source to each ear (Δx), resulting in interaural time difference (ITD) between the two ears.

around 20 dB, and humans can use such interaural intensity differences (IID) to localise the azimuth of a sound source (Feddersen et al. 1957). (ii) At low frequencies another mechanism is needed: the different distance between the sound source to the right and left ear, respectively, creates a difference in the arrival time of the sound wave (see Figure 8.5b). From such interaural time differences (ITD), the human ear can detect delays between the two ears in the range of 0.01–0.6 msec, which in air corresponds to a difference of about 3 mm between the distance between the sound source and the two ears (Stevens and Newman 1934). Both of these mechanisms critically depend on the separation of the two ears (about 15 cm), creating two distinct sampling points for sound waves. Note the similarity between auditory stereo (this name sounds familiar – your stereo system has two speakers!) and stereovision as discussed in Chapter 5 (compare the geometry sketched in Figure 8.5b and Figure 5.6). The smallest angular difference between two positions of a sound source in a horizontal plane, or the 'minimum audible angle' (MAA), that can be achieved with these two mechanisms can be as small as a few degrees.

Neither IID nor ITD can be used to detect vertical position, because all points in space that project with a similar angular difference on the two ears share a similar sound pressure and time difference. For estimating elevation, the pinnae are crucial (Middlebrooks and Green 1991), as can be easily demonstrated by the observation that performance is substantially reduced when using earphones. In more formal experiments, the sound reaching the two ears from loudspeakers at various elevations was recorded from the inside of the ear canals and then played back through headphones, and the specific spectra of these sounds allowed participants to identify where the loudspeakers had been positioned in the recordings, almost as accurately as in listening to the loudspeakers directly (Butler and Belendiuk 1977). Furthermore, these experiments demonstrate that the individual shapes of the pinnae are important – performance was reduced when a participant heard the sounds recorded from someone else's ears. Humans are also able to estimate the distance of a sound source under some conditions, although little is known about the underlying mechanisms. There is evidence that the familiarity with the sound source, that is, expectations about intensity and spectral composition, plays a crucial role in solving this task (Middlebrooks and Green 1991). In many of these more challenging situations strategies of active exploration are employed, by moving the head – this is a very simple trick used in many sensory systems to increase the number of spatial locations at which information is sampled (this point will be taken up more systematically in Chapter 12).

This variety of different mechanisms to extract particular spatial components of sound sources is combined in the brain to generate a coherent auditory representation of auditory space in three dimensions, which is needed to navigate and locate objects in space when the visual system is unreliable or unavailable, for instance in the dark. Whereas most of the basic mechanisms underlying such location are well understood, there are still a number of open questions that need to be answered before we can appreciate comprehensively how spatial hearing works. One example of such problems is how the auditory system is adjusted to changes in the layout of the sensor – during development from infant to adult the size and shape of the head and ears changes considerably, which requires the brain to recalibrate its analysis algorithms. We now have a growing body of evidence that the capacity for recalibrating auditory localisation continues well into adult life and involves a number of brain structures (King et al. 2001), although we also need to be aware that adjusting to a hearing aid, for instance, requires a lot of time and patience. When studying such challenging questions, it is once again help-ful to look at other biological systems. In the case of spatial hearing, major progress was made from investigations of barn owls, which have evolved highly specialised hearing functions that enable them to hunt in the darkness using acoustic information (Konishi 1986).

So far, we have only considered the localisation of isolated sound sources in space. In real life we are surrounded by multiple sound sources, as sketched in Figure 8.4, which need to be separated and grouped for perception. Perhaps one of the most astonishing phenomena is the ability to separate individual voices in a noisy crowded room, such as a classroom during break, or a pub on Friday afternoon. The 'cocktail party effect' refers to the fact that, at least for younger people, it is easy to single out a particular conversation or one particular voice from the noisy background while ignoring other voices and conversations (Cherry 1953). After the previous sections, we might be puzzled how can this be achieved, because the wild mixture of wavefronts that is hitting the ears at the same time has an overwhelming com-plexity. This is similar to tracing individual ripples on the surface of a pond in heavy rain back to individual raindrops! Perhaps less surprising than the effect itself is the fact that it is not unique to humans but can be observed in other animals, like penguins, living in large colonies (Aubin 1998). Identifying individual sounds is a fundamental problem for sensory information processing that goes along with social lifestyle. The core of the cocktail party problem is masking (see Chapter 7): the detection of a tone is impaired if another tone or noise is presented at the same time. Because masking depends on similarity in frequency and proximity in space, the process used to separate sound sources in space into individual streams can be described as binaural unmasking. If spatial distance or difference in frequency between competing sound sources increases, separation becomes easier. Because both of these cues are contained in the combined binaural information, sound sources can be separated by the interaction between the signals from the two ears. But this approach is only capturing the first processing steps, and it is clear that a range of high-level effects, like attention (Moray 1959), sequential grouping (Darwin 1997), the familiarity of a voice, its accent, the content of messages or the language used (Arons 1992) contribute to the solution of this information processing task. Furthermore, in challenging situations like such cluttered acoustic scenes, sensory fusion (see Chapter 12) is becoming increasingly important, with visual cues like facial movements or body language supporting the separation of conversations and voices.

AUDITORY ILLUSIONS

Finally, let us briefly return to the topic of illusions, which was so helpful to demonstrate in the visual domain the mechanisms underlying sensory information processing. Are there auditory illusions? The simple answer is yes, but many of these are not as obvious as in the visual system. There are discussions whether humans can experience auditory size constancy solutions, in which the relationship between perceived size and perceived distance determines what you hear, and it has been suggested that there is an auditory analogue to the Moon illusion (von Békésy 1949). Perhaps the most famous auditory illusion is Shepard's eternally rising tone (Shepard 1964). When a set of individual tones is continuously shifted to higher frequencies, while their amplitude is modulated by a constant envelope (see Figure 8.6a), the overall average frequencies remain roughly constant, although the individual tones are rising. In such a conflict between the local change of frequencies and the global constancy of frequencies, human participants perceive a sound with a frequency that does not stop rising – this eternally rising tone is an acoustic object that resembles the impossible geometric objects that we know from visual illusions like the eternally rising staircase (see Figure 8.6b), which demonstrate the conflict between a three-dimensional object and two-dimensional representation (cf. Figure 5.2a).

Figure 8.6

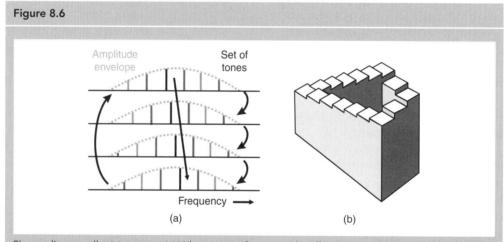

Shepard's eternally rising tone. (a) When a set of tones with different, constantly rising, frequencies (vertical lines with different shades of grey) is modulated in amplitude by a constant envelope (grey dotted line), a single sound is perceived, which appears to never stop rising in frequency. (b) The visual analogue of this illusion is an impossible object, the eternally rising staircase.

Take Home Messages

- spoken words generate complex patterns of frequency and intensity, which can be described and analysed as spectrograms that display frequency-intensity distributions as a function of time
- speech covers a considerable range of sound intensities and frequencies in the centre region of the audible spectrum; this finding helps us to appreciate the effects of natural and technical hearing impairments on communication
- sound can be localised by calculating intensity and phase differences between the two ears, and some subtle changes in the spectral properties of sound picked up by the outer ear

- in cluttered acoustic spaces auditory scenes, auditory localisation and the separation and grouping of sound sources is particularly challenging, but still possible, as demonstrated by the cocktail party effect
- can we create auditory illusions? Yes, we can!

Discussion Questions

- Discuss the causes and consequences of hearing impairments.
- How are the mechanisms underlying speech perception that are related to the auditory processing of music?
- Describe the two main auditory mechanisms of spatial localisation.
- What is the auditory processing problem commonly refereed to by the 'cocktail party effect'?

9 CHEMICAL SENSES: SMELL AND TASTE

OVERVIEW

For chemical senses, the physical, or better chemical, properties of sensory stimuli are the starting point to ask the same questions that we used to understand the relevance of other sensory modalities: What is the medium carrying the stimulus? How can it be detected? What are the limiting factors of detecting, discriminating and recognising stimuli? Are there any parallels to technical applications? The sense of smell is discussed in view of the sensor that is tasked with picking up chemicals from the air, which leads to an inherently narrow receptor tuning, and as a result of this to difficulties for a perceptual classification system for odours. The olfactory population code is explained as a highly evolved strategy to combine information from narrowly tuned receptors, allowing for the classification of a huge range of complex odours. Odour localisation is discussed as a typical example of active exploration, through sniffing. The sense of taste is discussed along the same line of thought – the basic sensor function, which again hinges on chemical binding of molecules, but now retrieving taste stimuli from a liquid medium; basic taste qualities; the dimensionality of this sensory space. The similarities and differences of the two chemical senses lead us to consider some aspects of smell–taste associations that are involved in the complex sensation of flavour. The experience of spicy food highlights a peculiar crosstalk between sensory channels, which gives the label 'hot' a new meaning. The predominance of olfactory and gustatory object-related recognition and classification is at the starting point of questioning the nature of perceptual experience in the chemical sensory domain, trying to assess the evolutionary benefit of opening up these sensory channels for humans.

THE NATURE OF 'OLFACTORY' PERCEPTION – SMELL

Imagine you are sitting at your kitchen table, eyes shut and ears plugged; without vision and hearing, you still can get some idea of what is going on. You smell the coffee, fried eggs and burning toast – and open your eyes to rescue whatever you can. And what is the significance of smell for everyday behaviour, outside of your kitchen? The sense of smell serves as a general alarm system, when you smell, for instance, gas, fire or smokers. Smell helps to assess the nature and quality of food, being a key component of perceived flavour. A recent discovery suggests that mammals, so far restricted to non-human species, are able to pick up the odours that signal cell damage and disease (Munger 2009). Smell can also be part of communication systems, picking up pheromones (chemical signals involved in social communication), or recognising odours that are tokens of family, gender or attractiveness. The scientifically rather obscure sense of smell is the basis of a multi-billion pound industry, selling fragrances to happy and beautiful customers all around the world. In many cases, olfactory communication stays completely below the radar of consciousness, so there was a lot of speculation whether humans could actually use odours to identify other individuals. In his groundbreaking experiment, M. J. Russel (1976) demonstrated that participants could recognise, by smelling T-shirts, their own body odour and the gender of other individuals' body odour. He also provided the first behavioural evidence that human infants in their first weeks of life can recognise their mothers by means of smell (for a review of similar studies, see Doty 1981). Generally, however, such detection thresholds are high and recognition performance is low. For other tasks, like the detection of airborne chemicals, human olfaction can be much more sensitive, and it can further benefit from combination with other sensory cues, in particular vision (Gottfried and Dolan 2003). Let the odorant be subtle or bold, soft or strong, ephemeral or long-lasting in your memory, the importance of smell in a social context and nutrition is witnessed by a large industry sector dedicated to the sale of fragrances and food!

Given the range of functional contexts, and the scope of information processing problems in the absence of straightforward unifying theoretical concepts, there are many questions to ask about olfactory perception, but rather few answers. Perhaps most pressingly in the quest of developing systematic experimental protocols, we need to ask, how can we classify odours? There are no simple physical dimensions for odours, as we know them from vision (brightness, colour) or hearing (loudness, pitch), and we tend to use descriptions by examples, such as 'this soap smells like Lavender'. Such challenges feed into experimental issues: how can we measure the intensity of odours, what are the lower limits of detecting them, can we localise them in space? For instance, it is very difficult to control the concentration of airborne molecules, and is even more difficult to capture the patterns of molecules floating in the air that have travelled a long distance from a source to the nose.

The sensory organ to capture olfactory information is the nose (see Figure 9.1), and olfaction is the most important function of the nose: apart from filtering and humidifying

Figure 9.1

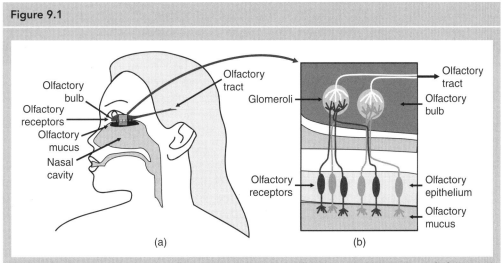

(a)   (b)

The nose is the sensory organ for olfactory perception. The olfactory epithelium at the roof of the nasal cavity (a) is covered by a mucus that contains the fine nerve endings of olfactory receptors (b) which bind odorant molecules (what makes them 'chemoreceptors') dissolved from the air flow passing through the nose. Chemoreceptor signals are pre-processed in glomeruli inside the olfactory bulb (b) and then transmitted through the olfactory tract into an extended network of neocortical and limbic brain regions.

the air before entering the lungs, its role is the gatekeeper of olfactory perception. Although the nose is sometimes regarded as a rather curious or crude protuberance of the face in need of embellishment, it presents a very intricate physical and biochemical design to support this dual function. The most relevant, although not the only, structure involved in converting airborne chemical signals into neural signals, is the olfactory epithelium and olfactory bulb at the roof of the nasal cavity (see Chapter 23 in Roberts 2002). When the air flowing through the nose is passing the sensory epithelium, the odorant molecules need to be captured from the air, by dissolving them in the olfactory mucus, which covers the epithelium. This mucus is a water-based solution of a number of biochemical substances, including enzymes to break down toxic substances, and proteins to bind odorants that would not dissolve in water (which are called 'hydrophobic'). Embedded in the mucosa are the fine nerve cell endings ('cilia'), which contain the chemoreceptors binding the odorants dissolved in the mucus. The axons of these olfactory receptors project into the glomeruli in the olfactory bulb, where the initial information processing is carried out. From there the olfactory information travels through the olfactory tract into the brain, where it is distributed into an extensive network of brain regions, in the limbic system, the thalamus and in neocortical areas (see Chapter 24 in Roberts 2002).

At first sight the mechanism of binding chemicals to receptors seems to be rather straightforward, but it immediately throws up two rather puzzling issues about strategies for encoding olfactory signals in neural systems. (i) Whereas the odorant molecules will remain in the mucosa for several minutes, we perceive odours on a much finer time scale: when you pass the espresso bar, the nice smell of coffee will fade within seconds! This suggests that in the olfactory system we should expect extensive suppression mechanisms. Interestingly, there are neuropsychological case studies of individuals who suffer from altered olfactory perception, which makes their sense of smell completely unselective and long-lasting – this rather irritating condition can be interpreted as loss of inhibition (see Chapter 18 in Sacks 1998). (ii) The chemical binding between the receptor and the odorant resembles the interaction between key and lock, with only a very small group of molecules connecting to a given receptor, and as such chemoreception is much more specific than the response of photoreceptors to light or the mechanoreceptors to sound. In consequence olfactory receptors have very narrow sensory tuning, and therefore we should not be surprised that a large number of different types of chemoreceptors have been found – over 1,000 receptor types have been described in the mouse and approximately 300–400 in humans. The Nobel Prize 2004 was awarded to Linda Buck and Richard Axel for their work on this exceedingly complex receptor system (Axel 2005).

RECOGNITION AND CLASSIFICATION OF ODOURS

With the large number of highly specific chemoreceptors, how many different odours can we identify and discriminate? This question is difficult if not impossible to answer, because there is no continuum of odours that can be discriminated, but particular substances that are stimulating particular receptors. In a strict sense, estimating the number of discriminable stimuli in such a categorical system of different sensory experiences would require presenting all possible odorants to a sufficiently large number of participants, under a wide range of experimental conditions, in an objective recognition task. Because this thought experiment is clearly not feasible in reality, and presumably also not overly exciting to carry out, nor really meaningful, we have to do some guesswork. So perhaps we could say with some reason that there are quite a few different odour categories, but certainly not millions.

When you want to test your sense of smell next time you visit one of the fancy soap shops on the high street, you might be surprised what a difficult task this is. Which brings us to the second question: how reliable is odour recognition? It has a simple answer: pretty bad! In a historic and quite heroic experiment Cain (1982) asked more than 200 participants to identify 80 common substances by smell. The proportion of correct identification varied between 90% and 20%, and overall performance was better for females than for males (see Figure 9.2). And, contrary to what most readers might expect, there are no clear patterns of olfactory experience: although men indeed tend to be better in recognising bourbon, sherry and beer, women almost reach the same 'performance' for beer, and the other few areas of male advantage (ammonia, mothballs, banana, mustard, raspberry syrup) hardly make a group of substances that would be associated with typically male activities and experiences. If we would really like to know whether there are gender-specific differences in olfactory perception, there would be no way to avoid an even more extensive, even more systematic, even more heroic experiment – so it might be worth asking seriously why we should expect such a difference.

From this type of experiments we can clearly recognise an emerging demand for some theoretical framework to study smell, which gives a rational basis for the classification of odours, similar to that of sound or colour. So can we identify a small basis set of fundamental odours that would generate a smell space? Usually olfactory stimuli and fragrances

Figure 9.2

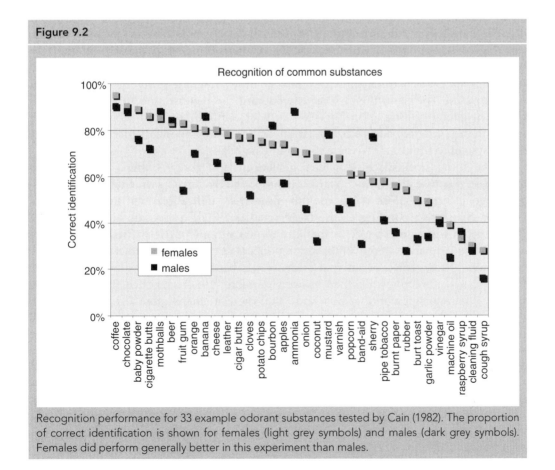

Recognition performance for 33 example odorant substances tested by Cain (1982). The proportion of correct identification is shown for females (light grey symbols) and males (dark grey symbols). Females did perform generally better in this experiment than males.

Figure 9.3

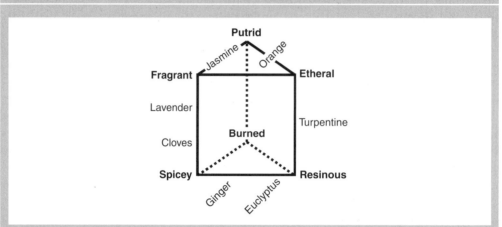

Odour prism as proposed by Henning (1916). The six primary odour qualities (bold labels) occupy the corners of this prism, and real olfactory stimuli are claimed to be positioned unambiguously on any of the nine axes (grey labels).

are described by object names, which need to be mapped onto such a smell space, where distance between any of two stimuli in a multi-dimensional map is inversely proportional to perceived similarity of these stimuli. Perhaps the most prominent attempt was made almost a century ago by H. Henning (Henning 1916), who designed a smell prism to arrange six primary (independent) odour qualities: fragrant, ethereal, resinous, spicy, burned, putrid. The claim then is that any odorant can be positioned on this prism in a unique neighbourhood relationship (see Figure 9.3), or in other words, that any olfactory sensation can be described as a combination of these six components (note the similarity of this system to the colour triangle shown in Chapter 4).

Although the 'smell space' depicted schematically in Figure 9.3 offers an elegant solution, there is debate on to what extent it is supported by any experimental evidence that goes beyond introspection. What would be needed are indications that there are specific receptor types corresponding to the basic small qualities, or specific anosmias ('smell blindness', in this case the specific inability to pick up one of the six basic qualities), or the selective adaptation of one of these components that would not affect any of the others. However, coherent experimental evidence has been thin on the ground, and there still are many more questions than answers. Amoore (1964) suggested that there seven primary odour qualities, and we now know that there are many more receptor types than the proposed independent perceptual qualities (Buck and Axel 1991). A recent computational attempt to determine the number of independent dimensions for odour recognition estimated around 32 to 64 (Mamlouk and Martinetz 2004). So the debate keeps moving on, though rather slowly.

At this stage it could be helpful to have another look at the neural systems involved in the processing of odour stimuli. If we could understand the fundamental principles of olfactory encoding, we might be able to develop a better theory of smell. So what is the olfactory code? Little is known about the physiology of olfactory processing in humans, but there are two threads of evidence from a wide range of biological systems, including mammals, about how the complex olfactory encoding can be deciphered. (i) The combinatorial matrix of activations in different receptor types and odorant molecules (Buck 2005) suggests a population code (schematically shown in Colour plate VI, Figure 3a): a specific pattern of activity that is distributed across a group of neurons reflects a given odour, and can be decoded from the distribution of activations (e.g. Koulakov et al. 2007). One of the most exciting aspects of such a population code is the fact that it joins together two prominent steps of olfactory processing: the decomposition of an odour into highly specific components at the lower level, and the completion of patterns in activity distributions at higher levels, which allows the sensory system to recognise an odour despite of the variation in the exact mix of components (Barnes et al. 2008). This design takes advantage from the general feature of distributed networks to be robust and 'error-resistant' (Minsky and Papert 1988). (ii) At other stages of the olfactory processing stream, we find neuronal activity patterns that suggest the existence of an olfactory map, in which different odours are represented at different locations in the neural network (for instance, in the olfactory bulb, schematically shown Colour plate VI, Figure 3b). This includes activations by airborne chemical stimuli like CO_2, which are not consciously perceived by humans but lead to distinct behavioural responses in animals (Axel 2005).

These two sets of observations offer no clue to support the idea that there is a reduced set of basic odorant qualities creating a simple smell space. However, they are based on evidence collected from simpler sensory systems than the human brain, and are restricted to comparatively early processing stages. So it could still be possible that the extensive redistribution of olfactory information across various structures in the human central nervous system (Chapter 23 in Roberts 2002) leads to different encoding strategies at higher levels.

ODOUR LOCALISATION: SNIFFING

Given that the function of the olfactory system is an alarm system and that it is involved in social communication, the localisation of odour sources is highly relevant. You might be rather interested to identify the person standing in a group who is wearing this attractive fragrance you did smell, and if you smell gas in your house you would like to know where it would be leaking from. Because odorant molecules are carried by air that usually is in flow, however, such localisation can be quite challenging. Furthermore, because of long-term and fast adaptation in the olfactory system (Dalton 2000) the exposure to an odorant can lead to a rapid decay in the information provided, which puts time constraints on detecting the source. So how well can humans localise the source of an odour? How do the underlying mechanisms compare to those of other sensory modalities, such as vision, hearing, touch? Because of the transient and spurious character of odorants carried by air, this is a problem much less easy to approach experimentally than in vision or hearing. Some researchers have invented ingenious setups to assess the performance at close range (see Figure 9.4a). Initial ideas about localisation focused on the fact that the differential information from the two nostrils could be used to localise a small, close source (von Békésy 1964). However, it soon became clear in such experiments that a key aspect to enhancing performance is active exploration. Human observers actively move their nose and inhale in bouts, possibly to maximise the number of molecules picked up and counteract adaptation effects. Still, even when employing such active exploration, as we all know from everyday experience, human performance is rather poor, and we can only observe with envy the sniffer dogs employed by Her Majesty's Customs Service, when detecting and tracing unwanted substances in the luggage of travellers.

Behavioural strategies, such as the 'olfacto-motor coordination' used by such sniffer dogs actively searching in great excitement through the luggage, can help to solve the localisation problem at a larger spatial scale, when odour traces become rather faint and spatially irregular. Such scanning movements are common in various animal systems. For instance, moths use odour cues for courtship navigation, and approach sources of airborne pheromones in characteristic zigzag flights (Kennedy 1983). A recent study demonstrated that humans develop very similar strategies when they were asked to trace a scent trail (such as a trace of chocolate on a sports ground, see Figure 9.4b) in the absence of other sensory cues, and that they are indeed capable of staying on track (Porter et al. 2007). When systematically trained for this job, just like sniffer dogs, these participants increased performance, by reducing the sideways deviations from the track, and increasing speed. It was also confirmed that sniffing patterns can support the completion of the task: the participants were moving faster when the frequency of sniffing was increased. Furthermore, when the entry points to the two nostrils were increased by small tubes attached to the nose, the performance increased; and when the both nostrils were supplied by the air from a single point, their performance was reduced. This gives further support to the early suggestion that there is an olfactory analogue to directional hearing or stereo vision. The most important conclusion from this study is the importance of active exploration (we will return to this issue in Chapter 12): by moving the sensor systematically through the environment, the sensory system can improve its efficiency tremendously.

Figure 9.4

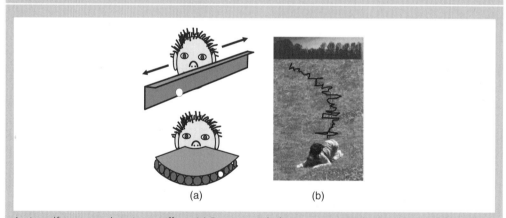

(a)   (b)

Active olfactory exploration: sniffing. (a) Boosting inhalation improves the localisation of an odour source (white disk) hidden in one of the small tubes arranged in fan-shape with the nose in the centre (bottom panel); sidewise scanning movements of the nose can help to locate the source of an odorant (white disk) hidden behind a ledge (top panel). (b) When humans, deprived of other sensory input, are challenged to track a scent trail, they develop behavioural patterns closely resembling those of sniffer dogs. (See http://www.nature.com/neuro/journal/v10/n1/suppinfo/nn1819_S1.html.) Reprinted by permission from Macmillan Publishers Ltd. Jess Porter et al. (2007). 'Mechanisms of Scent-Tracking in Humans', *Nature Neuroscience* 10, 27–9.

THE NATURE OF 'GUSTATORY' PERCEPTION – TASTE

In many ways, taste, or 'gustation', is the sibling of smell – it is another type of chemical sense, which helps us to discover dangers, such as poisoned or rotten food, and it is much more difficult to study than other senses such as vision or hearing, and therefore less is known about it. In other ways, taste is rather different from smell, because it picks up chemicals in solution, and therefore is sensitive to close sources but not to stimuli originating from a distance. It also appears to be possible to classify all tastes by a comparatively simple scheme of four basic components. So let us go through our standard set of questions that we ask for each sense, to paint a quick profile of gustatory perception. Why is it important to have a sense of taste? Taste serves as a safety system, making use of the fact that food that contains poisonous substances tastes different (because it might have been tampered with, or contaminated by random exposure, or simply changed through decomposition). Taste is vital for 'homeostasis', keeping a delicate balance of nutrients, minerals, fluids and acidity in the body, which can be controlled, mostly without being conscious about this at all, by selective eating and drinking. Obviously, and most prominently, taste is important for enjoyment and pleasure, an integral part of civilisation, and in specific cultural contexts an instrument to guide compliance with social conventions: the symbolical meaning of 'good taste' can be directly related to the expression of some well-trained sensory schemata. And why is taste an interesting scientific topic? Many aspects of taste perception so far remain rather obscure, if not mysterious, and in particular there is need of a unifying theoretical framework, similar to olfaction, but possibly less desperate because of a much-reduced number of receptor types. The sense of taste is less extensively investigated than visual or auditory system perception, and offers a wide range of questions to make important discoveries, in particular because it is of immense everyday relevance, being so closely related to food. Finally, there is a lot of financial interest because of the high economic relevance of gustatory perception – imagine how many extra tons of nasty junk food can be sold to happy customers, if there were a reliable method to get a grip on their taste perception!

The sensory system supporting human taste perception resides mainly in the tongue (Chapter 26 in Roberts 2002). The microscopic image of the surface of the tongue in Figure 9.5a shows, in a field of small cone-shaped ('filiform') papillae that serve a tactile function, some prominent large ('fungiform') papillae; these carry the taste buds, which are made up of a number of chemoreceptors (see Figure 9.5b). Additional taste buds are found in other regions of the mouth, such as the soft palate and pharynx, the entrance to the oesophagus. These sensory cells are in contact with the saliva, which carries the flavour molecules contained in food that will stimulate the receptors. The information captured by the chemoreceptors is transmitted by gustatory neurons through cranial nerves to the solitary nucleus in the brainstem and from there to various other brain regions, including the hypothalamus, thalamus and the sensory cortex. Here the information is further processed, possibly in the form of a distributed population code (as discussed above) and also interacts with olfactory information and other information to create the sensation of flavour. One interesting aspect of gustatory perception is that the highly sensitive taste buds are constantly exposed to many inadequate stimuli, including heat or aggressive chemicals, leading to substantial cell death and continuous regeneration. Note that this requires plasticity, i.e. the continuous rewiring of the connections between sensory cells and cortical projection areas to maintain reliable encoding of taste and subsequent sensory information processing.

Figure 9.5

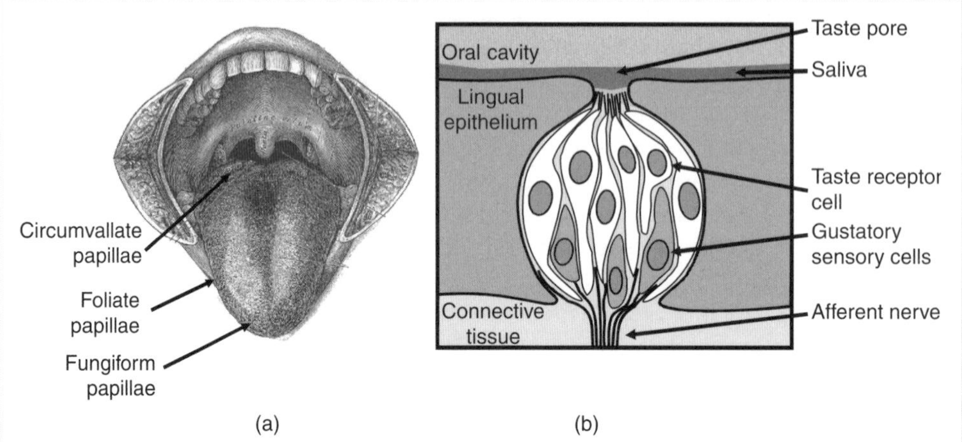

Taste sensors. (a) The tongue shown in this anatomical drawing (from 20th US edition of *Gray's Anatomy of the Human Body*, 1918) is covered with thousands of small papillae, which contain taste buds to pick up chemical signals dissolved in saliva when eating or drinking. (b) In taste buds, chemoreceptors are aggregated in groups, sending their axons through the cranial nerves into the brain.

CLASSIFYING TASTE: IS THERE A GUSTATORY SPACE?

There is a long tradition in assuming that there are four basic qualities of taste: sweet, sour, salty and bitter (Hänig 1901). These perceived taste qualities can be roughly related to four different types of chemoreceptors that pick up the chemical signals from sweet, sour, salty and bitter substances (see Figure 9.6a), and are commonly believed to be picked up preferentially at different locations of the tongue (see Figure 9.6b), although it is unclear what such a spatial representation would imply, because taste stimuli are carried by the fluid medium passing the tongue and therefore should be distributed rather evenly in the mouth. More recent experiments to estimate recognition thresholds and response magnitudes as a function of stimulus concentration for the four different taste categories found different patterns of preferred locations than the initial studies (Collings 1974). Furthermore, it has become clear in the last decade that, at least for various non-primate mammals such as rats, cats and rabbits, the receptor tuning to such chemical agents is much broader and not categorical as suggested by this classification (Pfaffmann 1955). Also, new evidence suggests the existence of a fifth taste category for certain amino acids that can be found in such food as mushrooms or cheese: 'Umami', which is sometimes also called 'savoury' (Nelson et al. 2002). Very recently, another taste receptor, for fatty acids, has been discovered (Laugerette et al. 2005).

Although current research, using behavioural, electrophysiological and molecular biological techniques suggests that the design of taste space, or in other words the sensory encoding of gustatory information, is more complicated than the initial picture might suggest, the representation of tastes in terms of four to six basic qualities still stands as a good first approximation (Scott and Chang 1984), if we do not expect that all possible experiences can be composed by combinations of the basic qualities (which was, for instance, possible for the encoding of colour from three primaries, as described in Chapter 4). The key observations to

Figure 9.6

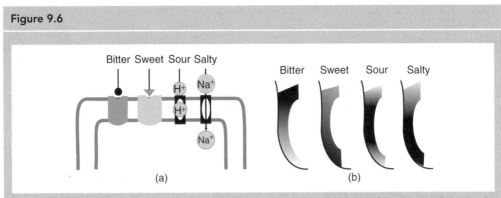

Taste sensors. (a) Four types of chemoreceptors in the taste buds, binding to four classes of chemicals, are believed to underlie the four basic taste qualities, bitter, sweet, sour, and salty. (b) The sensitivity for detecting the four basic gustatory categories varies considerably for different regions of the tongue (shown schematically for the right side of the tongue for bitter, sweet, sour, and salty taste, respectively: darker regions indicate more sensitive regions (after Hänig 1901)).

support the simplified image of four basic taste qualities are: (i) Mixtures of taste categories cannot be perceived, which means that a well-defined substance either tastes salty or sweet, but nothing in between. (ii) There is no cross-adaptation, so that after the adaptation to a sweet stimulus there is no change in sensitivity to bitter, for instance. (iii) Nevertheless, we can experience after-effects that suggest some more complicated kind of opponency processing. For example, participants report that pure water tastes sweet after they had been adapting to bitter/sour stimuli (Breslin and Spector 2008).

One of the more puzzling aspects of gustatory perception is related to individual differences. It is commonplace to say that taste can be a very individual sensation, in two ways. (i) Taste is a private experience, which is almost impossible to talk about – you know how a strawberry tastes for you, but can you describe it to someone else and find out whether it tastes the same for them (without diving into the fanciful poetry of food journalists who mostly rely on similes from other sensory domains)? (ii) The perceived gustatory strength of a particular substance can vary considerably between individuals. One aspect that is investigated extensively is the bitter taste of the chemicals phenylthiocarbamide (PTC) and propylthiouracil (PROP), which can be famously detected as bitter by parts of the population ('tasters'), but not by others ('non-tasters'), and in another group has very intense, and often repellent effect ('super-tasters'). These different groups are distinguished by differences in the density of taste receptors (Bartoshuk et al. 1994), and there are indications that these anatomical differences as well as the specifically enhanced sensitivity, and food preferences resulting form these differences, are genetically mediated (Drewnowski and Rock 1995). It could be interesting to speculate whether the bitter, metallic taste experienced by some people for a couple of days after eating pine nuts of South-East Asian origin that contain certain triglycerids (Mostin 2001) could be related to such differences in the taste receptor inventory. Recent research seems to indicate that there also more general variations in the sensitivity to a range of taste stimuli, which might be related to overall taste receptor density (Reed 2008).

In everyday life, however, gustatory perception tends to be rather more complicated. Still at the level of basic categories, we find the perceived intensity for different qualities to develop differently in time, such that mixtures of two stimuli can be perceived first as one quality, and then as the other (Kelling and Halpern 1983). This could be the physiological and perceptual basis of what the food and drink industry calls a taste profile. Such dynamic changes of the taste sensations while eating or drinking a single substance can be the result of multiple interactions between a range of different aspects of the complex information contained in food, at various levels of subcortical and cortical processing (Katz et al. 2002). Unfortunately, this phenomenon is very difficult to investigate psychophysically, because the description of the dynamic changes of perceived taste under real-life conditions depends largely on careful introspection, which obviously is subjective and can easily be misled. You can try this yourself and will see how difficult it is to describe precisely the sensations you experience one after the other when you drink your next cappuccino. Most importantly, indicating massive reorganisation of the perceptual representation of tastes, we tend to use qualitative descriptions and refer to objects when try to characterise tastes – you would say something like 'this jelly bean tastes like strawberry', rather than listing the combinations of basic qualities, and how they might change with time while you are chewing your treat.

Finally, we should have a brief look at the interaction and cross-talk between the chemical senses, and with other senses. In general, there are very close interactions between different sensory modalities when enjoying food, and the term 'flavour' is used to describe the combination of different sensory modalities, including taste, smell, temperature, softness, tactile texture, etc. (Chapter 26 in Roberts 2002). There are complex interactions between such different sensory cues in the representation of olfactory information in the primate orbitofrontal cortex, which could provide hints about the mechanisms of encoding flavour relationships in the nervous system, and its relationship to perceived pleasure (Rolls 2000). Because it has been shown that smell–taste associations, for instance, can be learned, it can be assumed that perceived flavour is the product of life-long experiences with food (Stevenson et al. 1998). More direct interaction of chemical senses with other perceptual modalities can be observed as direct sensory cross-talk, which corresponds to inadequate stimulation at the receptor level. A well-investigated aspect of taste perception demonstrating such an effect is hot food, which suggests that sensory boundaries can be crossed at the earliest processing level. Hot chilli peppers contain a chemical called 'capsaicin', which activates nociceptive C fibres, pain receptors that usually would respond to heat (Caterina et al. 1997). The effectiveness of this chemical in truly activating a different sensory system is demonstrated by the fact that capsaicin can elevate pain thresholds by adaptation of pain receptors!

Take Home Messages

- the two chemical senses, smell and taste, share some properties, like their ecological significance and highly variable sensitivity, but respond to different (airborne or dissolved, respectively) stimuli, which can correspond to distant or close sources
- olfactory perception (smell) is characterised by a complex dimensionality based on a large number of specific chemoreceptors in the nose, which is best accounted for by population coding of odorants
- active exploration strategies, such as sniffing patterns, are employed to improve the localisation of odorant sources
- gustatory perception (taste) is understood to rely on a small number (4–6) basic qualities, which roughly correspond to the filter properties of the chemoreceptors in the mouth
- smell and taste interact with each other, and with other sensory modalities, in the perception of flavour

Discussion Questions

- Describe the attempt to classify different odours in a simple 'smell space'.
- Why is sniffing like a sniffer dog such a successful strategy in localising the source of an odour?
- Discuss the evidence for and against the common assumption that there are four basic components of taste perception.
- What makes hot chilli peppers hot?

10 BODY SENSES: FROM THE CONTROL OF POSTURE TO TOUCH

OVERVIEW

The somatic sensory system includes a group of senses that we are usually completely unaware of, because they are not organised around prominent organs like the eye or the ear, and because they are, to a large extent, dealing with information about the internal state of the body (interoception) rather than being exclusively directed at the external world (exteroception). Despite being hidden, somatosensory perception is of great importance for maintaining the physical control and integrity of the body. You might want to know, for instance, where your left foot is at the moment, and whether the chair underneath your back does support your weight. The proprioceptive and the vestibular sense will be introduced as systems to monitor and maintain static and dynamic stability in space. Temperature and pain sensitivity are considered as archetypical alarm systems that keep humans out of danger and prevent or minimise damage. The focus in this chapter will be on touch, with a more obvious exteroceptive, wide-ranging and everyday significance for navigation in darkness, exploration of objects in the close environment, and social communication. Starting from the physics of 'tactile' stimuli and the biological design of sensors, we will look at the basic and more advanced mechanisms of encoding and higher-level processing of tactile information in the nervous system. We will revisit fundamental processing concepts that we know from other sensory modalities such as receptive fields, adaptation or active exploration. The comparatively low spatial resolution of touch is considered with respect to how it varies in different regions of the body surface. The existence of a somatosensory map, the homunculus, is introduced as another instance of topographic cortical representation, together with the plasticity of remapping observed during growth and after loss of parts of the body, leading to 'phantom limbs'.

BODY SENSES – SOMATOSENSORY INFORMATION

Whereas all of the sensory systems covered so far are collecting well-defined information about the outside world, and are recognised by a distinct sensory organ such as the eyes or ears, we now turn to a sensory system, which is based on sensors that are widely distributed across the whole body, and which is largely tuned to the internal body states and is used indirectly to control the body relative to the outside world. These somatic senses are monitoring the physical state of the body, based on a variety of information, such as pressure, stress or strain, temperature and pain. Proprioceptors are used to monitor and control the position and posture of body and limbs, further supported by the vestibular system, which indicates movement and acceleration of the body and space; temperature sensors are important to monitor and control body homeostasis, and pain receptors are crucial to detect and avoid noxious stimuli and injury. Finally, the tactile system is based on mechanosensors in the skin, which pick up information about the contact with other objects and thus their location and shape, and the properties of surfaces.

Somatosensory perception is very peculiar, and there are some weird stimuli, such as tickling, which lead to very mysterious responses such as laughter (Blakemore et al. 1998). To start with, information about the body is impossible to share with others – you can see the same movie and hear the same song as your classmates and can arrive at a reasonable agreement about your experiences, but you cannot feel their pain. Different from other sensory channels such as hearing or vision, most of the time we are completely unaware of the rich sensory information provided by the somatic senses. And yet this information source is absolutely crucial to live a normal life, and one couldn't even imagine how it would be to survive without this information. You might get a glimpse of this when your vestibular system is malfunctioning during a very bad cold, and you are having difficulties to stay upright and start swaying when you try walk straight, or you are unable to control your speech after visiting the dentist, who gave you local anaesthetics. Now imagine you are losing all the control over your body posture, any sense of movement, and cannot feel anything you touch, like the spoon in your hand or even the clothes on your skin – your whole body would be like a sagging container of water. Partial or complete loss of somatic senses is a very rare event (however, see Chapter 3 of Sacks 1998), so luckily it is very unlikely that you will ever experience such a condition. Interestingly, it is the somatosensory sense that is absolutely crucial for our bodily awareness, linking imagination and the Self (Smith 2006). If there are conflicts between the somatosensory and other information sources, humans can experience very curious states of consciousness, such as the apparent disownment of limbs, or the acquisition of an animated object as part of their body, as demonstrated in the rubber hand illusion (Tsakiris and Haggard 2005). Somatic senses are crucial to maintain the integrity of the body, both in a direct physical sense, and in a psychological sense of 'ownership'.

PROPRIOCEPTION AND VESTIBULAR SYSTEM

When you are closing your eyes, how do you know which direction your eyes are looking, where your foot is in space, or whether your thumb is extended or bent? All over your body, in the muscles, in the tendons connecting muscles with bones, and in the joints between bones, there are hundreds of mechanoreceptors that provide the brain with information about position, or angles between parts of the skeleton that define posture, and about changes in the muscoskeletal system or movement (see Chapter 20 of Roberts 2002). These receptors are called 'proprioceptors' because they are picking up the body's own position and movement (from Latin *proprius*, which means 'one's own'), and are sometimes distinguished as inward-looking receptors ('interoception') from all major sensory systems, which are directed to the outside world ('exteroception'). Proprioceptors are responsible for getting into an upright position in the morning and maintaining balance for much of the day. They trigger the stretch reflexes (such as the knee-jerk reflex), which clinicians use to test the function of the central nervous system (Sherrington 1907). Proprioceptors are monitoring the muscle tone that controls general tension and relaxation of the body when it is involved in different levels of activities (from lying in the hammock, or doing yoga, to lifting weights). By measuring the tension in abdominal connective tissue, they tell you when your stomach has reached capacity limits and you should stop eating. Proprioceptors are instrumental in putting the jigsaw fragments, which you capture with your eyes when you look in different directions, together into a uniform coherent image by letting the brain know in which direction your gaze has shifted at any time (Wade and Tatler 2005). Although we are completely unaware of the proprioceptive sensory information, the information about the internal states and position relationships of our body parts is fundamental to operating a body, and developing technical systems to provide and process such information is one of the most challenging engineering tasks when designing articulated robots or sophisticated prosthetics (Brooks 2003).

The most important somatosensory information that is crucial for maintaining static and dynamic balance, and for sensing self-motion, is captured by the vestibular system. The vestibular system allows us to realise we are being turned on an office chair in the dark, to give one example, and is responsible for noticing that our train starts moving after we close our eyes. Together with the cochlea (see Chapter 7), the vestibular system forms the labyrinth, a system of tunnels that are filled with a viscous fluid (endolymph), which constitutes the inner ear (see Figure 10.1). There are two parts of the vestibular organ. (i) The two otolithic organs, the utricle and saccule, enable us to detect static position, like being upright, in a horizontal position or upside down; and linear acceleration, such as experienced when increasing speed in a car or braking. (ii) The three semicircular canals detect the rotation of the head around any of the three possible axes. Just like the organ of Corti in the cochlea of the hearing system, the physiology of the vestibular system is based on the stimulation of mechanoreceptors, tiny hair cells, by the movement of the endolymph (see Chapter 7 in Roberts 2002). It is interesting to note that both the auditory and the vestibular system evolved from the lateral line organ that fish use to detect vibrations and movements in the water surrounding them (Van Bergeijk 1966). The vestibular system is essential for motor control, from getting up in the morning, moving around, to lying down in the evening, without swaying, stumbling or falling over; it allows us to walk or run, to jump or ride a bicycle, without getting hurt, and it enables acrobats to do the most amazing tricks up high in the circus tent. Only when things go wrong, for instance after a middle ear infection, alcohol intoxication or a stroke, and control over the body is lost, does the constant and reliable operation of this highly sophisticated sensory system become apparent.

Figure 10.1

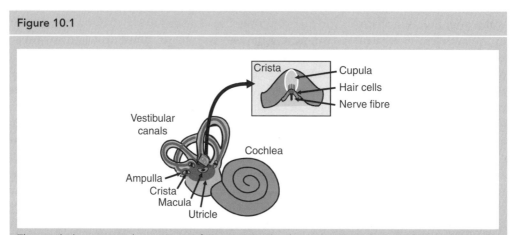

The vestibular organ in the inner ear (cf. Figure 7.4). The three ring-shaped 'vestibular canals' and the 'utriculus' are filled with endolymph, which is accelerated by movement of the head and consequently leads to stimulation of tiny 'hair cells' (mechanoreceptors) attached to a small sensory surface in the 'macula' and three 'cristae' that are sitting in the 'ampulla' at the end of each of the three canals.

The information from the vestibular system is transmitted by neurons based in Scarpa's ganglions into the brainstem vestibular nuclei, which connect to other parts of the brainstem, including the oculomotor nuclei that connect to the eye muscles. One particularly interesting aspect of the vestibular system is its involvement in the control of eye movements. The information from the inner ear about the movement of the head is used to generate eye movements in the opposite direction, which helps to stabilise the images on the retina (see Colour plate VII, Figure 1). This so-called vestibulo-ocular reflex (VOR) can be easily experienced, by moving the book you are reading leftwards and rightwards at such a speed that the letters become blurred from the movement, showing the limits of stabilising the image by tracking the moving book with the eyes. However, when you shake your head at the same speed, you will notice that the letters will not be blurred. The reason for this sharp image is the fact that the vestibular information about head movement is used by the brain to drive compensatory eye movements, which stabilise the retinal images (Angelaki 2004). There are a number of well known and rather irritating phenomena such as vertigo or motion sickness, which can be explained by a discrepancy between the visual and the vestibular information driving eye movements.

TEMPERATURE AND PAIN

Sensors for temperature were briefly mentioned in Chapter 9 in the context of taste, as a means of protecting the body against food or drink that is too hot. Temperature control, and therefore temperature sensors, have a much wider relevance in protecting the complete body against overheating or temperature loss. Sticking your fingers into the flame of a candle, getting grilled by the relentless sun on some southern beach, or freezing your fingers and toes in ice and snow is far from a healthy lifestyle, although some fire-eaters and Arctic explorers seem to make a living out of it. Blisters from sunburn, as well as frostbite are to be avoided, because they are symptoms of cell death in surface or deeper layers of the skin, and therefore clear signals of exposure to dangerous environmental temperatures. Warm-blooded animals such as humans and other mammals also require thermal homeostasis to maintain a comparatively narrow range of body temperature around 37 degrees. To avoid the pathological consequences of deviating from this required temperature, the whole body is populated with temperature sensors (see Figure 10.2), which not only provide an alarm system for extreme exposure that is an immediate threat to the body's integrity, but are also involved in physiological mechanisms to control general body temperature, by adjusting blood flow or breathing, burning extra fuel, or changing wardrobe. It is clear from these examples that temperature stimuli can either arise from contact with hot or cold objects, or they can be generated by distant sources, like the sun, and transmitted by radiation – in both cases it is the temperature sensors in the skin that pick up the information. Traditionally it has been believed that perception of heat or cold and pain is picked up by separate sensors and transmitted through separate neural pathways, but there is growing evidence that there is a strong overlap between these three types of sensation (Green 2004).

Pain sensors (see Figure 10.2), in a natural alliance with temperature and other somatosensors like those responsible for pressure or stretch, provide input to a second-tier alarm system, which detects conditions that pose a serious threat of damage to the body, when the heat is getting too strong or muscles over-strained – and obviously pain also signals existing tissue damage such as a cut in the skin or a broken bone. The urgency to protect the body against serious or further harm is the reason why pain leads to very strong behavioural responses that often are difficult to control, such as the withdrawal reflex when you burn your fingers (or tears in the eyes). Most

Figure 10.2

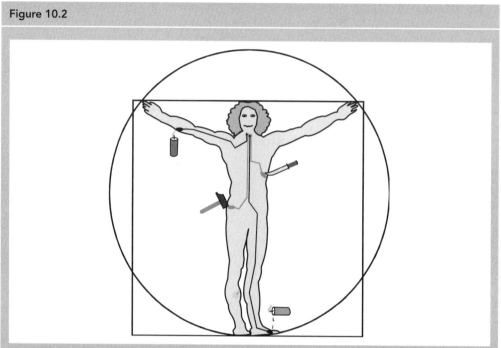

The human body (here illustrated with a caricature of Da Vinci's famous drawing of the 'Vetruvian man') contains a dense network of specialised receptors to pick up temperature and pain, which connect through high-speed nerve fibres to the brain, eliciting very fast and strong behavioural responses. Both of these stimuli are key indicators of potential damage of the body (burning, injury), and therefore need to be linked to quick and appropriate action.

importantly, pain is a perception that differs fundamentally in that it can be fully dissociated from the stimulus (see Chapter 22 in Roberts 2002). After the initial strong pain following an injury, the sensation of acute pain disappears rapidly, by means of peripheral adaptation and synaptic reorganisation in the central nervous system, and will only recover as part of the healing process. Inversely, patients can complain about – and perceive – chronic pain in the absence of any tissue damage. This reminds us how difficult it is to measure the intensity of pain objectively, a rather tricky issue for the medical profession. Chronic pain affects sufferers in all aspects of their life, and is a problem of outstanding clinical relevance that motivates great research activity about the molecular and neural mechanisms underlying the perception of pain. Sharp and dull pain sensations are originating from fast and slow pain receptors, also called 'nociceptors', in two particular types of free nerve endings that can be found in all kinds of tissues (Millan 1999). These signals are transmitted into the spinal chord where they are modulated through descending (i.e., top-down) pathways, and from there into the thalamus and into various parts of the cortex where they further interact with other sensory information. The complexity of the perceptual quality of pain, its interactions with other sensory modalities, and its unusual plasticity makes pain an extremely challenging and exciting, but still puzzling sense to study. With new imaging technologies, we now slowly begin to understand the wide distribution of sensory information about pain in the cortex (Hofbauer et al. 2001; Treede et al. 2000), and in particular how pain intensity relates to cortical responses (Coghill et al. 1999) – could we be on the way to an objective assessment of perceived pain?

TOUCH: USING THE BODY SURFACE AS SENSORY ORGAN

The body sense most people would be immediately aware of is the sense of touch, also known as 'tactile' perception. Different from the other somatosensory channels, tactile perception is a dedicated extraneous sense, collecting information about the outside world. This most immediate, physical interaction with the environment is the reason why the tactile sense is so significant for orientation, exploration and communication. Touch is important for organising behaviour when moving around, in particular for navigating through a cluttered world. Obviously, when trying to find the way around the house in the dark, you use your hands to 'see' whether there are any chairs or closed doors in your way, and blind people learn to use the cane to expand their operating range in such exploratory behaviour. But equally you use your touch sensors when sitting down to find out when your back has found support – you don't need to turn around and look for the chair! Using your fingers to recognise objects and find out about their properties, such as testing the texture and softness (the 'feel') of a new jumper or the crispiness of a slice of toast, is an everyday activity, called 'haptic' exploration. Often forgotten but rather important, touch can be a major component of communication, in particular in the context of social systems. There is a lot people 'tell' each other by physical contact, so there is a lot of information that is being picked up from tactile sensations. Touch even plays a role in the organisation of social system, and there usually are strict rules that the higher-ranking individual may touch a lower-ranking individual, but not the other way around. Figure 10.3 shows the infamous moment in 1992 when the Australian Premier of that time got too close with Her Majesty (10.3a), earning himself the nickname the 'Lizard of Oz', and a more recent incidence of political intimacy (10.3b), a meeting between the new American and British foreign secretaries, which we still need to make sense of. Rituals at

Figure 10.3

(a)   (b)

Touch in social communication. (a) How inappropriate was it of the Australian Premier, Paul Keating, to touch the Queen (Photographer News Ltd Copyright© Newspix/News Ltd/3rd Party Managed Reproduction & Supply Rights Date Taken Monday, 24 September 2001). The tabloids called him the 'Lizard of Oz'! (b) A meeting of minds: The foreign secretaries of the UK and the US are reinvigorating the special relationship between their countries. What are David Miliband and Hillary Clinton up to (Getty Images 2009)? Note that in these images we use our perception to construct narratives from the (limited) visual information given about the use of tactile information in social communication.

small and large scales, from rubbing shoulders, or exchanging a hug between friends, to the pre-fight war dances of sports teams, are embedded into a culture that needs physical contact as reassurance about personal relationships and group alliances.

The adequate stimuli for the tactile sensory system are simple physical events such as pressure, deformation or stress of the skin. To measure such forces, humans have a large number of mechanoreceptors embedded in their skin tissue, distributed all over the body. The main four different types of mechanoreceptors (see Figure 10.4 for a schematic representation) respond to different physical conditions (see Chapter 18 of Roberts 2002). (i) Merkel discs, embedded in the top layers of the skin, are comparatively slow and respond to light touch, that is, slow changes of the pressure on the skin (best response at approximately 1 Hz frequency). (ii) Meissner corpuscles are activated by light touch and vibration (flutter) at medium frequencies (approximately 10 Hz). (iii) Ruffini cylinders are embedded in the deeper layers of the skin and are mainly activated by fast stretch (approximately 100 Hz). (iv) Pacinian corpuscles are found in the neighbourhood of tendons and muscles (Adrian and Umrath 1929), as well as in the deeper layers of the skin, where they are preferentially activated by heavy pressure, and fast vibrations (approximately 400 Hz). It should be noted that each of these receptor types is specifically tuned to the physical quality and a temporal frequency of a stimulus. They also have spatial receptive fields, as will be discussed in the next section, and specific profiles of adaptation effects (Johansson et al. 1982). All of these aspects are standard elements of neural encoding of sensory information, which we know from other sensory modalities. The combination of information from these different mechanoreceptors can be used to create more abstract representations of force patterns, such as the direction of a force on the fingertip (Birznieks et al. 2001), and it creates the unitary perception of touch, which can be used in a wide range of behavioural contexts.

Figure 10.4

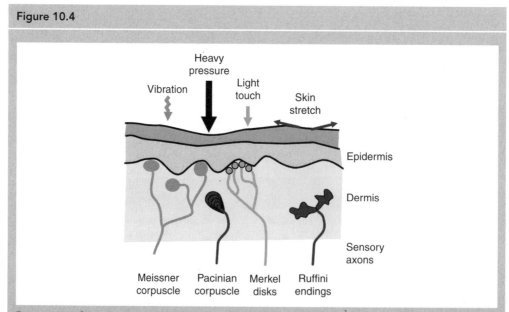

Four types of touch sensors that are embedded in the lower layers of the human skin (bottom, indicated by different shades of grey: Meissner corpuscle, Paccinian corpuscle, Merkel disks and Ruffini endings) respond to different types of tactile sensation (top), thus monitoring the status of the body surface.

TACTILE SPACE

Each of the mechanoreceptors in the skin is characterised by its location, optimum temporal frequency and its spatial receptive fields. Tactile receptive fields can be studied by applying two pressure points (for instance, the two tips of a compass tool separated by a small distance), which can only be perceived as separate if they are stimulating the receptive fields of different mechanoreceptors (see Figure 10.5a) – if they are positioned within a single receptive field they cannot be discriminated from a single pressure point (Johnson and Phillips 1981). Conversely, the receptive field size determines the spatial resolution in a particular region of the skin, which is the number of pressure points that can be detected in a given skin area, and corresponds to the tactile grating resolution. By applying such stimuli with different separation the tactile resolution, corresponding to receptive field size, can be shown to vary considerable for different areas of the body surface (see Figure 10.5b): resolution on the fingertips is better than palm of the hand, which is better than that on the arm, which is better than on the shoulder, and so forth. Two-point resolution of touch is in the range of millimetres on the fingertips and amounts to several centimetres on the back (Weinstein 1968). This resolution can change with age and experience – for instance, it appears to be much higher in blind individuals (Stevens et al. 1996). Similar regional patterns are described for the absolute sensitivity to tactile stimuli, such as the minimum pressure that can be detected (Sekuler et al. 1973). The highest sensitivity and resolution is found for the fingertips and lips, which could be interpreted in the context of our evolutionary history as an indication of how important it is to manipulate food between fingers and lips. Equally, one might speculate whether the growing significance of manual handling and speech production for humans led to optimisation of tactile resolution for these critical regions of the body surface, although this would not explain why other animals have similar specialisations.

Figure 10.5

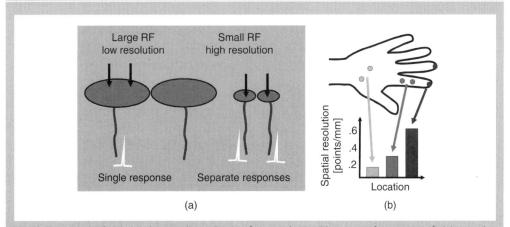

(a)   (b)

Tactile receptive fields and spatial resolution for touch. (a) The size of receptive fields can be tested in a 2-point-resolution task: two pressure points can only be discriminated if they stimulate separate (i.e., small) receptive fields; left: two close stimuli (black arrows) stimulate the same receptive field (grey horizontal ellipse) and therefore elicit only a single response (white spike), as if there were only a single stimulus; right: two separate receptive fields are stimulated, leading to separate responses (spikes). (b) The spatial resolution (number points that can be discriminated per millimetre) for such tactile stimuli varies for different regions of the hand – it is highest at the tip of the index finger.

The psychophysical approach to test the spatial limits of touch perception (Loomis 1981) can go beyond the question of how many tactile stimulus points can be resolved on the skin, by studying the smallest distance of two objects touching the skin that can be discriminated (see Figure 10.6a). This performance limit can be compared to the limit of how well the position of an object touching the skin can be detected relative to others (see Figure 10.6b). Indeed, localisation acuity is by about an order of magnitude better than the spatial resolution limit. The assessment of tactile perception in terms of spatial resolution with two-point stimuli and gratings (Johnson and Phillips 1981), and comparing this with localisation acuity by using position shift stimuli (Loomis 1981), or sensitivity for movement, closely resembles the procedures to describe the spatial performance of the visual system (cf. Chapters 3, 6), and suggests that there are commonalities in the underlying encoding strategies. This analogy goes even further, as demonstrated by experiments with multiple pressure points, which suggest that lateral inhibition mechanisms operate in the tactile system as well (von Békésy 1967). Furthermore, there are similar strategies to expand the sensitivity limits of touch and of vision by moving the fingertips, similar to moving the eyes. This element of active exploration is crucial for the detection of tactile texture, for which humans can reach outstanding sensitivity, using basic qualities like smooth/rough, soft/hard or sticky/slippery (Hollins et al. 2000). Patterns of pressure changes can be detected when moving the fingertips across different materials, like glass, silk or sandpaper (see Figure 10.6c), which correspond to depth variations reflecting the texture of a surface. If these variation of depth span as little as a few tens of micrometres, textures can be detected and discriminated as long as the fingertips are moving across them (Bensmaia and Hollins 2005)! The latest research in this area suggests that the tiny ridges on the skin that generate fingerprints and improve grip by increasing friction are crucial to achieve such a performance, by amplifying the vibrations generated when brushing the surface with the fingertips (Scheibert et al. 2009).

Figure 10.6

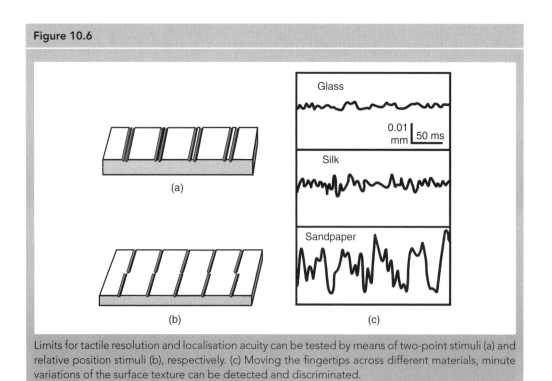

Limits for tactile resolution and localisation acuity can be tested by means of two-point stimuli (a) and relative position stimuli (b), respectively. (c) Moving the fingertips across different materials, minute variations of the surface texture can be detected and discriminated.

CORTICAL REPRESENTATION

How is the local somatosensory information, for instance, the pressure distribution arising from the fingertips brushing a surface, represented in the cortex? Tactile information from all over the body is transmitted through the spinal chord (and the trigeminal nerves for face regions) into the brainstem and thalamus, and finally into the somatosensory cortex (see Figure 10.7a), where all the information needed for tactile perception is further processed and joined together (Chapters 18 and 19 in Roberts 2002), to create a representation of the complete body surface. Similar to what we know from the functional architecture of cortical representations of other sensory domains (cf. Chapter 2), a map is formed on the cortical surface such that the neighbourhood relations in the brain correspond to those on the sensory surface. This 'somatotopic' representation means that a map of the body surface itself is created – and a little person can be outlined on the cortical surface (see Figure 10.7b), representing the sensory input from the body, which is called the 'homunculus' (Penfield and Rasmussen 1950). Interestingly, there is a second homunculus, on the other side of the central sulcus in the primary motor cortex. This motor map in the cortex represents locations of motor outputs in the body, and is involved in motor control, which obviously can benefit greatly from the close neighbourhood of sensory information.

The amount of space on the cortex surface, or cortical volume, in the somatotopic map dedicated to a particular region of the body surface differs widely between different body areas in such a way that the scale of the map reflects the somatosensory resolution in these areas. Wherever the density of separable touch points (number of points per skin area) is large, a large cortical area is dedicated to this somatosensory information (see large fingertips and lips on the homunculus shown in Figure 10.7b). This scaling of the cortical representation area according to the number of sensory sampling points dedicated to the

Figure 10.7

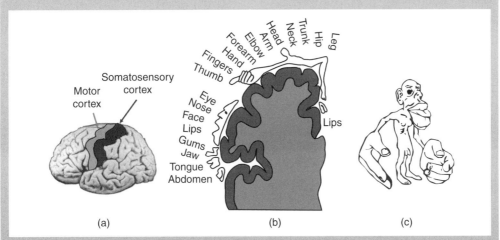

(a)   (b)   (c)

The homunculus. (a) The somatosensory cortex sits in close proximity to the primary motor cortex, and both are organised in terms of somatotopic maps. (b) In somatosensory maps neighbouring body regions are projecting to neighbouring regions on the cortical surface, scaled with the spatial resolution of the somatosensory sampling at that location. (c) The reconstruction of a resolution-scaled homunculus demonstrates the relative importance of particular body parts to somatosensory perception in terms of 'cortical magnification'.

various body parts (see Figure 10.7c) gives 3D models of the homunculus a very curious appearance (such a model can be seen in the Science Museum in London).

Knowing about the cortical organisation of somatosensory perception, we can make an attempt to explain a very puzzling phenomenon – the experience of phantom sensations – following from the loss of limbs or other body parts after surgical removal. After amputation, the majority of patients report a range of sensations including pain, warmth, cold, itching, squeezing, tightness or tingling. These sensations are impossible to control because they arise from a part of the body that physically no longer exists, hence the name 'phantom' (see Figure 10.8a). They can be best understood as cortical plasticity, resulting from the reorganisation of somatosensory maps that connect the orphaned projection regions to neighbouring sensory input fibres. Such plasticity in mapping the sensory surface onto the cortex (see Figure 10.8b) following amputation has been demonstrated in animal models (Merzenich et al. 1984), which can lead to stable novel maps in the long term (Manger et al. 1996). In humans, rapid cortical reorganisation was observed together with sensitivity changes for touch as consequence of cutaneous anaesthesia (Björkman et al. 2009). In all of these cases, brain regions originally dedicated to the severed body region seem to be connected to other peripheral regions – through such rewiring tactile information is no longer going to the correct destination and can be misinterpreted, as phantom sensations! A particularly stunning example has been described by Ramachandran and Rogers-Ramachandran (2000) of a patient who localises individual fingers of his amputated hands on particular regions of the face, such that a map of the phantom hand can be drawn on his face (see Figure 10.8b). It is tempting to speculate that the absence of sensory input from the amputation stump that originally represented the hand, results in invasion of input connections from the neighbouring somatosensory regions representing the face (these neighbourhood relationships can be seen in Figure 10.7b), which then can be perceived as stimuli to the phantom limb.

Figure 10.8

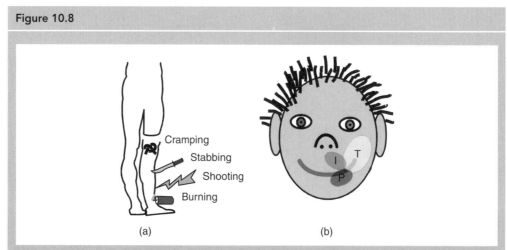

(a)   (b)

Rewiring the brain. (a) After amputations, many patients suffer from vivid somatosensory sensations, phantom experiences such as pain, itching or burning. (b) By touching specific regions of the face, tactile sensations can be triggered in the phantom hand, which are localised to particular fingers (t = thumb, I = index finger, P = pinky) and specific to the type of sensation (the phantom hand can be tickled!).

HAPTICS: ACTIVE EXPLORATION

It was mentioned above in the context of tactile texture recognition that tactile exploration improves performance tremendously. The active deployment of the sensory organ in fingers, haptic exploration, is a very powerful and constantly used behavioural strategy to collect information – we talk about 'handling' objects. Lateral motion across a surface to scrutinise its texture, increase of contact surface to sample object temperature, following contours or enclosing an object to assess its overall shape, applying pressure to feel its softness, or just picking and holding it up to estimate its weight, are just a few examples of how the interaction between the main somatosensor array – the hand – and the environment is used to maximise the information that is collected. Precise coordination between the sensory and the motor processes is needed to make reliable information available, and it is no surprise that we experience illusions when using the sense of touch, like the haptic Müller-Lyer illusion, very similar to some phenomena known from the visual system (Heller et al. 2002).

Haptic exploration has a very special relevance, because it is the basis of reading Braille by using the fingertips (Foulke 1982). Braille letters are specifically designed symbols for stimulating the fingertips by punching them into the paper. They are easier to identify at the low spatial resolution that limits the tactile sense (Loomis 1981) than embossed conventional characters. By using a raster of well-spaced points to define a set of spatial relationships that carry the information to be read, rather than conventional letters such as Roman characters, a system is developed that is less susceptible to blur. This is demonstrated in Figure 10.9b, where two lines of Roman (lines A) and Braille (lines B) characters are blurred in order to simulate low spatial resolution of the sensory system picking up such information. It is clear that blurred Roman characters (lines C) are amorphous blobs that can barely be discriminated from each other, whereas blurred Braille (lines D) retains characteristic patterns that can be easily identified and discriminated. But why would it not be simpler just to use larger

Figure 10.9

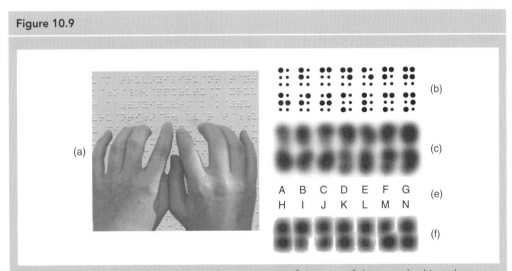

(a) Reading Braille code is based on tactile recognition of patterns of dots punched into the paper, and therefore needs to be resistant against blurring from low spatial resolution. A set of six dots in a cell define the letters of the Braille alphabet, as shown in two lines for the first 14 letters (b), just as the characters in (e) compose the Roman alphabet; when blurred, the Roman characters turn into blobs that are difficult to discriminate (f), whereas the Braille characters retain their distinct patterns (c).

Roman characters, in order to cope with the low spatial resolution of touch? Whereas such a technique indeed could overcome the problem with discriminability, now the overall size of each character would be much larger, and a new problem would be created. Because of the restricted size of fingertips, which acts like a restricted field of view for tactile information, very few characters could be touched at the same time, and more hand movement, and more coordination between the motor and the sensory system would be necessary to read a text – which would make it much more difficult to learn to read by touch. Just imagine if you were to read a book through a mask that only allows you to read one letter at a time! It can be concluded that the design of the communication technology, the Braille characters in this case, needs to take into account the sensitivities and the limitations of the sensory processing mechanisms, in this case the spatial resolution of the tactile system, to make communication reliable, efficient and reasonably easy to learn.

Take Home Messages

- the somatosensory system provides information about the internal physical state of the body and collects information about the external world through the body surface
- pain and temperature contribute to homeostatic and alarm systems that are responsible for the physical integrity of the body
- the proprioceptive and the vestibular system provide information about body posture and motion that is crucial for various stabilisation reflexes
- touch is a spatial sense with a range of biological functions; in many aspects tactile perception makes use of very similar neural encoding mechanisms and data collection strategies to those of other sensory systems
- active exploration is crucial to overcome the low spatial resolution of touch perception; haptics is a powerful tool to explore the outside world and communicate

Discussion Questions

- Describe briefly the design and function of the vestibular system.
- How can we measure the spatial resolution of the tactile sensory system?
- What is meant by somatosensory map?
- Discuss in what ways the Braille alphabet, developed to enable blind people to read, is well adapted to the limitations of the tactile sense.

11 FOCUS OF INTEREST: ATTENTIONAL MODULATION OF PERCEPTION

OVERVIEW

Presenting the brain with sensory information from so many different sources, collected in highly efficient ways with the aim to maximise the information throughput, there is a clear danger of information overload. In technical systems, parallel transmission and processing strategies are used to optimise the use of limited CPU capacity, memory and channel bandwidth. Biological systems employ similar strategies, but in addition are using highly specialised mechanisms to select relevant information: attention processes. Pre-attentive and attentive vision is illustrated by phenomena of parallel and serial search and pop-out of salient objects. Based on these phenomena, some conceptual aspects of attention are discussed and related to the neural substrate underlying the control of attention. Change detection and change blindness are used as a starting point to discuss issues of attention, awareness and consciousness. Strategies to guide attention (overt and covert attentional tracking) and the failure of attention processes are presented in a practical context, such as navigating through dense traffic. The chapter will close with an example of a highly specialised practitioner of manipulating attention – with a little glance into the magician's bag of tricks.

WHAT IS ATTENTION, WHY DO WE NEED IT?

In his famous *Principles of Psychology*, William James provides an insightful description of attention: 'Everyone knows what attention is. It is the taking possession by the mind, in clear and vivid form, of one out of what seem several simultaneously possible objects or trains of thought. Focalization, concentration, of consciousness are of its essence' (James 1890). As convincing as this sounds, for the scientist this definition raises a lot of questions, which might end with a suspicion that nobody really knows what attention is. (And yet, this might be the fault of scientists rather than of everyone else – although everyone knows what light is, for instance, scientists can debate the nature of light for centuries.) So what is attention, how does it work, why can we lose it, why do we need it?

The sensory system, as portrayed in this book, is a massive information-processing device that is used for extensive data mining. Humans collect information about their external world persistently and effortlessly. It is difficult to precisely estimate the amount of information captured, or the processing capacity (bandwidth), although we may want to attempt a rough guess for the visual system, based on the number of photoreceptors (approx. 10^8) in each retina, and similar measurement can be used for the other sensory streams. If each photoreceptor has 256 discriminable states of activation and is updated 10 times per second, it would collect 10 bytes (0.01 KB) per second – and each eye would collect 10^6 KB (1000 MB, or 1 GB) per second. By comparison, a typical modem operates at approx 10 KB per second, and a reasonable broadband connection gives you access to the Internet with 12.5 MB per second. The disk of the laptop I am writing on at this very moment would be completely filled up by the information picked up by a single eye after about 4 minutes of data streaming! Obviously, this wouldn't work, and we, or our brains, need some clever data compression mechanisms (as discussed in previous chapters) and some efficient data selection. When you read a newspaper, or browse webpages, you would not attempt to read everything from the first to the last letter, but would try to focus on what you are interested in, and ignore the rest. This is exactly what the sensory system does for us, according to the 'bottleneck theory' of early selective attention (Broadbent 1958) in order to prevent overload and hitting the capacity limits for transmission, processing and storage. It is perhaps surprising how small the number of items is that we can attend to simultaneously – about four (somewhat depending on experimental conditions, Scholl et al. 2001), which roughly corresponds to the three to seven items that we are able to hold simultaneously in the short-term memory (Miller 1956).

In order to deal with the capacity limits for processing information, selectivity is required or, in the technical terminology introduced in Chapter 2, 'filters' that remove information that is redundant, or unimportant, for the control of behaviour. This may sound like a straightforward idea, but understanding the mechanisms of selecting information at an early level in the sensory stream turns out to be a major challenge, because we are not talking about a simple filter process that removes certain stimulus components from the image like red colour, or everything else but red. The conundrum of selective filtering is that in many situations it would be difficult to know what should be filtered from the stimulus without knowing the contents of the stimulus. Therefore usually two mechanisms are distinguished that are involved in attentive selection. In top-down selection, voluntary attention directs processing resources towards particular aspects of the incoming information. In bottom-up selection, external events that are highly 'salient' attract attention in an automatic, involuntary manner (Itti and Koch 2000). In the latter case one might want to know, however, what kind of implicit mechanism is hiding behind the definition of 'saliency'. So do we know what attention is, and how it works? Let us start with some simple experiments to study this phenomenon under controlled conditions.

A SIMPLE EXPERIMENTAL APPROACH

A very simple experiment demonstrates the role of attention in segmentation, as illustrated in Figure 11.1. Different regions of this image are defined by local elements, such as Ls, Ts or tilted Ts. The boundary between the T region and the tilted-T region on the right is immediately visible – it 'pops out' automatically and therefore is believed to be the result of a pre-attentive segmentation process based on local orientation that is highly salient. On the other hand, the boundary between the T region and the L region, on the left, is much less salient, and requires the observer to check one element after the other, guided by attention in a 'serial search' process that categorises each element on the basis of the junction type that is defined by the relative position of the intersection between the horizontal and vertical line segment (Treisman 1986). This is because L and T use the same orientations, whereas the tilted T shares no orientations with the upright T.

The difference between pre-attentive and attention-driven processes become even more obvious in a visual search paradigm (Treisman 1986), asking the participant to identify a single target element (the 'singleton') that is different from all the other randomly structured elements (the 'distracters'). As illustrated in Colour plate VII, Figure 2, it is easy to find the target in a set of distracters that differ in a single simple property, such as shape or colour, suggesting

Figure 11.1

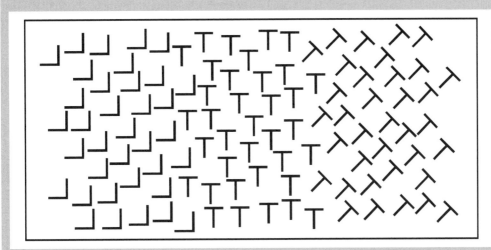

Some texture contours 'pop out' (e.g. when defined by local orientation, right), others don't (e.g. when defined by type of junction, left).

fast parallel processing that does not require attentional control. Searching for a single target among distracters that differ in a single property (shape in Colour plate VII, Figure 2a, or colour in Colour plate VII, Figure 2b) is fast and simple. If each distracter differs in one of two possible properties (shape or colour in Colour plate VII, Figure 2c), the search task is much more difficult, takes longer and requires attention. The idea that in this case the image is serially searched for the target is strongly supported by the observation, and under such conditions the search time increases with the number of distracters (Colour plate VII, Figure 2d).

These segmentation and search tasks are a simple tool to study the function of attention in a quantitative way. (a) Pre-attentive processing based on elementary features leads to fast pop-out and operates in parallel such that the number of distracters does not affect search time. (b) Discrimination based on conjunctions of simple features involves logical operations to assess object attributes, and therefore requires attention to guide the search in a serial manner from element to element. This leads to a distinct fingerprint for attentional processing in search paradigms: the time to make a decision increases with the number of distracters.

CONCEPTUAL ASPECTS OF ATTENTION

A straightforward way to think about attention would lead to the suggestion that attention is a mechanism to enhance processing at a particular location in the sensory environment, which facilitates faster and more accurate responses and lowers detection thresholds. In the 'spotlight model' developed by Posner (1980) the key idea is that attention can be directed to a particular location by a cue before stimulation and this increases performance in this task at the cued location, but not in other locations. Attention acts like a spotlight that allocates extra processing resources in the regions within its beam. Posner's basic cueing paradigm is illustrated in Figure 11.2: participants are asked to fixate the centre of a screen and to respond with pressing keys, or to make a saccade towards a target when it appears right or left to the

Figure 11.2

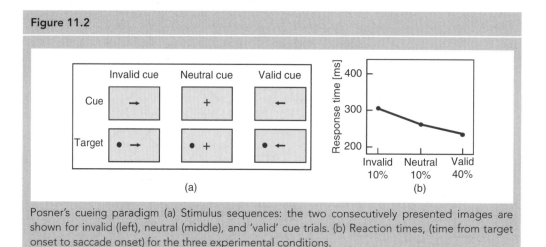

Posner's cueing paradigm (a) Stimulus sequences: the two consecutively presented images are shown for invalid (left), neutral (middle), and 'valid' cue trials. (b) Reaction times, (time from target onset to saccade onset) for the three experimental conditions.

fixation spot. In 50% of the trials the fixation cross is replaced by an arrow pointing right or left to indicate the side of the stimulus field on which the target can expected to appear. Participants can use this cue to direct their attention to the predicted target region, but are not allowed to move their eyes until the target appears. When the target is appearing at the cued position ('valid' condition, used in 40% of all trials) the reaction time from target onset to saccade onset is decreased as compared to the situation when no direction cue is provided ('neutral' condition, in 50% of all trials). When the target is appearing on the uncued side ('invalid' condition, in 10% of all trials) reaction times are increased. These results suggest that attention directed to the cued area speeds up the response to a target in this region but slows down the response to targets elsewhere.

By shifting the focus of the 'attentional spotlight' in space we can actively search for objects of interest. We can choose to move our attention voluntarily under top-down control, or it can be drawn to a location or object involuntarily in a bottom-up process. Not only are objects processed better in the spotlight, but other objects outside the spotlight get ignored. In the experiment described in Figure 11.2, the eyes are kept still before target onset, looking at the centre of the screen, to study shifts of attention independent of eye movements. When attention is directed in this way to a region outside of the fovea without fixating the attended area, we speak about 'covert' attention. Usually, however, we deploy attention by moving our eyes around to fixate the object, or the region, we are attending to – which is called 'overt' attention. Under some experimental conditions, the spotlight of attention can be larger or smaller, or can be even split between locations (Castiello and Umilta 1992).

In transparent motion stimuli groups of randomly distributed dots are moving in two or more directions, at the same time and within the same region of the visual field (Treue et al. 2000) – in this rather complex stimulus human observers can focus their attention on a particular motion direction independent of location (Felisberti and Zanker 2004), suggesting that there is more to focussing attention than a directing spotlight to a region in visual space. Selectivity of attention for features rather than space is not uncommon at all. The ability to select parts of a scene to be processed preferentially on the basis of visual features such as motion direction or colour is referred to as 'feature-based attention'. A typical demonstration that is regarded as evidence that attention can be allocated to stimulus features rather than

Figure 11.3

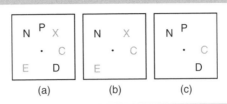

(a)   (b)   (c)

Feature-based attention. When participants need to report the black letters in very briefly presented sets of grey and black letters (a), accuracy decreases with the number of black letters (b) but is unaffected by the number of grey letters (c), suggesting a selective processing of the attended colour of letters.

locations is illustrated in Figure 11.3. Participants are asked to report just the black letters in very briefly displayed sets of grey and black letters. The response accuracy (proportion of correctly reported letters) decreases with an increasing number of target letters, but is unaffected by the number of distracter letters, which demonstrates that there is a selective advantage for the feature that needs to be attended, irrespective of location (Desimone and Duncan 1995).

As mentioned in the previous section, attention is focussed in a serial search strategy on individual elements in a display when performing a conjunction search, in order to bind the properties at any given location (Treisman and Gelade 1980). The process of binding element properties in a conjunction search is called 'feature integration'. At very short presentation durations, observers can experience illusory conjunctions, while attention is diverted elsewhere. Because such conjunction errors are more frequent than incorrect reports of colour or shape in isolation, they are believed to reflect genuine exchange of component properties rather than simply misperceptions of a single object. The phenomenon of illusory conjunctions has been taken as evidence that selective attention plays a role in solving the binding problem (Treisman 1998). These properties of binding features together along the lines of feature integration theory is of special interest for studying consciousness because of their role in the experiencing of visual objects as unified perceptual wholes located in a world perceptually unified world, rather than as a collection of unrelated features (Revonsuo and Newman 1999).

NEURAL CORRELATES OF ATTENTIONAL MODULATION

The perceptual changes induced by attention are not restricted to indirect effects like the improvement of detection and recognition performance, there are indications of increased contrast sensitivity and spatial resolution, as a result of attention at an early level of the visual system. Direct effects of attention on the appearance of a stimulus have been demonstrated, suggesting that perceived contrast is enhanced by paying attention to a stimulus (Carrasco et al. 2004). These behavioural results correspond to the neurophysiological observation that attention increases the salience of stimuli. Single-cell recordings from neurons in the lateral intraparietal area (LIP) of the monkey cortex (Colby et al. 1995) show that responses of individual neurons increase when the monkey attends to the region in which their receptive field is located (see Figure 11.4). This single-cell physiology result

Figure 11.4

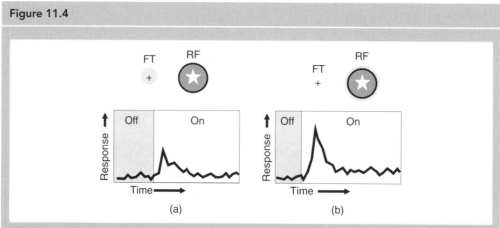

Attentional modulation of single neuron activity (schematically, after Colby et al. 1995). The response of single neuron in area LIP with a receptive field (RF) in the periphery of the fovea (indicated by Fixation Target, see spatial sketch above response traces) is plotted as function of time (lower panels) for a presentation of a stimulus inside the receptive field (off-on). When the monkey is instructed to attend the receptive field region (b), the response is strongly enhanced from the control condition of attending the fixation target (a).

corresponds to observations made in neuroimaging experiments with humans that demonstrate a strong effect of attention on the local activity in a range of cortical regions in the visual stream. When attending to a quadrant of the visual field, the regions corresponding to this quadrant in the retinotopic map of these cortical areas increase their overall level of activity, and decrease if another quadrant is attended to (Tootell et al. 1998). From these different threads of evidence it appears that the changes of neural activity in the brain that process information from attended regions of the visual field can be best described as a modulation of neural gain factors, which could be a direct neurophysiological basis for the perceptual effects of attention.

Additional evidence about the neural mechanism of attention comes from a neuropsychological condition that leads to a massive attentional deficit, which is called 'hemispatial neglect' (Bisiach et al. 1979; Husain and Rorden 2003). After damage to one hemisphere of the brain, usually on the right side, for instance after suffering a stroke, patients are fully unaware of the opposite (usually left-hand) side of space. This condition is most directly expressed as visual neglect, although it can extend to other sensory domains. Although these patients ignore the left side of their world, sometimes to the extent that they 'forget' to shave or put on make-up on the left side, they can turn their gaze to the left side and have not lost complete sensitivity on the left side. When asked to report what they see in a room, they present detailed descriptions of all the objects that are located in their right side but don't talk about the left side (Bisiach 1993). Such attention deficits also affect visual memories. Bisiach asked patients to report what they remember seeing when standing on the Piazza del Duomo in Milan: when they imagined standing on the square at the entrance of the Galleria, facing south, they did not remember that there is the cathedral on their left side, but when they imagined entering the square from the opposite side, facing north, they gave a clear description of the cathedral on their right (Bisiach and Luzzatti 1978). Some clinical tests to characterise hemispatial neglect are illustrated in Figure 11.5.

Figure 11.5

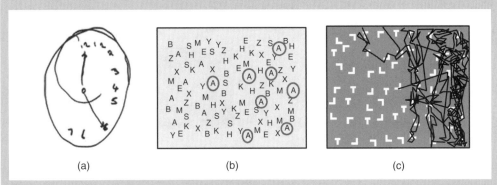

(a)   (b)   (c)

Clinical tests for hemispatial neglect. (a) When drawing a clock from memory, some neglect patients omit the left (contra-lesional) side. (b) In the cancellation test, patients are asked to circle a target letter (A) and fail to do this on the left (contra-lesional) side, but perform well on the right side. (c) Fixational eye movements are restricted to the right (ipsi-lesional) side and are further characterised by many revisits of the most peripheral targets. Reprinted by permission from Macmillan Publishers Ltd. Husain M. and Rorden C. (2003).'Non-spatially lateralized mechanisms in hemispatial neglect', *Nature Reviews Neuroscience* 4, 26–36.

Right-hemisphere damage in the parietal lobe can also lead to a similar, but less severe, condition of attentional loss, called 'extinction' (Driver and Vuilleumier 2001; Rees et al. 2000). These patients are able to detect an object when presented on the left side of the visual field if the right visual field is empty. As soon as an object is placed on the right side, however, they ignore the left visual field and report only the contents of the right field. Both of these conditions, hemispatial neglect and extinction, suggest that the (right) parietal network is involved in guiding visual attention, because damage in this brain region impairs the ability to notice regions of space despite intact eyes and other visual brain regions.

INATTENTIONAL BLINDNESS

If selective attention plays a role in solving the binding problem and binding is required for a unified conscious percept, we may ask ourselves what would be perceived when something happens outside the spotlight of attention. It turns out that even rather substantial changes can happen to a scene, when attention mechanisms are engaged elsewhere, a phenomenon usually referred to as 'inattentional blindness'. A most stunning demonstration of this effect is change blindness displays (Rensink et al. 1997), such as shown schematically in Figure 11.6. In the simplest version, a sequence of four images is shown, alternating a blank screen with two images from a natural scene, which undergoes a major change in the background. When presented as a sequence, the change remains invisible to a naïve observer for quite some time until they actively attend to the railing. The interleaved blank frames interrupt the presentation by a strong flicker sensation, so that the change cannot be perceived as motion, while the observer tends to focus their attention on the foreground of the scene. The same effect can be achieved when instead of the blank frame the two edited versions of the natural scene are interleaved with some strong distracters superimposed, called 'mud splashes' (O'Regan et al. 1999).

There are many different examples of such change blindness stimuli, and corresponding phenomena can be observed in other sensory domains (Gallace et al. 2006), and they never

Figure 11.6

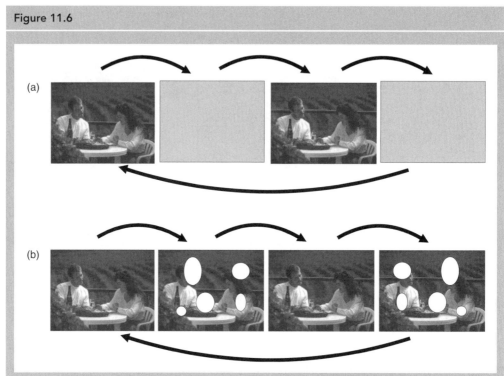

Change blindness. When observers see sequences of these images (presentation sequence indicated by black arrows), the obvious change in the background of this natural scene remains unnoticed for a long time, because attention is disrupted. Top: flicker paradigm; bottom: mud splash paradigm. Reprinted by permission from Macmillan Publishers Ltd. O'Regan et al. (1999). 'Change-Blindness as a result of "mudsplashes"', *Nature* 398, 34.

fail to surprise the viewer who has not seen them before. Normally such obvious changes in the scene would attract your attention, but a big change in between is enough to disrupt the normal detection process. Even more surprising, if your attention is distracted, you may fail to see major events in unedited movie sequences, such as changes of actors, clothing or stage props, which become the hobby horse of some cinema enthusiasts to spot in badly made movies. Should we ever trust an eyewitness? For a controlled study of such effects, Simons and colleagues produced a short movie, in which a gorilla or a woman with an open umbrella walks slowly through two teams of students bouncing a basketball – when participants are asked to count silently the aerial and bounce passes of the ball for one of the teams they often did not notice the strange appearance at all, because their attention was fully engaged with the rather demanding counting task (Simons and Chabris 1999). The probability of detecting the gorilla or woman with an umbrella depends on the attentional selectivity, the difficulty of the task, the salience of the misfit event, as well as the expectations of the observer. The fact that we may miss such massive disruptions of a natural dynamic scene should make us wonder how much we might miss when driving a car through busy traffic – and makes us aware that there are good reasons to ban the use of mobile phones by car drivers!

The exact relationship between the attended primary task (e.g. count the bounces of the basketball) in the example above and the unattended secondary task (detect the gorilla) can be investigated more formally and quantitatively in an 'inattentional blindness cross-task procedure' with simple stimuli that can be systematically manipulated (Mack and Rock 1998). In such an experiment, for instance, participants were shown a cross with two of the arms having different colours, and two of the arms having different lengths, and had to report either which arm was longer (difficult, 'high-load' condition) or which of the arms had a particular colour (easy, 'low-load condition). In the final presentation of a set of trials a task-irrelevant outline square was presented in the background of the cross (critical condition). The probability to detect the square in the critical condition was substantially reduced for the high load primary task (Cartwright-Finch and Lavie 2007). A corresponding effect of task difficulty, or perceptual load, can be found in a range of similar experiments to test selective attention, and is driving a debate whether such a selection of the relevant stimulus components happens at early processing stages, such that irrelevant components are not represented perceptually, or whether it happens at a late stage, such that irrelevant components are retained at higher perceptual levels and are only suppressed in preparing the relevant response (Lavie 1995). The importance of perceptual load on the primary task for ignoring the secondary task supports the idea of an early selection process, whereas manipulating the cognitive control load (for instance, by manipulating working memory) weakens the selection process, which suggests that for a selective attention task resources are required at higher level as well (Lavie 2005). This interpretation of stimulus selectivity being affected by the capacity limits of mental processing on different levels is consistent with an engineering perspective about the optimal use of limited transmission and processing capacity to manage a huge flow of information.

CROSS-MODAL AND SOCIAL ATTENTION: MAGIC

Does attention operate separately within each sensory modality, or are there cross-modal links between sensory systems for the control of attention? This is a very important question to relate behavioural data to underlying neural processes. The direct way to investigate this question is to find out whether shifts of attention in one modality can speed up responses to a stimulus in a different modality. This was tested in a visual elevation judgement task (Driver and Spence 1998) where participants, while fixating a central target, had to decide as fast as possible whether a light appeared in the upper or lower visual field, irrespective of whether this happened in the right or left periphery, without making eye movements. A sound that was irrelevant to the task, produced on the left or right side, preceded the visual stimulus. When the sound came from the side where the visual stimulus was presented, decisions were faster than when it came from the other side, suggesting that attention was drawn to the side of the sound, and thus demonstrating a cross-modal link between sensory modalities for the control of covert attention. When participants are asked to make saccadic eye movements to visual targets, their reaction times are also reduced when the attention is drawn to the target location by an auditory stimulus (Frens et al. 1995), so the cross-modal link seems also to apply to the control of overt attention. Similarly, visual discrimination is faster and more accurate if it follows a task-irrelevant tactile cue given on the side where the visual stimulus is presented. Even more surprisingly, when the arms are crossed over and the tactile cue is given to the right hand (now on the left side), it is the position in space, not the position relative to body coordinates that directs attention to the side of the visual stimulus – suggesting that the neural system controlling attention has the ability to remap tactile space in relation to limb position (Kennett et al. 2002).

We finally will apply our knowledge about the mechanisms involved in the control of attention to reveal some of the methods used by magicians to baffle their audience. Kindly enough,

Figure 11.7

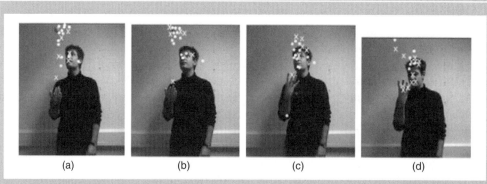

(a)   (b)   (c)   (d)

The psychology of magic. Through his body language, and in particular his eye movements, the magician distracts the gaze, or overt attention, of the audience (indicated by white crosses) from the hand where the ball disappears in this trick (last image in sequence a–c) and thus makes it invisible; if the magician does what would be expected from him, looking at the hand and drawing the audience attention to it (see control condition in (d)), the trick would fail (after Kuhn and Land 2006).

some professional magicians are supporting such ambitious plans by being scientists studying the mechanisms of attention in such 'real-life' environments themselves (Kuhn and Tatler 2005), or revealing some aspects of their arts to the scientific community (Macknik et al. 2008). The key to many magic tricks is the misdirection of the audience's attention, which makes this topic scientifically accessible to empirical study by measuring eye movements as a token of overt attention (Kuhn et al. 2008). Whereas the initial fixations of an object, which the magician wants to disappear without a trace, are driven by the saliency of the object (let's say a bright red juggling ball), the magician uses distracters to direct the audience to irrelevant events, while the object does disappear from their attention first, and then from their sight. Making use of the fact that attention can be directed by social cues like the gaze of another person (Langton et al. 2000), misdirection can be based on surprisingly subtle cues, such as the magician looking in a direction where he wants the audience to lose the joggling ball while he hides it in a location outside the spotlight of attention (Kuhn and Land 2006). This phenomenon is illustrated in Figure 11.7.

Take Home Messages

- attention is a highly sophisticated selection method to control information flow in the nervous system and avoid flooding the brain with irrelevant information (information overload)
- the perceived components in cluttered scenes can be selected in a reflexive, bottom-up fashion driven by the sensory information collected (i.e., based on salience), or can be guided voluntarily in a top-down fashion
- perceptual effects can be related to both spatial attention linked to locations in sensory space and to feature-based attention linked to stimulus properties
- attention is reflected by modulations of activity in the sensory cortex; it can benefit from cross-modal connections
- selective attention means that our awareness of the environment is rather limited, which can pose risks in complex environments and provide opportunities for magicians to trick their audience

Discussion Questions

- Describe how pre-attentive and attention-driven processes can be investigated in search tasks.
- What is meant by covert and overt attention?
- How can we study the neural correlates of attention?
- Discuss the role of attentional mechanisms that are used by magicians to perform their tricks.

12 MANAGING INFORMATION FLOW THROUGH INTEGRATION OF SENSORY AND MOTOR SYSTEMS

OVERVIEW

So far, we have been studying sensory systems in isolation, as if they were completely separate channels to collect information, which do not interact with each other and the environment. Not surprisingly, there is much more to perception, and we now turn to two very important strategies to maximise 'data mining'. Firstly, evolution has created a multitude of highly sophisticated mechanisms to make full use of the senses by interacting with the environment. The advantage that moving sensors have over static ones, incorporated in strategies of exploration, will be described as a starting point to look into some examples of sensory–motor integration to control information flow. The specific function of eye movements such as nystagmus, smooth pursuit, saccades, vergence and accommodation is discussed in the context of behaviour, and extended to the issues of eye and head coordination and other types of active sensing. Secondly, we will consider how the different sensory modalities are combined in the brain to channel them into a holistic experience of our environment – after all, we are not living in separate visual and acoustic worlds! In technical systems, for instance in man–machine interfaces or in robots, 'sensory fusion' is regarded as a major problem, which currently attracts a lot of research. The combination of sensory information is accomplished by multisensory neurons in multisensory brain regions, with audio-visual speech integration being a particularly interesting example. It will be shown how perception can be affected through sensory integration, from a very basic level of abstract stimuli to the meaning of spoken words. Together, these aspects of integration demonstrate how the use of sensory information can be optimised for the control of behaviour in a complex environment, and more generally help us to understand the design of flexible and efficient agents.

ACTIVE SENSING

A static sensory system would miss out on a lot of that is happening in its surroundings, and as a result could easily be a dead system. If an animal is depending on food that is not delivered to its mouth – which would hold for most if not all of them – it cannot survive without starting to forage, that is, actively search for food. In effect, the animal moves its sensors (eyes, ears, nose) through the environment to pick up signals that can indicate, among many other crucial external conditions, threat or food, be it the smell of a carrot for the rabbit, or the shape of a rabbit for the fox. Highly developed strategies of active exploration, which can be found for all sensory domains, and are vital for many aspects of behaviour, are very good examples of sensory–motor integration, where sensory signals and motor action work together in so-called feedback loops to guide the agent (fox) to the target (rabbit). Such feedback loops are crucial for the control of behaviour on all levels, from navigation and orientation tasks (follow the smell of coffee to find the mug) to manipulating objects (pick up a needle from the floor). The interaction between sensory information and motor action, which changes the sensory signal, has been the subject of extensive experimental and theoretical analysis creating a very powerful framework, which is usually called 'control theory' or 'cybernetics' (Wiener 1948).

Arguably the prime example of sensory–motor control can be found in eye movements – it is obvious how the movement of the eye changes the sensory signal (the image is displaced across the retina). One of the most simple, and most puzzling, experiments (see Wade and Tatler 2005) demonstrates the difference between passive and active eye movements, which in terms of feedback correspond to an 'open loop' and a 'closed loop' condition. When you touch the eyelid very gently with your finger (while keeping the eye open) and move the eye ever so slightly with the finger, that is, passively, you can see the world moving – which should be expected because the retinal image of the world is displaced when the eye is moving. However, when you execute exactly the same eye movement actively by the use of your eye muscles, the world seems to be static despite the fact that the effect you generated on the retina is the same as in the passive case. One way to resolve this apparent paradox is the idea that sensory signals about the eye movements themselves, which Helmholtz called 'a measure of the effort to move the eyes' (von Helmholtz 1924), can be used to predict the image shift from the eye movement and correct the perceived image (Guthrie et al. 1983). This 'efference copy' would drive a feedback loop to stabilise the perceived image during active eye movements. In reverse there are a number of feedback loops to minimise the shift of retinal images by 'gaze stabilisation', when moving the body through the environment, or to stabilise the retinal image of a moving object (Collewijn and Tamminga 1984), which will be described below.

Smooth pursuit eye movements are executed when an observer follows an object moving at moderate speed (see Colour plate VII, Figure 3a). This would happen when you track a target such as a bird flying in the sky or a car on the motorway. In this case the angular velocity of the eye matches that of the moving target such that the image of the target is kept in the foveal region of the retina where the spatial resolution is highest (Robinson 1965). During episodes of smooth pursuit, as long as the target does not accelerate or decelerate, eye velocity remains approximately constant, hence the label 'smooth'. One interesting aspect of such pursuit eye movements is that the static background in the scene (for example, the road, street lights and buildings in case of the traffic scene) is perceived as static, although its image is shifted across the retina.

A completely different pattern of eye movements is generated when an observer explores a static scene, such as a painting or a photograph. In *saccadic scanning* (see Colour plate VII, Figure 3b) the eye fixates key regions of the picture in turns and frequently jumps between such locations with very brief and fast eye movements, called saccades (Yarbus 1967). Perhaps the most astonishing example for saccadic scanning is reading: our eyes move across the text in a pattern of saccades that fixate individual words (see Figure 12.1), or parts of long words, at intervals that roughly depend on reading speed (Rayner 1998). Despite the large image shifts caused by saccades, the image is perceived as static, and the observer is completely unaware of the fast displacements. Functionally, this is a crucial feature of this eye movement strategy, because such image shifts would be very disruptive for any image analysis process. In contrast, when an observer is fixating a target on a screen while an image is displaced behind the target in a pattern that mimics the image shift during saccadic scanning of the static image, motion blur is observed and it is very difficult for the observer to see any detail in this image during the movement. The absence of such disruptive effects on perception during actively generated saccades is often interpreted as 'saccadic suppression' of vision (Burr et al. 1994).

Figure 12.1

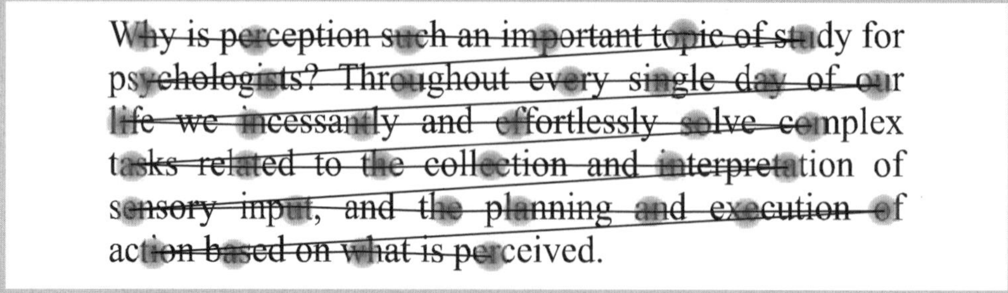

Why is perception such an important topic of study for psychologists? Throughout every single day of our life we incessantly and effortlessly solve complex tasks related to the collection and interpretation of sensory input, and the planning and execution of action based on what is perceived.

Schematic sketch of scanning eye movements during reading at moderate speed. Periods of fixation (indicated by grey dots) are separated saccades, the eye moving rapidly on to one of the next words, or to the beginning of the next line. The pattern of re-fixation changes substantially at higher reading speed.

When you sit on a train travelling through the countryside and watch the landscape passing by through the window, you generate a peculiar pattern of eye movements that prevent the image blurring owing to the fast motion. Episodes of slow pursuit, during which some part of the outside scene is stabilised on the fovea, are interleaved by large and very fast saccadic movements in the opposite direction, which you do not notice at all, resetting the gaze position (relative to the head) to an angle close to where it started from (see Colour plate VII, Figure 3c). As a result of this slow–fast zigzag displacement, which is called 'Opto-kinetic Nystagmus', or OKN (Die and Collewijn 1982), you are able to see the world gently passing by, you can pick up details in the scene, and thanks to the return saccades you don't rotate your eyeballs infinitely in their sockets. Obviously one doesn't need to sit on the train to generate nystagmus eye movements, but this is the regular response of the eye control system to any continuous motion of the observer, such as being turned on an office chair, or steadily moving images that cover large areas of the visual field, such as watching an extensive camera pan on a large movie screen.

In the eye movement types discussed so far, the two eyes usually move together in the same direction and at the same speed. Only when the eyes fixate the far distance, however, is the line of sight for the left and the right eye in parallel, but they will converge as soon as an object at close range is fixated (see Chapter 5). If an observer fixates a looming object, such as the football sketched in Colour plate VII, Figure 3d, and the angle between the left and right direction of gaze increases when the distance of the fixated object from the observer is decreasing, such movement of the two eyes in opposite directions is called 'vergence'. As the similarity of the geometric configuration of these eye movements to that of disparity changes used for stereoscopic depth perception suggests (cf. Figure 5.7), vergence is a direct cue for distance estimation (Tresilian et al. 1999). This depth cue is further supported by accommodation, which is the change of the optical power of the eye's lens, which keeps the approaching object in focus.

Apart from these four major functional types of eye movements, there are some much smaller displacements of the eyes, the function of which is less obvious. Apart from random jitter and slow drifts of the eye position during fixation, the eyes frequently execute small jumps to new positions, which are called 'microsaccades' (Martinez-Conde and Macknik 2007) and are believed to be the cause for some puzzling motion illusions perceived in static patterns (Zanker and Walker 2004). To further complicate the picture, in natural operating conditions eye movements need to be considered in the context of head and body movements, which requires additional coordination of motor programmes (Brouwer et al. 2009). Specific head movements, such as the head-bobbing of pigeons (Frost 1978) or the sideways movements of the head (peering) in insects (Collett 1978), are specialised visuo-motor strategies to make optimal use of the eyes. Apparently simple tasks, like pointing at objects, reaching and grasping, catching a ball, or avoiding it, require the careful coordination of arm and hand and body movements under the guidance of moving eyes. Sports professionals such as cricket batsman can reach astounding precision in sensory–motor coordination (Land and McLeod 2000). Recent studies have demonstrated the complex control task sequences involved in everyday activities, some of which we usually regard as rather trivial, such as making a cup of tea (Land 2006).

The movement of the eyes is often compared with that of a surveillance camera, which moves its viewing direction and zooms in on objects of interest, usually under the control of a human operator. Although some auto-piloting cars and cutting-edge robots have been designed to move around autonomously, and move their camera eyes without human control as well, it is the effectiveness of visuo-motor coordination and the sophistication of image analysis that makes biological systems far superior to these man-made agents. The core functions of eye movements, image stabilisation and active exploration, using visual sensors that are closely interacting with the environment, have evolved to a level of robustness, versatility and efficiency that are far from being matched by the performance of any technical system. This section has focussed on sensory–motor aspects in the visual system, because here the interactions are most obvious, but similar strategies of active sensing are also found in other sensory domains, such as moving the ears (which can be easily observed in dogs or horses), or active sniffing (see Chapter 9). In general, the phenomena briefly described here demonstrate how the loop is closed from the sensory systems collecting information about the world to successful and meaningful interaction with static objects and mobile creatures in the world, which in return affects the information collected.

THE COMBINATION OF SENSORY INFORMATION

The sensory system is generally believed to be organised in sensory modalities or channels (see Chapter 1), and so far this book has been treating them in isolation. Whereas in the tradition of Aristotle (Everson 1997) we talk about five senses of vision, hearing, touch, smell and taste, there are a number of somatic senses of which we are less aware (see Chapter 10), and in Chapter 13 you will read about several sensory domains which humans have no access to. In all of these cases, however, it is clear that the sensory system is organised in separable modules. Modular design is a standard method that humans apply to building things: these days it is rare that a house is carved out of a single rock, and quite often the conventional technique of laying brick by brick is replaced by assembling prefabricated modules. Modular design is used everywhere, from your mobile phone to an airplane, because it has the advantage that you don't have to rebuild from scratch when something breaks but simply exchange the faulty module, and the components can be added or exchanged if the size or function of the construct needs to be adjusted to the changing circumstances. Because of this functionality it is not surprising that evolution led to sensory systems organised in modules, which transmit information about different aspects of the environment in separate channels. But is there more to the sensory system? In the context of the control of eye movements, we already noticed in passing that a range of sensory information is driving the oculomotor system (Collewijn and Kowler 2008): somatosensory signals from the eye muscles, movement information from the vestibular system, and visual information about object position and motion (see above). It turns out that cross-modal combination of information is a very common and powerful property of the human sensory system. In the case of smell and taste, the cross-talk between the two sensory modalities can be so strong that it is difficult to separate the two components contributing to a given flavour (see Chapter 9).

So what is the function, and what is the advantage of combining the different modalities of sensory information? Alarm systems can improve their sensitivity and selectivity by making optimal use of all the sensory information that is available. In the twilight of the jungle, for instance, sounds and odours are crucial in disambiguating spurious visual cues, and equally in modern traffic we are using sound (such as squeaking brakes, or the horn of other cars) to guide the visual system in picking up particularly dangerous situations. In many different contexts, the reliability of object identification increases considerably if the information from two different sensory channels can be combined (a function which develops very early in the human infant, see Figure 12.2). In moonlight we would not be able to recognise the colour of an orange, but the smell immediately indicates that the spherical object on the garden table is an orange. The combination of auditory and visual information can be particularly helpful for localisation and recognition of objects that are partially hidden or positioned in the peripheral regions of the visual field, where a spatial resolution is low. The combination of interoceptive body senses with exteroceptive sensors, in particular vision, plays a major role in the control of locomotion. This was described in the previous section for the control of eye movements, and similar cross-modal combination of sensory information takes place in many other contexts.

Figure 12.2

The combination of sensory information – in this example vision, touch and taste – is crucial for controlling some of the earliest and strongest emotions acquired by human infants.

An interesting case in point is the cross-modal adaptation between the visual system and the proprioceptive system in the perception of one's own running speed (Pelah and Barlow 1996). The least obvious, but arguably most important, function of multi-sensory interaction is to generate an internal representation of a coherent world: we do not perceive there to be separate visual and acoustic spaces around us but a unitary and physically coherent environment. The tendency to create a unified presentation is so strong that some cases of cue conflict can create even physiologically aversive reactions – when the vestibular information about our own movement is in conflict with the visual information, we experience motion sickness. Because of this high importance of multi-sensory integration, there is a large interest from the engineering disciplines in understanding the basic underlying mechanisms. Sensory fusion is a hot topic in robotics, virtual reality and in particular, video games, which live from a convincing recreation of physical reality. So how do nervous systems combine sensory information from different modalities and in such an efficient way?

Multi-sensory neurons have been described in single-cell recordings from subcortical regions of the mammalian brain, for instance the superior colliculus (Stein et al. 1993), suggesting by its early appearance in the information processing stream a fundamental role in the functional architecture of sensory processing. These neurons receive input from a range of other brain regions that process visual, auditory, somatosensory and motor signals (see Figure 12.3a). One of the most intriguing aspects of this sensory integration on the level of individual neurons is the alignment of receptive fields. As shown in Figure 12.3b for the example of such collicular neurons in the cat, there is an overlap of the region in space from which a neuron can be stimulated by sound and by vision, or by vision and touch, etc. – in these brain regions we find integrated multi-sensory maps of the environment. Individual neurons can operate as 'coincidence detectors', if they respond preferentially to the combination of cues. For instance, a particular neuron may only respond if the cat is picking up simultaneously a visual and an auditory stimulus from the same location in the environment, such as a little mouse running through the leaves on the ground. This example illustrates how cross-modal integration can be a highly adapted mechanism to match a particular environment and lifestyle of an animal.

Figure 12.3

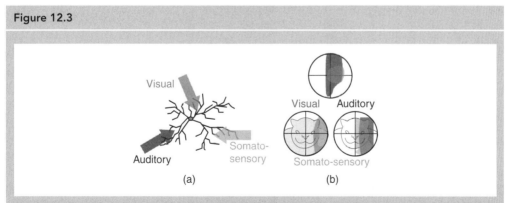

Multisensory neurons in the superior colliculus of the cat. (a) An individual neuron (grey cell body and black dendrites) may receive information different sensory modalities such as the visual, auditory or somatosensory system (indicated by arrows in different shades of grey). (b) The receptive fields of multi-sensory neurons in the visual, auditory and somatosensory space (indicated by regions of different shades of grey) overlap.

How and where are the different senses integrated in the human brain? As we know from the previous chapters about individual sensory modalities, each of them has a unique area in the cortex into which the particular information is transmitted. If sensory signals arise from a common event, they should be related to the same location in space and moment in time for each of the sensory modalities. This coincidence can therefore be used to link the modality-specific information from different brain areas. Fast progress in MRI imaging techniques allows us to investigate such interactions in the human cortex (Macaluso and Driver 2005). Such studies suggest in a first approximation that modality-specific, or 'unimodal', regions are located in the early sensory streams, feeding into 'heteromodal' regions, which thus receive multi-sensory input. More surprisingly, multi-sensory interactions can also be found in unimodal brain regions, which requires the revision of a simple, bottom-up processing model. It is clear, however, that heteromodal brain regions, which are sensitive to spatial and temporal coincidence of stimuli from several sensory domains, are likely to be the neural substrate of cross-modal object identification. Understanding the specific feed-forward, feedback and integration mechanisms between sensory information from different modalities, however, requires extensive physiological work on animal model systems (Driver and Noesselt 2008).

INTERACTION OF VISION AND TOUCH

Handling objects under visual control is a common and frequent task for humans, which requires close interaction between hand and eye movements, and between visual and somatosensory information. So it is not surprising to find strong interactions between visual and tactile systems. This is also a cross-modal interaction, which is comparatively straightforward to investigate experimentally. In such experiments participants are asked to make judgements about objects, using information from one or the other or both domains, making use of conflicting conditions in which the visual information is systematically distorted. For instance, a lens is used to reduce the visual image of a small block, which leads to a then incorrect estimation of object size; haptic exploration of the very same object in the dark allows a participant to correctly estimate its size. When the participant is allowed to handle that object in the light while looking at it, such that both the reduced size image and the correct haptic information are available, the visual image dominates the perceived size and the haptic size information is largely ignored (Rock and Harris 1967). In another typical experiment, participants are tasked to recognise objects by exploring them with their hands behind a screen, or with their eyes without touching them, or looking at their hands while handling the objects. Again visual was superior to haptic performance, with haptic recognition being improved by vision, but not the other way round (Millar 1971). The dominance of the visual system can be easily understood by its much higher special resolution and robustness against noise, as compared to a rather coarse sense of touch (see Chapter 10).

With new display technologies becoming available, the interaction between haptic and visual information has recently attracted new interest. Using three-dimensional visual stimuli generated in a virtual reality setup, which can be systematically manipulated, together with presenting physical objects for haptic inspection (see Figure 12.4a), performance for judging the size of such objects was tested for different levels of visual noise introduced into the virtual reality image of the object (Ernst and Banks 2002). When participants were asked to judge size without visual stimulation they achieved a certain performance level on completing this task, but this was lower than that reached with visual stimulation in the absence of visual noise.

Figure 12.4

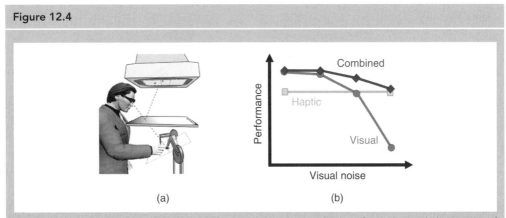

(a)   (b)

Interaction between touch and vision. (a) Independent manipulation of visual stimuli, by means of a three-dimensional virtual reality set-up (top), and tactile stimuli presented through a mechanical device (bottom). (b) When the noise in the visual stimuli is increased, performance decreases for purely visual stimulation, is unaffected for haptic stimulation and corresponds to the best of the two isolated performance levels for combined stimulation.

However, with increasing visual noise levels performance dropped dramatically when only visual information was available. When participants had access to both sources of information, performance corresponded approximately to that observed for the sensory input that would yield higher performance in isolation at this noise level (see Figure 12.4b). It appears that by using two combinations the sensory system is making use of the best information available, which then determines the limit of performance. The underlying process of such a cross-modal integration is called 'maximum likelihood estimator', which is an optimal strategy for the combination of several information sources with different reliability to generate a robust percept (Ernst and Bülthoff 2004). With emergence and fast proliferation of a wide range of medical imaging technologies (comparable to different senses) in recent years, the intelligent fusion of different sources of information, and relating this information to semantic knowledge bases (in other words, recognition), has become increasingly important for assisting the medical professional with diagnostic procedures and the planning and execution of surgery. Using biological systems as models to design such cross-modal integration and object recognition mechanisms offers the potential to design particularly robust artificial systems (Möller et al. 2008).

INTERACTION OF VISION AND HEARING

Are other types of cross-modal interaction driven by the same strategies of combining different information sources? Combining visual and auditory information, and expanding the approach described for haptic and visual interaction, leads to an experiment to estimate the speed, corresponding to arrival time at a predetermined location, of a visual target and an auditory target moving around the participant (sketched in Figure 12.5a). This experiment was dubbed 'catching auditory mice' (Hofbauer et al. 2004). When the movement of the target was continuously visible, or audible, or visible and audible, but superimposed with visual or auditory noise, the performance for the condition where both sensory modalities were available was twice as good as in either of the conditions when the stimulus was presented in only one modality. However, when the stimulus was switched

Figure 12.5

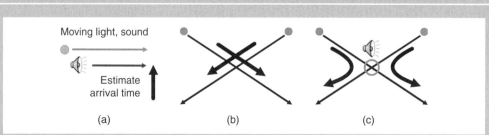

Moving light, sound

Estimate
arrival time

(a)   (b)   (c)

Low-level interaction between hearing and vision. (a) The type of integration of auditory and visual information for estimating the speed (here, arrival time) of a moving object depends on the exact nature of the task. (b) Two dots are perceived as 'streaming' across each other when they move simultaneously and continuously on a straight diagonal path across a screen. (c) When a brief sound is added to the stimulus at the time when the paths of the two dots cross over, the dots are perceived as 'bouncing' off each other.

off for a brief period before it reached its final destination, and the participant needed to extrapolate the movement of the target from the stimulus history, performance was not significantly improved by combining the two stimulus sources, and participants relied largely on the visual information. These observations suggest that there might be a variety of methods to combine stimulus information from different sensory domains, which depend on the nature of the task to be solved.

Another kind of low-level interaction between visual and auditory information is demonstrated by the so-called 'streaming and bouncing' experiment (Sekuler et al. 1997). When two simple dots appear on a display and move diagonally in opposite directions across the screen such that their movement paths cross over somewhere in the middle of the screen (see Figure 12.5b), observers see two dots moving on the screen on straight paths and streaming across each other halfway ('streaming'). If, however, a short sound is played when the two motion paths intersect, the percept changes dramatically (see Figure 12.5c): now observers report that two dots are colliding with each other in the centre and, just like billiard balls, continue their journey in another direction ('bouncing'). The interesting observation in this experiment is that sound not only has a quantitative effect on visual perception, but can lead to categorical changes of what is seen. We also should note that this bouncing effect of a brief stimulus is not restricted to auditory stimuli, but can also be elicited by a tactile stimulus (Shimojo and Shams 2001).

The most important integration between visual and auditory information is related to the perception of speech. In this context we find some high-level interactions between complex visual stimuli related to facial expression, in particular lip movements, and complex sound signals related to the phonemes that are the building blocks of human speech (see Chapter 8). Usually we assume that speech is largely transmitted through the auditory channel, and we are not aware that we are picking up visual signals in order to understand spoken language. Only when we try to follow a speaker in an acoustically cluttered environment (remember the cocktail party effect) do we start focussing on the face and lips of a speaker when trying to select their voice and follow them. The visual–auditory interaction is shown most dramatically in the McGurk effect, which demonstrates that coherence between visual *and* auditory information is needed to understand speech correctly (McGurk and MacDonald 1976). Again, the crucial experiment involves a cue–conflict situation, by separating the image

Figure 12.6

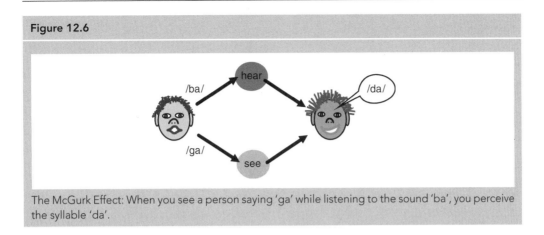

The McGurk Effect: When you see a person saying 'ga' while listening to the sound 'ba', you perceive the syllable 'da'.

sequence in video clips of a person speaking a syllable from the corresponding sound trace: when participants saw a person saying 'ga' while they were listening to the sound 'ba', they perceived the syllable 'da' (see sketch in Figure 12.6). This paradoxical result clearly indicates that auditory information and visual information are carefully integrated in the decoding of speech. Brain imaging studies have shown that in a particular region in the human brain, the superior temporal sulcus (STS), the neuronal activity depends on the congruence of speech signals: when lip movements correspond to the sounds presented, the activity in this region is increased, as compared to the sum of the responses to separate signals, and it is suppressed when there is a discrepancy between visual and auditory information (King and Calvert 2001). This result suggests that the binding of visual and auditory components of speech is located in the STS.

The connectivity between visual and auditory brain areas raises further interesting questions, such as the use of auditory processing areas in deaf people who communicate using sign language (see Figure 12.7a). Nishimura and colleagues (1999) studied the activity in the primary auditory cortex and the auditory association area in the supratemporal gyrus (STG) in a congenitally deaf individual watching video clips showing sign language words. This stimulus elicited clear responses in the STG, suggesting that this auditory region has been taken over to process visual information, a striking case of neural plasticity. In a control experiment, after receiving a cochlear implant that led to restoration of auditory function (but not to speech recognition), meaningless sound led to activation of the primary auditory cortex, and meaningless visual signing led to activation of the visual cortex, without any activation of the STG (see Figure 12.7b). This is interpreted as evidence that the primary auditory does not benefit from the same cross-modal plasticity as the auditory association area, and that the latter area is specifically dedicated to language processing. Other imaging studies involving deaf signers add further evidence that brain regions commonly believed to be auditory areas for speech processing may be dedicated more generally to language processing. These brain regions therefore are not exclusively to one sensory modality but instead can act as multi-modal network that computes aspects of language on the basis of both auditory and visual input (Petitto et al. 2000).

As a final aspect of interaction between the visual and auditory system, let us consider an inverse effect of language on visual face perception. A most striking effect of cross-modal binding between emotional content of a voice and facial expression was demonstrated in a study assessing the perceived happiness of faces in a psychophysical rating experiment (de Gelder and Bertelson 2003). Participants were asked to judge the emotional expression of

Figure 12.7

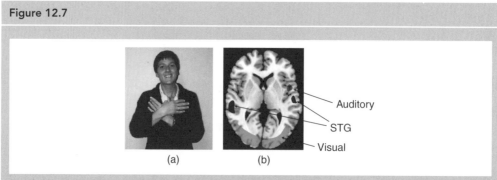

Sign language with the auditory cortex. (a) Example for sign language: 'butterfly'. (b) Activation of the auditory association area (STG, dark grey regions) by sign language in a congenitally deaf individual, in the visual cortex (light grey) during meaningless signing, and in the primary auditory area (medium grey) by sound after restoration of basic hearing function by means of a cochlear implant.

Figure 12.8

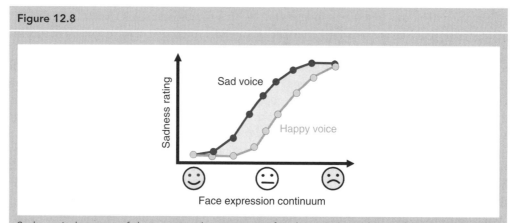

Sadness judgement of the emotional expression of sad, neutral and happy faces (indicated by symbols along the x-axis) accompanied by a sad voice (dark grey dots) or happy voice (light grey disks) demonstrate a shift of the psychometric curve, indicating that the same face is perceived as more sad when accompanied by a sad voice.

photographs of real faces, which span a range of happy, neutral and sad expressions, on an artificial scale of sadness. The results of this experiment are shown in Figure 12.8 as sadness ratings, which follow a 'psychometric curve' from low to high for happy to sad faces. When the visual display is combined with a sad or happy voice, the psychometric curve is shifted to higher or lower sadness ratings, respectively. The emotional content of the voice affects the categorisation of facial expression.

CROSS-SENSORY ASSIGNMENTS

The connectivity between the different sensory domains can lead to strong illusions in which the percept from one domain is assigned to another domain. Perhaps the best-known illusion of this kind is ventriloquism (Bertelson and Radeau 1981). In this case of perceptual fusion the sound originating from the ventriloquist is captured by the dummy, which is acting through the hands of the artist in a way that it is perceived as the sound source. For a convincing performance dynamic signals, that is, the movement of the dummy, are crucial (Soto-Faraco et al. 2002).

A wide range of other puzzling perceptual assignments of perceptual features across different dimensions within a sensory domain or across sensory domains can only be experienced by a limited number of people. In a condition known as 'synaesthesia', a person called a 'synaesthete' has reliable associations between unrelated phenomena such as coloured shapes or sounds, or particular colours that elicit the sensation of sound, or shapes that are connected to a particular taste, sounds that elicit sensations of odour, etc. (Ramachandran and Hubbard 2003). This phenomenon is generally believed to be the result of an unusual mixing of senses that does not reflect physical reality, whereby cross-modal connections between normally separate brain areas have been established that lead to cross-activation going beyond the normal perceptual binding of different object features (such as the peculiar smell of a particular flower). A comparatively common form of synaesthesia is known as the grapheme–colour relationship whereby black letters or numbers are perceived to have a specific colour (Simner et al. 2006). An illustration of a condition in this category is shown in Colour plate VIII, Figure 1, where three simple shapes are associated by the synaesthete with three basic colours. Interestingly, this particular colouration scheme was investigated experimentally, in a simple questionnaire study, by the Bauhaus artist Kandinsky, who believed it to be a natural preference for colour–shape associations that is shared by the majority of the population. There is evidence that Kandinsky himself was a sound–colour synaesthete, who could see colours in music and hear sounds arising from colours and forms, and his painted 'compositions' clearly are very evocative of musical experiences (Ione and Tyler 2003). It has been speculated whether sound–colour synaesthesia is an experience that is accessible to 'all of us' (Ward et al. 2006). Certainly, we are only at the beginning of understanding the experience of synaesthesia and its neurological basis, but what we know so far seems to suggest that there is a continuum of perceptual association that should warn us to be very careful when using the label 'normal'.

As final example of cross-modal assignment, we should consider sensory substitution. Research in recent decades has seen various attempts to replace a missing or lost sense with some other sense. The biggest efforts have been made to develop artificial visual systems for blind people by translating video images into a tactile matrix that is attached to the tongue, for instance (Bach-y-Rita et al. 1998), or into sounds (Auvray et al. 2007). In order to be able to 'see with the tongue' or 'see with the ears' by making use of such devices, the individual needs to go through an extensive training programme. The necessary redirection of somatosensory or auditory information into cortical areas, which can build spatial representations corresponding to the images translated into tactile or auditory signals, requires the same potential for cortical plasticity, which has been mentioned in the previous section in the context of mapping sign language, and which might be the basis of some synaesthetic experiences. This ability to make new cortical connections is undoubtedly also the basis for the most interesting case study of echolocation in humans (Stoffregen and Pittenger 1995), which reports the amazing case of the Californian teenager Ben Underwood who learnt after the loss of sight to use the echoes of sharp clicks for safe navigation through his environment and for basic object recognition, without the help of any technical devices!

Take Home Messages

- to make optimal use of the sensory system, it needs to be integrated with behavioural strategies of active sensing, which requires sensory–motor coordination
- although we usually regard the different sensory modalities as separate, there is a range of cross-modal integration that optimise the use of the sensory system for organising behaviour
- combining sensory information requires multi-sensory neurons and multi-sensory areas in the cortex, in which the different sensory information is joined together
- visuo-haptic sensory integration improves recognition performance, in particular in conditions of low signal-to-noise ratios
- audio-visual integration sensory integration plays a major role in speech perception, including lip reading, and has interesting implications for the processing of sign language
- different types of sensory information can be associated with each other, leading to synaesthesia, and being the basis for sensory substitution that makes use of cortical plasticity

Discussion Questions

- What do engineers mean by a 'feedback loop', and why is this concept so important for the understanding of biological sensory–motor systems?
- Describe the main types of eye movements.
- Discuss the most prominent case of interaction between visual and auditory information processing.
- How can we interpret the phenomenon of synaesthesia in terms of brain architecture?

MAKING SENSE: THEORETICAL APPROACHES TO PERCEPTION

OVERVIEW

Each organism has a highly specific sensory make-up, reflecting a sophisticated adaptation to a particular ecological niche – the performance and the limitations of the human sensory system clearly reflect the environment and lifestyle of early hominids. Looking at the 'task space' is one way of understanding and comparing how human and non-human sensory systems are adapted to behaviour and environment, leading to some extraordinary pieces of sensory equipment. An overarching framework, which is based on concepts of ecology and evolution, links perception on the one hand to the computational analysis of the underlying information processing and on the other to the physiological study of the neuronal implementation of such mechanisms. This dominating contemporary view, the 'information processing approach', to studying perception has developed from a number of theoretical positions that have been discussed by scholars for more than a century as larger frameworks that can join together a range of perceptual phenomena. Three major historical concepts of perception will be introduced here: Gestalt Theory (the mind follows certain laws to extract perceptual configurations), Constructivist Approaches (the mind constructs the most likely external world from limited and unreliable data), and the idea of Direct Perception (the sensory input is used to directly to control behaviour). The merit of these ideas about how perception is organised, and their heritage in contemporary thinking about perception, is considered by assessing the behavioural, neuroscientific and computational aspects of our current knowledge about sensory systems to the question of how evolution optimises particular designs to solve particular tasks in particular environments.

THE PROBLEM OF PERCEPTION

As discussed in Chapter 1 in some detail, the purpose of sensory and perceptual systems is to convert the physical, external world into an internal, mental world, so that it can be used for interpretation of the surroundings and control of action. Not surprisingly, any mapping from one to another domain implies transformation, and possibly distortion, of the information, loss of signal components and addition of noise (see Chapter 2). Perception can suffer from systematic distortion, for instance, to the colour space in individuals with colour vision deficiencies (Backhaus et al. 1998), or to the full range of sensory experience in autism (Bogdashina 2003). It also can be shifted dramatically in response to extended exposure to unorthodox environmental conditions, such as weightlessness in space, or just by wearing glasses (Kohler 1962). Even in the most simple case of taking a photograph, much too often you discover a loss of spatial detail, distortions of colours and the introduction of random image elements or motion blur, as you know from many disappointing photographic prints. All of these problems, and many more, are relevant when we look with our eyes at the external world – and yet the world always looks 'better', that is, more natural or more realistic, when we look at it with our eyes than looking at (unedited) photographs. One possible answer to this puzzle could be that the perceptual image of the world is more than a simple snapshot, never being just a pixel-by-pixel representation, but an image that is smartly encoded and sophistically interpreted (see Chapters 3 to 5). Figure 13.1 illustrates how the perceptual improvement, which distinguishes a mental image from a plain copy of the image of the scene we look at, starts right at the beginning in the visual processing stream. The image projected on the retinae covers a very wide visual field (about 180 degree horizontally and 120 degree vertically), comparable to that of a fisheye lens for a camera. Projected on a flat plane, like this printing page, the image would appear highly distorted (see Figure 13.1a). Nevertheless, the world usually does not look distorted to us, which means that we have to assume that the perceived image is reconstructed from the initial sensory information. Not a big deal for the visual system, because this is exactly its job, and it does it all the time, starting with images that are upside down (see Figure 1.2)! The ability of the visual system to reconstruct flat-plane projections of the outside world from distorted images may be the reason why we can interpret the geometry of architectural environments from drawings even when they are not seen from the correct viewing angle (Hagen 1980).

Attentive readers of this book will have noticed that there is a little fudge in this argument about image distortions in the retina, because there obviously is no flat image plane onto which the neural image is projected, and the mapping of retinal images (projected on a spherical plane) onto the folded cortex (retinotopic maps) introduces much more complex distortions than the projection geometry in the eye, such as those resulting from cortical magnification or anatomical deformations of the cortical surface (Hoffmann et al. 2009). These observations, however, only underline the need for advanced image processing that includes the reconstruction of spatial relationships, in order to allow 'the mind' to interpret the sensory information in such a way that it is an accurate representation of the external world.

Figure 13.1

(a)   (b)

The mental representation of the physical world. (a) An impression of the image of an old college building as projected on the retinae of the visual system – due to the large field of view (visual field) there are substantial geometric distortions, and straight lines in the world can bend considerably in the image. (b) An impression of what we perceive when looking at the very same scene – geometric distortions are corrected and proportions look approximately rectangular.

How the conscious mind does access all this information for interpretation is the matter of a lively philosophical debate that goes far beyond this book. Sometimes the metaphor of a 'Cartesian Theatre' is used to describe the display of all sensory information to the individual's mind – the outcome of sensation and perception (Dennett 1992). And finally we have to ask ourselves, what actually is an 'accurate' representation of the many facets of the world surrounding us? Irrespective of the unresolved philosophical issues around such misrepresentations and corrections of physical properties of the world, after the previous chapters the reader can appreciate that we are exposed to substantial perceptual errors in a wide range of contexts. Most strikingly, illusions have been depicted time and again throughout this book as illustrations of how misperceptions of the physical reality can be used as a key to reality, because they help us understand fundamental processing mechanisms, such as adaptation, opponency and redundancy reduction. (see Chapters 2–4, and 6). The big question will be how far this approach to interpreting illusions in the context of simple information processing mechanisms can take us in the understanding of a large variety of illusions, or whether there are alternative approaches to conceptualise perception.

Scientists try to find similarities and regularities – they want to identify order in the world. Arranging numbers in a linear sequence, or recording the size of leaves or ears, is straightforward enough. But describing the similarity and differences in the designs of leaves or hearing organs turned out to be a much more complicated feat, and usually leads to constructs of relationships resembling trees. Bringing order in seriously complex phenomena such as brain function, or the plethora of perceptual illusions (Coren and Girgus 1978), poses a real challenge to scientific intuition and to evidence-based reasoning. Often we end up with network structures describing such relationships (van Essen et al. 1992). When you look at a range of brightness illusions, such as shown in Figure 3.6, or at a variety of geometric illusions such as shown in Figure 13.2, there are similarities, like the judgement of one feature relative to another, suggesting commonalities in possible explanations such as encoding of features in

Figure 13.2

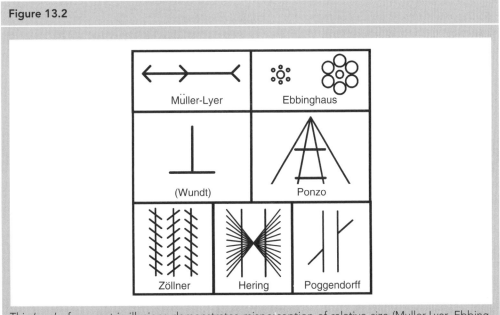

This 'zoo' of geometric illusions demonstrates misperception of relative size (Muller-Lyer, Ebbinghaus, Wundt, Ponzo), relative orientation (Zöllner, Hering) or location (Poggendorf).

relationship to their neighbourhood – but there could be rather different ways of interpreting such illusions, and indeed there are rather different ways to think about perception than the functional approach pursued in this book, which looks from the perspective of an engineer at the highly effective designs that did evolve for the neural processing of sensory information. So let us review in the next sections some of the classical approaches to understanding perception in the context of a larger conceptual framework.

GESTALT PSYCHOLOGY

Gestalt theory has its focus on the principles of perceptual organisation, which are derived from a systematic attempt to define the crucial aspects of object recognition. The German word 'Gestalt' used by Wertheimer (Wertheimer 1923) could be best translated as 'shape', 'form' or 'figure'. The central tenet of this theory concerns the way figures emerge perceptually from their components, summarised in the famous phrase 'the whole is more than the sum of the parts', illustrated in Figure 13.3. In opposition to the dominating scientific view of the early twentieth century that complex phenomena need to broken down into small components, Gestalt psychologists investigated a wide range of perceptual phenomena (Koffka 1935; Köhler 1947) to demonstrate that perception is more than passive acquisition of sensory information, but an active process to create meaningful percepts. This work led to a small number of 'laws' of perceptual organisation, which will be briefly summarised in the following. A new twist to the interpretation of the Kanizsa figure as a case in point of Gestalt Psychology arises from experiments (Van Hateren et al. 1990) demonstrating that honeybees – which as insects are usually regarded as comparatively simple animals that do not employ higher-level cognitive processes – do 'perceive' the same illusion.

- *Praegnanz*, or 'good Gestalt': of several geometrical possible organisations, the most simple and stable will be perceived (Figure 13.4a).
- *Good continuation*: the tendency to perceive smooth contours ('inertia') leads to simpler interpretations of given configurations (Figure 13.4b).
- *Closure*: the interpretation of incomplete lines is dominated by the tendency to complete shapes (Figure 13.4c).

Figure 13.3

The 'Kanizsa triangle' in this version is made up of six components, three small black lines and three black disks from which a 60 degree sector has been cut out ('pacmen'). What you see, however, is more than these parts, namely a white triangle, on top of lines converging to the centre and three full disks (Kanizsa 1979).

Figure 13.4

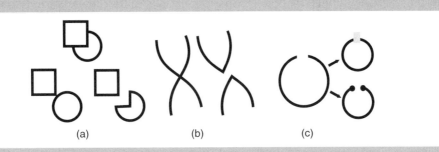

(a)   (b)   (c)

Gestalt laws of perceptual organisation – shapes. (a) Praegnanz: The drawing at the top is interpreted as a square on top of a circle (bottom left), not as a square and a pacman (bottom right). (b) Good continuation: The left drawing is interpreted as two curved lines intersecting, rather than two pointed shapes (right) touching each other at their tips. (c) Closure: The drawing on the left is not interpreted as an unfinished circle (right bottom), but as a full black circle superimposed by an object (right top).

Figure 13.5

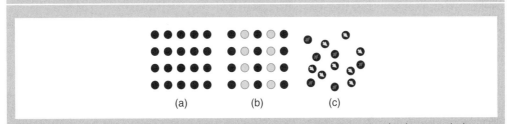

(a)   (b)   (c)

Gestalt laws of perceptual organisation – groups. (a) Proximity: Because the horizontal distance between the dots is smaller than the vertical distance, you perceive four horizontal rows of dots. (b) Similarity: When the same set of dots is characterised by different shades of grey, you perceive five vertical columns of dots, alternating in dark and light grey. (c) Common fate: A randomly distributed set of dots can be easily separated into two groups, if they are moving in two different directions (indicated by arrows in different shades of grey).

- *Similarity*: the tendency to perceive elements that are similar (e.g. in terms of form, colour, depth) as a group (Figure 13.5a).
- *Proximity*: the tendency to group elements together that are close to each other (see Figure 13.5b); this is also crucial for the perception of ambiguous apparent motion stimuli (see Chapter 6).
- *Common fate*: elements that share a history of temporal change or movement (see Chapter 6) are perceived as a group.

Although these 'laws' of perceptual organisation are certainly a good approach to describe phenomena surrounding the recognition and grouping of objects, one might ask two questions. (i) Do these 'laws' have the same status as other laws in science that describe fundamental properties of our world, such as Newton's laws of motion? (ii) While these 'laws' do provide some good descriptions of perceptual phenomena, do they offer an explanation in terms of a possible mechanism?

CONSTRUCTIVIST APPROACH

Starting from the seminal work of von Helmholtz (1924) and his notion of 'unconscious inferences' there is another theory emphasising top-down processes in perception, which however goes beyond purely descriptive rules proposed by Gestalt psychologists in suggesting an abstract mechanism for such processes. Helmholtz's principle states that the visual system reconstructs the most probable object from the sensory data, which can account for visual illusions: 'Objects are always perceived as being present in the field of vision as would have been there in order to produce the same impression on the nervous system, the eyes being used under ordinary normal conditions' (Gregory 2007). The constructivist approach to perception claims that the perceptual system tries to make the best sense of sensory input when incomplete or ambiguous data are provided, by applying previous knowledge about the external world (Gregory 1997). The interaction between higher-level aspects of the human mind and perceptual processes becomes apparent in the relation between perception and emotion: emotional memories can affect perceptions (like musical tunes being connected to important events in your life, or the association of beauty with pictures), and perceptions can obviously affect emotions (just think of a disgusting photograph or a repulsive screeching noise). In a similar sense there is a lot of abstract knowledge connected to all kinds of sensory information, like the perspective geometry of space, the black and yellow stripes you associate with wasps, or the tunes of your mobile phone indicating an incoming call or an alarm. The iterative comparison of the sensory input with internally stored knowledge, be it abstract meaning or emotional association, develops and refines hypotheses about the external stimulus configurations that can support recognition in noisy stimuli, such as the photograph shown in Figure 13.6. And the other way round, we can find that expectations based on previous

Figure 13.6

The Dalmatian (R. C. James, as shown in Marr 1982). If you have not seen this photograph before, it is very difficult to make sense of it. Once you have been made aware that it shows a Dalmatian dog sniffing the ground in the central area of the picture, you will be able to outline the shape of the dog and you will never have any difficulties to recognise it when you see the photograph in the future.

experience can generate specific errors, or 'cognitive' illusions (Gregory 1998): many of the depth and size illusions discussed in Chapter 5, most prominently the Ames room, are usually explained by assuming that knowledge about perspective cues drives misperceptions in unorthodox stimulus conditions. It should be noted that Gregory is fully aware that this is only an explanation for some of the illusions, pointing out 'that *physiological* illusions tell us about the *brain*, and *cognitive* illusions tell us about the *mind*' (Gregory 1998: 248). Most importantly, this is an active, top-down process that constructs percepts from sensory data that do not offer an immediate and unique solution (Neisser 1968).

Obviously it would be important to strengthen the validity of this approach by identifying a physiological basis of such top-down processes, but given the nature of its crucial components, such as previous knowledge and iterative approximation, this could be a tall order. On the other hand, recent progress in the field saw a mathematical framework emerge, in the form of Bayesian estimation techniques (Westheimer 2008) that describe how solutions to ambiguous sensory data analysis problems can be derived by use of assumptions about how likely it is that certain stimulus configurations would be arising from external events, so-called priors. This statistical method gave a new thrust to constructivist approaches, by providing quantitative predictions that can be tested (e.g. Hürlimann et al. 2002), and indeed can be related to properties of sensory neurons (e.g. Lee 1995).

DIRECT PERCEPTION: AN ECOLOGICAL APPROACH

Another conceptual framework for perception, seemingly from the other end of the spectrum, is the concept of 'direct perception' that was spearheaded by Gibson (1950). The basic idea is in direct opposition to constructivist theories by emphasising bottom-up processing, claiming that for many perceptual judgements, and in particular for the control of action, it is not necessary at all to 'synthesise' meaningful objects from sensory signals encoded at early stages of the sensory system, but the overall pattern of such signals can be used directly to extract the essentials of an environment. In the visual system, this holds in particular for the perception of three-dimensional space, which does not need to be reconstructed by 'inferences' or 'reasoning' such as suggested by constructivist theory, but can be established through a direct and comprehensive correspondence between the overall pattern of stimulation, called 'optic array', and the situation of the observer (Gibson 1979). The visual system exploits the richness of the environmental information encoded in sensory arrays, like perspective cues arising from local orientation, gradients of size and texture, and patterns of local motion. Patterns of local motion, called 'flowfields' (see Figure 13.7), are arguably the most impressive way to illustrate this point – they provide comprehensive, unambiguous and immediate information about the spatial layout of the environment (due to motion parallax, see Chapter 7) and the movement of the observer in this environment, which can be used for navigation. Equally, for individual objects it is believed that low-level features provide a direct indication of the meaning of such objects in a behavioural context, their so-called 'affordances'. More generally, this concept brings us back to the question of what the 'accurate' representation of the world is. For the 'direct perceiver' this is not a really relevant question, as for them it does not matter whether the retinal or mental image of the apple tree is heavily distorted, or whether the colour of the red apple is composed from an ambiguous set of wavelengths – the only thing that matters is to reach the apple tree without incident, to find the sweetest apple, and to be able to grasp it and have a bite. 'Accurate' in this context means nothing more, or less, than being accessible to successful action!

There is now a large body of behavioural (Lappe et al. 1999) and electrophysiological (Wall and Smith 2008) evidence in support of such an ecological approach suggesting that patterns

Figure 13.7

A sketch of the flowfield experienced by a pilot approaching a runway (after Gibson 1979). The characteristic pattern of motion signals (indicated by grey arrows) from the complete visual field gives a direct indication of the three-dimensional layout of the environment (close runway, distant mountains) and the movement of the pilot (towards the horizon, i.e. overshooting the runway if the pilot does not correct their flight path).

of local signals such as flowfields are directly used in navigation tasks used not only by humans but also by a wide range of animals (Huston and Krapp 2008). Although direct perception and constructivist theory are often seen as in competition, it has already been pointed out by Gregory that they are complementary strategies to account for different aspects of perception (Gregory 1998). This combined view was further developed into a dual-process approach to visual perception, where the dorsal visual stream carries direct ecological processes, which the observer is incorporating into guiding unconscious behavioural reactions, and the ventral visual stream is the substrate for constructivist processes, which reach conscious perception (Norman 2002). Other authors discuss a similar dichotomy of visual representations in the ventral and dorsal stream for the planning of action making use of cognitive information and the online control of action using low-level visual signals (Glover 2004). The complexity of processing in these schemes corresponds to the speed with which the information needs to be extracted for driving the task.

SENSORY ECOLOGY

The ecological theme introduced by direct perception leads to another concept that helps us to understand the design and function of sensory systems. The following brief survey of nonhuman senses demonstrates how many animals were adapted by evolution to live in environments in which humans need technical devices in order to survive. The sensory make-up of an animal corresponds to its particular ecological niche, and sensory systems co-evolve with behaviour, to allow the occupation of specific environments. The limitations of human sensory systems can best be demonstrated by looking at the 'sensory ecology' of ultraviolet and infrared vision, and sensitivity to polarised light, electricity or magnetic fields (Endler 1992).

Exposure to UV light, with wavelengths below 400 nm, can have immediate and long-term damaging effects on human eyes. Photokeratitis resembles a painful sunburn on the front surface of the eyes (for instance, in snow blindness), but many animals use UV vision by using screening mechanisms in the retina to protect against damage. In consequence, many birds and fish see the world in a very different way from humans, as illustrated for the example of Damsel fish shown in normal colour and in UV spectrum in Colour plate VIII, Figure 2. The ability to detect UV light affects the behaviour of these animals, for instance in terms of recognising facial patterns that are invisible to humans, which is used in inter- and intra-specific communication, in particular territorial (Siebeck 2004) and mating systems (Bennett et al. 1996). In this context, various theories based on co-evolution have been developed about the function of animal and plant coloration, including mimicry, fruit colours etc. The ability to detect UV signals is also found in many insects, which is important for them in the context of food selection and orientation towards particular targets, like other insects.

Other animals, particularly invertebrates, have evolved sensitivity to the plane of polarised light, the preferred orientation of electromagnetic waves relative to the direction of a light beam, which provides them with an extra dimension of visual information. The functional significance of polarised light is poorly understood, but it is generally believed to play an important role in navigation as some kind of polarisation compass (Dacke et al. 1999). Dung beetles, for instance, live on firm sand surfaces in burrows, and have the ability to return to their burrows along the shortest possible route from extended foraging trips, which usually follow highly irregular paths. In this environment visual landmarks are very scarce, and the beetles need to rely on cues in the sky to find their way back. Using their polarisation-sensitive photoreceptors in the regions of their eyes which are directed upward, they can make use of polarisation patterns that indicate the position of the sun or moon, even if the sun is invisible in haze or behind clouds (Dacke et al. 2003). Highly specialised polarisation sensitivity also appears to play an important role in recognising coloration patterns among other animals (Land 2008). Humans are completely blind to this property of light, but the advanced lens technology used in polarising sun glasses helps them to eliminate surface glare and reduce unwanted reflections, which can be very helpful in activities like fishing.

Rattlesnakes and other pit vipers have evolved the ability of visualising heat, which is usually referred to as 'infrared vision', with wavelengths above 700 nm. The heat-sensing 'loreal' pits behind each nostril (Colour plate VIII, Figure 3a) are highly effective organs detecting differences in temperature at large distances. This ability is crucial for hunting warm-blooded animals in the dark, and equally as protection against large predators. The infrared images from the loreal pits are integrated with visual images in the brain (Newman and Hartline 1982). Humans, once again, need to use tools for infrared vision, such as thermal imaging cameras, which are often used to trace leaks in heat insulation, or electrical and mechanical malfunctions that are accompanied by heat loss (see Colour plate VIII, Figure 3b for a thermal image of a dog). As in the case of infrared vision in snakes, this technology is used in particular by humans for night vision equipment.

There are many other sensory domains that animals have occupied, which are closed to humans. Fish, turtles, insects and birds are known to sense magnetic fields, which can be used as a compass for long-distance navigation (Etheredge et al. 1999). They exploit the magnetic field of the earth like sailors using a magnetic compass needle. Little is known about the location and function of magnetic sensors and the strategies to exploit such signals. A number of fish living in muddy waters (Nelson and MacIver 1999), and also the Australian platypus, can generate electric fields and/or detect electric fields, which are used for active or passive orientation ('electrolocation') and communication. Finally, the human range of hearing (see Chapter 7) is extended substantially in the animal kingdom. Elephants and whales use infrasound for communication (Payne et al. 1986), and bats use ultrasound for orientation and foraging (Neuweiler 1984), similar to echolocation in submarines or ultrasound imaging systems used in medical imaging.

THE INFORMATION PROCESSING APPROACH

After the survey of some classical conceptual frameworks of perception in the previous paragraphs, and a brief note on the ecological context of sensory systems, we are now prepared to revisit the functional perspective chosen in this book as a basis to understand perception. Does such a combination of ecological, neuroscientific and computational approaches provide the unifying vision to join together all the phenomena, all the different aspects of perception that have been covered in the 12 previous chapters? The notion of information processing indeed offers a powerful framework to comprehend the sensory and perceptual aspects of the human nervous system. Equally, information processing connects on one side to the ecology of the environment, providing 'sensory data' with a well-defined statistics, and on the other side with the behavioural repertoire of the organism living in such an environment, implementations of control mechanisms, and cognitive processes in terms of management of abstract knowledge and decision-making. All these different aspects of perception converge in the idea that such information processing can be expressed in computational models, and can be experimentally investigated by studying perceptual performance in close connection to the neural substrate that is responsible for carrying out the necessary computations. This approach has been extraordinarily successful in recent decades, leading to impressive progress in understanding how the human brain, and the human mind, works. Across the different specific designs of sensory systems, that is, different sensory modalities, there are a variety of common and central concepts, which demonstrate the explanatory power and the 'transferable' nature of the functional approach. These include:

- receptor: responsible for the transformation from environmental to neural signals
- filter: the basic element for encoding information, and for tuning to specific properties
- receptive field: the physiological basis for localisation and spatial tuning
- serial and parallel processing: different schemes to organise and traffic data
- representation: projecting features from sensors onto cortical activity (mapping)
- illusion: the results of processing mechanisms that misrepresent physical conditions
- active sensing: sensory systems link with exploratory behaviour to catch more signals.

The previous 12 chapters, on the other hand, equally should have demonstrated that our understanding of perception remains rather rudimentary, and that there are evolutionary designs and adaptations of perceptual systems that still need a huge amount of observation, measurement and thought to become accessible to the human mind.

References

Adams, A. J., Wong, L. S., Wong, L., and Gould, B. (1988). 'Visual Acuity Changes with Age: Some New Perspectives' *American Journal of Optometry and Physiological Optics*, 65 403–406.

Adelson, E. H. (2000). 'Lightness Perception and Lightness Illusions', in M. S. Gazzaniga (Ed.) *The New Cognitive Neurosciences* (Boston: Boston) pp. 339–351.

Adelson, E. H. (2001). 'On seeing stuff: The perception of materials by humans and machines', in B. E. Rogowitz and T. N. Pappas (Eds) *Proceedings of the SPIE Vol. 4299, Human Vision and Electronic Imaging VI*, pp. 1–12.

Adelson, E. H. and Bergen, J. R. (1985). 'Spatiotemporal energy models for the perception of motion' *Journal of the Optical Society of America*, A 2 284–299.

Adelson, E. H. and Movshon, J. A. (1982). 'Phenomenal coherence of moving visual patterns' *Nature*, 300 523–525.

Adrian, E. D. and Umrath, K. (1929). 'The impulse discharge from the pacinian corpuscle' *J. Physiol*, 68 139–154.

Albers, J. (1975). *Interaction of Color* (New Haven, CT: Yale University Press).

Amoore, J. E. (1964). 'Current status of the steric theory of odor' *Annals of the New York Academy of Sciences*, 116 457–476.

Anderson, B. L. (1997). 'A theory of illusory lightness and transparency in monocular and binocular images: The role of contour junctions' *Perception*, 26 419–453.

Angelaki, D. E. (2004). 'Eyes on Target: What Neurons Must do for the Vestibuloocular Reflex During Linear Motion' *J Neurophysiol*, 92 20–35.

Anstis, S. M. (1970). 'Phi Movement as a Subtraction Process' *Vision Research*, 10 1411–1430.

Anstis, S. M. (1980). 'The perception of apparent movement' *Philosophical Transactions of the Royal Society*, B 290 153–168.

Anstis, S., Rogers, B. and Henry, J. (1978). 'Interactions between simultaneous contrast and coloured afterimages' *Vision Research*, 18 899–911.

Arons, B. (1992). 'A review of the cocktail party effect' *Journal of the American Voice I/O Society*, 12 35–50.

Aubin, T. (1998). 'Cocktail-party effect in king penguin colonies' *Proceedings of the Royal Society B: Biological Sciences*, 265 1665–1673.

Auvray, M., Hanneton, S., and O'Regan, J. K. (2007). 'Learning to perceive with a visuo-auditory substitution system: Localisation and object recognition withThe vOICe' *Perception*, 36 416.

Axel, R. (2005). 'Scents and Sensibility: A Molecular Logic of Olfactory Perception (Nobel Lecture)' *Angewandte Chemie International Edition*, 44 6111.

Bach-y-Rita, P., Kaczmarek, K. A., Tyler, M. E., and Garcia-Lara, J. (1998). 'Form perception with a 49-point electrotactile stimulus array on the tongue: A technical note' *Development*, 35 427–430.

Backhaus, W., Kliegl, R., and Werner, J. S. (1998). *Color Vision: Perspectives from Different Disciplines* (Walter de Gruyter).

Barlow, H. B. and Mollon, J. D. (1982). *The Senses* (Cambridge, London, New York: Cambridge University Press).

Barnes, D. C., Hofacer, R. D., Zaman, A. R., Rennaker, R. L., and Wilson, D. A. (2008). 'Olfactory perceptual stability and discrimination' *Nature Neuroscience,* 11 (12) 1378–1380.

Bartoshuk, L. M., Duffy, V. B., and Miller, I. J. (1994). 'PTC/PROP tasting: Anatomy, psychophysics, and sex effects' *Physiology & Behavior,* 56 1165–1171.

Behrens, R. R. (1987). 'The Life and Unusual Ideas of Adelbert Ames Jr.' *Leonardo,* 20 273–279.

Bellamy, J. C. (2000). *Digital Telephony* (New York: John Wiley & Sons Inc.).

Bennett, A. T. D., Cuthill, I. C., Partridge, J. C., and Maier, E. J. (1996). 'Ultraviolet vision and mate choice in zebra finches' *Nature,* 380 433–435.

Bensmaia, S. and Hollins, M. (2005). 'Pacinian representations of fine surface texture' *Perception & Psychophysics,* 67 842–854.

Berlin, B. and Kay, P. (1999). *Basic Color Terms: Their Universality and Evolution* (Stanford: CSLI Publications).

Berrien, F. K. (1946). 'The effects of noise' *Psychological Bulletin,* 43 141–161.

Bertamini, M., Yang, T. L., and Proffitt, D. R. (1998). 'Relative size perception at a distance is best at eye level' *Perception and Psychophysics,* 60 673–682.

Bertelson, P. and Radeau, M. (1981). 'Cross-modal bias and perceptual fusion with auditory-visual spatial discordance' *Perception & Psychophysics,* 29 578.

Bhattacharya, J. and Petsche, H. (2001). 'Universality in the brain while listening to music' *Proceedings of the Royal Society B: Biological Sciences,* 268 2423–2433.

Birznieks, I., Jenmalm, P., Goodwin, A. W., and Johansson, R. S. (2001). 'Encoding of Direction of Fingertip Forces by Human Tactile Afferents' *J. Neurosci.,* 21 8222–8237.

Bisiach, E. (1993). 'Mental representation in unilateral neglect and related disorders: The twentieth Bartlett Memorial Lecture' *The Quarterly Journal of Experimental Psychology Section A,* 46 435–461.

Bisiach, E. and Luzzatti, C. (1978). 'Unilateral neglect of representational space' *Cortex,* 14 129–133.

Bisiach, E., Luzzatti, C., and Perani, D. (1979). 'Unilateral neglect, representational schema and consciousness' *Brain,* 102 609–618.

Björkman, A., Weibull, A., Rosén, B., Svensson, J., and Lundborg, G. (2009) 'Rapid cortical reorganisation and improved sensitivity of the hand following cutaneous anaesthesia of the forearm' *European Journal of Neuroscience,* 29 837–844.

Blake, A. and Bülthoff, H. H. (1990). 'Does the brain know the physics of specular reflection?' *Nature,* 343 165–168.

Blakemore, C. (1977) *Mechanics of the Mind* (Cambridge: Cambridge University Press).

Blakemore, S-J., Wolpert, D. M., and Frith, C. D. (1998). 'Central cancellation of self-produced tickle sensation' *Nat Neurosci,* 1 635–640.

Blakeslee, B. and McCourt, M. E. (1997). 'Similar Mechanisms Underlie Simultaneous Brightness Contrast and Grating Induction' *Vision Research,* 37 2849–2869.

Bogdashina, O. (2003). *Sensory Perceptual Issues in Autism and Asperger Syndrome: Different Sensory Experiences, Different Perceptual Worlds* (London: Jessica Kingsley Publishers).

Boomsliter, P. and Creel, W. (1961). 'The Long Pattern Hypothesis in Harmony and Hearing' *Journal of Music Theory,* 5 2–31.

Borst, A. (2007). 'Correlation versus gradient type motion detectors: The pros and cons' *Philosophical Transactions of the Royal Society B: Biological Sciences*, 362 369–374.

Borst, A. and Egelhaaf, M. (1989). 'Principles of visual motion detection' *Trends in Neuroscience*, 12 297–306.

Boycott, B. B. and Wässle H. (1974). 'The morphological types of ganglion cells of the domestic cat's retina' *J. Physiol*, 240 397–419.

Boynton, R. M. and Olson, C. X. (1990). 'Salience of chromatic basic color terms confirmed by three measures' *Vision Research*, 30 1311–1317.

Bracewell, R. N. (1986). *The Fourier Transform and its Applications* (Singapore: McGraw Hill).

Bradbury, J. W. and Vehrencamp, S. L. (1998). *Principles of Animal Communication* (Sunderland, MA: Sinauer Associates).

Bradley, D. C., Chang, G. C., and Andersen, R. A. (1998). 'Encoding of three-dimensional structure-from-motion by primate area MT neurons' *Nature*, 392 714–716.

Braitenberg, V. (1984). *Vehicles: Experiments in Synthetic Psychology* (Cambridge, MA: MIT Press).

Breslin, P. A. S. and Spector, A. C. (2008). 'Mammalian taste perception' *Current Biology*, 18 R148–R155.

Broadbent, A. D. (2004). 'A critical review of the development of the CIE1931 RGB color-matching functions' *Color Research & Application*, 29.

Broadbent, D. E. (1958). *Perception and Communication* (London: Pergamon Press).

Brooks, R. A. (2003). *Robot: The Future of Flesh and Machines* (London: Penguin Books Ltd).

Brouwer, A-M., Franz, V. H., and Gegenfurtner, K. R. (2009). 'Differences in fixations between grasping and viewing objects' *Journal of Vision*, 9 1–24.

Buck, L. and Axel, R. (1991). 'A novel multigene family may encode odorant receptors: A molecular basis for odor recognition' *Cell*, 65 175–187.

Buck, L. B. (2005). 'Unraveling the Sense of Smell (Nobel Lecture)' *Angewandte Chemie International Edition*, 44 6128–6140.

Bülthoff, H. H. and Mallot, H. A. (1990). 'Integration of Stereo, Shading and Texture', in A. Blake and T. Troscianko (Eds) *AI and the Eye* pp. 119–146.

Burr, D. (2000). 'Motion vision: Are "speed lines" used in human visual motion?' *Current Biology*, 10 R440–R443.

Burr, D. C., Morrone, M. C., and Ross, J. (1994). 'Selective suppression of the magnocellular visual pathway during saccadic eye movements' *Nature* 371 511–513.

Butler, R. and Belendiuk, K. (1977). 'Spectral cues utilized in the localization of sound in the median sagittal plane' *The Journal of the Acoustical Society of America*, 61 1264–1269.

Cain, W. S. (1982). 'Odor identification by males and females: Predictions vs performance' *Chem. Senses*, 7 129–142.

Campbell, F. W. and Kulikowski, J. J. (1966). 'Orientational selectivity of the human visual system' *J. Physiol*, 187 437–445.

Campbell, F. W. and Maffei, L. (1974). 'Contrast and Spatial Frequency' *Sci. Am.*, 231 106–114.

Campbell, F. W. and Robson, J. R. (1968). 'Application of fourier analysis to the visibility of gratings' *J. Physiol.*, 197 551–566.

Carrasco, M., Ling, S., and Read, S. (2004). 'Attention alters appearance' *Nature Neuroscience*, 7 308–313.

Cartwright-Finch, U. and Lavie, N. (2007). 'The role of perceptual load in inattentional blindness' *Cognition*, 102 321–340.

Castet, E. and Zanker, J. M. (1999). 'Long-range interactions in the spatial integration of motion signals' *Spatial Vision*, 12 287–307.

Castiello, U. and Umilta, C. 1992 'Splitting focal attention' *J. exp. Psychol. [Human Perception&Perf.]*, 18 837–848.

Caterina, M. J., Schumacher, M. A., Tominaga, M., Rosen, T. A., Levine, J. D., and Julius, D. (1997). 'The capsaicin receptor: A heat-activated ion channel in the pain pathway' *Nature*, 389 816–824.

Chatterjee, S. and Callaway, E. M. (2003). 'Parallel colour-opponent pathways to primary visual cortex' *Nature*, 426 668–671.

Chen, M. J. and Cook, M. (1984). 'Representational drawings of solid objects by young children' *Perception*, 13 377–385.

Cherry, E. C. (1953). 'Some experiments on the recognition of speech, with one and with two ears' *Journal of the Acoustical Society of America*, 25 975–979.

Coghill, R. C., Sang, C. N., Maisog, J. M., and Iadarola, M. J. (1999). 'Pain intensity processing within the human brain: A bilateral, distributed mechanism' *Journal of neurophysiology*, 82 1934–1943.

Colby, C. L., Duhamel, J-R., and Goldberg, M. E. (1995). 'Oculocentric Spatial Representation in Parietal Cortex' *Cereb. Cortex*, 5 470–481.

Collett, T. S. (1978). 'Peering – A locust behaviour pattern for obtaining motion parallax information' *J. exp. Biol.*, 76 237–241.

Collewijn, H. and Kowler, E. (2008). 'The significance of microsaccades for vision and oculomotor control' *Journal of Vision*, 8 1–21.

Collewijn, H. and Tamminga, E. P. (1984). 'Human smooth and saccadic eye movements during voluntary pursuit of different target motions on different backgrounds' *J. Physiol.*, 351 217–250.

Collings, V. B. (1974). 'Human taste response as a function of locus of stimulation on the tongue and soft palate' *Perception & Psychophysics*, 16 169–174.

Coren, S. and Girgus, J. S. (1978). *Seeing is Deceiving: The Psychology of Visual Illusions* (Hillsdale: L. Erlbaum Ass.).

Cornsweet, T. N. (1970). *Visual Perception* (Orlando: Academic Press).

Corwin, J. T. and Oberholtzer, J. C. (1997). 'Fish n' Chicks: Model Recipes for Hair-Cell Regeneration?' *Neuron*, 19 951–954.

Cox, T. J. (2008). 'Scraping sounds and disgusting noises' *Applied Acoustics*, 69 1195–2004.

Crick, F. (1995). *The Astonishing Hypothesis* (London: Touchstone).

Croy, H. (1918). *How Motion Pictures are Made* (New York: Harper & Bros.).

Cuddy, L. L. (1968). 'Practice Effects in the Absolute Judgment of Pitch' *The Journal of the Acoustical Society of America*, 43 1069–1076.

Czigler, I., Cox, T. J., Gyimesi, K., and Horváth, J. (2007). 'Event-related potential study to aversive auditory stimuli' *Neuroscience Letters*, 420 251–256.

Dacke, M., Nilsson, D-E., Scholtz, C. H., Byrne, M., and Warrant, E. J. (2003). 'Insect orientation to polarized moonlight' *Nature*, 424 33.

Dacke, M., Nilsson, D. E., Warrant, E. J., Blest, A. D., Land, M. F., and O'Carroll, D. C. (1999). 'Built-in polarizers form part of a compass organ in spiders' *Nature*, 401 470–473.

Dalton, P. (2000). 'Psychophysical and Behavioral Characteristics of Olfactory Adaptation' *Chem. Senses*, 25 487–492.

Darwin, C. J. (1997). 'Auditory grouping' *Trends in Cognitive Sciences*, 1 327–333.

Daugman, J. G. (1988). 'Complete Discrete 2-D Gabor Transforms by Neural Networks for Image Analysis and Compression' *IEEE Trans. Acoust. Speech, Signal Proc.* 36 1169–1179.

Davidoff, J. (2001). 'Language and perceptual categorisation' *Trends in Cognitive Sciences*, 5 382–387.

Davidoff, J., Davies, I., and Roberson, D. (1999). 'Colour categories in a stone-age tribe' *Nature*, 398 203–204.

De Gelder, B. and Bertelson, P. (2003). 'Multisensory integration, perception and ecological validity' *Trends in Cognitive Sciences*, 7 460–476.

DeAngelis, G. C., Ohzawa I. and Freeman R. D. (1995). 'Receptive-field dynamics in the central visual pathways' *Trends in Neuroscience*, 18 451–458.

Dennett, D. C. (1992). 'Time and the observer: The where and when of consciousness in the brain' *Behavioral and Brain Sciences*, 15 183–247.

Deregowski, J. B. (1972). 'Pictorial Perception and Culture' *Scientific American*, 227 82–88.

Descartes, R. (1644). *Principia Philosophiae* (Amsterdam: Elzevir).

Descartes, R. (1664). *Treatise on Man* (Cambridge: Cambridge University Press).

Desimone, R. and Duncan, J. (1995). 'Neural mechanisms of selective visual attention' *Annual Review of Neuroscience*, 18 193–222.

DeValois, R. L. and Jacobs, G. H. (1968). 'Primate color vision' *Science*, 162 533–540.

Die, G v. and Collewijn, H. (1982). 'Optokinetik Nystagmus in Man' *Human Neurobiol.*, 1 111–119.

Doddridge, D. (1753). 'Postscript of a Letter from the Rev. Dr. Doddridge at Northampton, to Mr. Henry Baker F. R. S. of One, Who Had No Ear to Music Naturally, Singing Several Tunes When in a Delirium' *Philosophical Transactions (1683–1775)*, 44 596.

Dorward, F. M. C. and Day, R. H. (1997). 'Loss of 3-D shape constancy in interior spaces: The basis of the Ames-room illusion' *Perception*, 26 707–718.

Doty, R. L. (1981). 'Olfactory communication in humans' *Chem. Senses*, 6 351–376.

Drayna, D., Manichaikul, A., Lange, M. D., Snieder, H., and Spector, T. (2001). 'Genetic Correlates of Musical Pitch Recognition in Humans' *Science*, 291 1969–1972.

Drewnowski, A. and Rock, C. L. (1995). 'The influence of genetic taste markers on food acceptance' *American Journal of Clinical Nutrition*, 62 506–511.

Driver, J. and Noesselt, T. (2008). 'Multisensory Interplay Reveals Crossmodal Influences on "Sensory-Specific" Brain Regions, Neural Responses, and Judgments' *Neuron*, 57 11–23.

Driver, J. and Spence, C. (1998). 'Cross-modal links in spatial attention' *Philosophical Transactions of the Royal Society B: Biological Sciences*, 353 1319–1331.

Driver, J. and Vuilleumier, P. (2001). 'Perceptual awareness and its loss in unilateral neglect and extinction' *Cognition*, 79 39–88.

Duck, M. J. (1988). 'Newton and Goethe on colour: Physical and physiological considerations' *Annals of Science*, 45 507–519.

Endler, J. A. (1992). 'Signals, Signal Conditions, and the Direction of Evolution' *The American Naturalist*, 139 S125–S153.

Ernst, M. O. and Banks, M. S. (2002). 'Humans integrate visual and haptic information in a statistically optimal fashion' *Nature*, 415 429–433.

Ernst, M. O. and Bülthoff, H. H. (2004). 'Merging the senses into a robust percept' *Trends in Cognitive Sciences*, 8 162–169.

Escher, M. C. (1971). *Graphik und Zeichnungen* (München: H. Moos Verlag).

Etheredge, J. A., Perez, S. M., Taylor, O. R., and Jander, R. (1999). 'Monarch butterflies (Danaus plexippus L.) use a magnetic compass for navigation' *Proceedings of the National Academy of Sciences*, 96 13845–13846.

Evans, E. F. (1982a). 'Functional anatomy of the auditory system', in H. B. Barlow and J. D. Mollon (Eds) *The Senses* (Cambridge, MA: Cambridge) pp. 255–306.

Evans, E. F. (1982b). 'Functions of the auditory systems', in H B Barlow and J D Mollon (Eds) *The Senses* (Cambridge, MA: Cambridge) pp. 307–331.

Everson, S. (1997). *Aristotle on Perception* (Oxford: Clarendon Press).

Exner, S. (1876). 'Über das Sehen von Bewegungen und die Theorie des zusammengesetzten Auges' *Sitzgsber. Akad. Wiss. (Wien)*, 72 156–191.

Eysenck, M. W. (2006). *Fundamentals of Cognition* (Hove: Psychology Press).

Fahle, M. (2002). *Perceptual Learning* (Cambridge, MA: MIT Press).

Fechner, G. T. (1860). *Elemente der Psychophysik 1* (Leipzig: Breitkopf & Haertel).

Feddersen, W. E., Sandel, T. T., Teas, D. C., and Jeffress, L. A. (1957). 'Localization of High-Frequency Tones' *The Journal of the Acoustical Society of America*, 29 988.

Felisberti, F. M. and Zanker, J. M. (2004). 'Does attention affect transparent motion perception?' *Perception*, 33 S 124.

Fiorentini, A., Baumgartner, G., Magnussen, S., Schiller, P. H. and Thomas J. P. (1990). 'The Perception of Brightness and Darkness: Relations to Neuronal Receptive Fields', in L. Spillmann and J. S. Werner (Eds) *The Neurophysiological Foundations of Visual Perception*.

Fisher, N. and Zanker, J. M. (2001). 'The Directional Tuning of the Barber Pole Illusion' *Perception*, 30 1321–1336.

Formisano, E., Kim, D-S., Di Salle, F., van de Moortele, P-F., Ugurbil, K., and Goebel, R. (2003). 'Mirror-Symmetric Tonotopic Maps in Human Primary Auditory Cortex' *Neuron*, 40 859–869.

Foulke, E. (1982). 'Reading braille', in W. Schiff and E. Foulke (Eds) *Tactual Perception: A Sourcebook* (Cambridge: Cambridge University Press) p. 168.

Freeman, M. O. (1993). 'Wavelets: Signal Representations with Important Advantages' *Opt. & Photonics News*, 8 8–14.

Frens, M. A., Van Opstal, A. J., and Van der Willigen, R. F. (1995). 'Spatial and temporal factors determine auditory-visual interactions in human saccadic eye movements' *Perception and Psychophysics*, 57 802–816.

Frisby, J. P. (1979). *Seeing: Illusion, Brain, Mind* (Oxford: Oxford University Press).

Frost, B. J. (1978). 'The optokinetic basis of head-bobbing in the pigeon' *Journal of Experimental Biology*, 74 187–195.

Gallace, A., Tan, H. Z., and Spence, C. (2006). 'The Failure to Detect Tectile Change: A Tactile Analogue of Visual Change Blindness' *Psychonomic Bulletin and Review*, 13 300.

Gegenfurtner, K. R. and Rieger, J. (2000). 'Sensory and cognitive contributions of color to the recognition of natural scenes' *Current Biology*, 10 805–808.

Gibson, E. J. and Walk, R. D. (1960). 'The "Visual Cliff"' *Scientific American*, 202 64–71.

Gibson, J. J. (1950). *The Perception of the Visual World* (Cambridge, MA: The Riverside Press).

Gibson, J. J. (1979). *The Ecological Approach to Visual Perception* (Hillsdale, New Jersey: Lawrence Erlbaum Associates).

Gierer, A. (1983). 'Relation between Neurophysiological and Mental States: Possible Limits of Decodability' *Naturwissenschaften*, 70 282–287.

Gilchrist, A. L. (1979). 'The Perception of Surface Blacks and Whites' *Scient. Am.*, 240 88–97.

Gingras, B. (2003). 'Johannes Kepler's Harmonice mundi: A "Scientific" version of the Harmony of the Spheres' *Royal Astronomical Society of Canada*, 97 228–231.

Glover, S. (2004). 'Separate visual representations in the planning and control of action' *Behavioral and Brain Sciences*, 27 3–24.

Goldstein, E. B. (2007). *Sensation and Perception* (Belmont: Thompson Wadsworth).

Gombrich, E. H. (1977). *Art and Illusion* (Oxford: Phaidon).

Gombrich, E. H. (1982). *The Image and the Eye* (London: Phaidon Press Ltd).

Gonzalez-Crussi, F. (1990). *The Five Senses* (London: Picador).

Gopen, Q., Rosowski, J. J., and Merchant, S. N. (1997). 'Anatomy of the normal human cochlear aqueduct with functional implications' *Hearing Research*, 107 9–22.

Gottfried, J. A. and Dolan, R. J. (2003). 'The Nose Smells What the Eye Sees: Crossmodal Visual Facilitation of Human Olfactory Perception' *Neuron*, 39 375–386.

Green, B. G. (2004). 'Temperature perception and nociception' *Journal of Neurobiology*, 61 13–29.

Greenwood, D. D. (1961). 'Auditory Masking and the Critical Band' *The Journal of the Acoustical Society of America*, 33 484–502.

Gregory, R. L. (1968). 'Visual illusions' *Scientific American*, 219 66–76.

Gregory, R. L. (1997). 'Knowledge in perception and illusion' *Philosophical Transactions of the Royal Society*, B 352 1121–1128.

Gregory, R. L. (1998). *Eye and Brain* (Oxford: Oxford University Press).

Gregory, R. L. (2007). 'Helmholtz's principle' *Perception*, 36 795–796.

Gregory, R. L. and Gombrich, E. H. (1973). *Illusion in Nature and Art* (London: Duckworth & Co. Ltd.).

Gregory, R. L. and Harris, J. P. (1984). 'Real and apparent movement nulled' *Nature* 307 729–730.

Gregory, R. L., Harris, J. P., Heard, P., and Rose, D. (1995). *The Artful Eye* (Oxford: Oxford University Press).

Gross, C. G. (1998). *Brain Vision Memory – Tales in the History of Neuroscience* (Cambridge, MA: MIT Press).

Gulick, L. G., Gescheider, G. A., and Frisina, R. D. (1989). *Hearing: Physiological Acoustics, Neural Coding, and Psychoacoustics* (New York: Oxford University Press).

Guthrie, B. L., Porter, J. D., and Sparks, D. L. (1983). 'Corollary Discharge Provides Accurate Eye Position Information to the Oculomotor System' *Science*, 221 1193–1195.

Hagen, M. A. (1980). *The Perception of Pictures* (New York: Academic Press).

Haines, M. M., Stansfeld, S. A., Job, R. F. S., Berglund, B., and Head, J. (2001). 'Chronic aircraft noise exposure, stress responses, mental health and cognitive performance in school children' *Psychological Medicine*, 31 265.

Hänig, David P. (1901). 'Zur Psychophysik des Geschmackssinnes' *Philosophische Studien*, 17 576–623.

Harris, J. P. and Calvert, J. E. (1989). 'Contrast, spatial frequency and test duration effects on the tilt aftereffect: Implications for underlying mechanisms' *Vision Research* 29 129–135.

Hartline, H. K. and Ratliff, F. (1957). 'Inhibitory Interaction of receptor units in the eye of limulus' *J. Gen. Physiol*, 40 357–376.

Hebert, L. E., Scherr, P. A., Bienias, J. L., Bennett, D. A. and Evans, D. A. (2003). 'Alzheimer Disease in the US Population: Prevalence Estimates Using the 2000 Census' *Arch Neurol*, 60 1119–1122.

Heller, M. A., Brackett, D. D., Wilson, K., Yoneyama, K., Boyer, A., and Steffen, H. (2002). 'The haptic Muller-Lyer illusion in sighted and blind people' *Perception*, 31 1263–1274.

Henning, H. (1916). *Der Geruch* (Leipzig: J. A. Barth).

Herbert, S., Braun, M., Hill, P., and McCormack, A. (2004). *Eadweard Muybridge: The Kingston Museum Bequest* (The Projection Box).

Herholz, S. C., Lappe, C., Knief, A., and Pantev, C. (2008). 'Neural basis of music imagery and the effect of musical expertise' *European Journal of Neuroscience*, 28 2352–2360.

Hess, R. F., Field, D. J, and Watt, R. J. (1990). 'The puzzle of amblyopia', in C. Blakemore (Ed.) *Vision: Coding and Efficiency* (Cambridge: Cambridge) pp. 267–280.

Hess, R. H., Baker, C. L. Jr., and Zihl, J. (1989). 'The "motion-blind" patient: Low-level spatial and temporal filters' *J. Neurosci.*, 9 1628–1640.

Hildreth, E-C. and Koch, C. (1987). 'The analysis of visual motion: From computational theory to neuronal mechanisms' *Annual Review of Neuroscience*, 10 477–533.

Hill, H. and Bruce, V. (1993). 'Independent effects of lighting, orientation, and stereopsis on the hollow-face illusion' *Perception*, 22 887–897.

Hofbauer, M., Wuerger, S. M., Meyer, G. F., Roehrbein, F., Schill, K., and Zetzsche, C. (2004). 'Catching audio–visual mice: Predicting the arrival time of auditory–visual motion signals' *Cognitive, Affective, & Behavioral Neuroscience*, 4 241–250.

Hofbauer, R. K., Rainville, P., Duncan, G. H., Bushnell, M. C. (2001). 'Cortical representation of the sensory dimension of pain' *Journal of Neurophysiology*, 86 402–411.

Hoffmann, M. B., Stadler, J., Kanowski, M., and Speck, O. (2009). 'Retinotopic mapping of the human visual cortex at a magnetic field strength of 7T' *Clinical Neurophysiology*, 120 108–116.

Hollins, M., Bensmaia, S., Karlof, K., and Young, F. (2000). 'Individual differences in perceptual space for tactile textures: Evidence from multidimensional scaling' *Perception and Psychophysics*, 62 1534–1544.

Horridge, G. A. (1966). 'Direct response of the crab Carcinus to the movement of the sun' *J. exp. Biol.*, 44 275–283.

Howard, I. P. and Rogers, B. (2008). *Seeing in Depth* (Oxford University Press, USA).

Hubel D. H. (1963). 'The Visual Cortex of the Brain' *Scient. Am.*, 209 54–63.

Hubel, D. H. (1979). 'The Brain' *Scientific American*, 241 39–47.

Hubel D. H. (1988). *Eye, Brain and Vision* (New York: Freeman & Co.).

Hubel D. H. and Wiesel T. N. (1962). 'Receptive fields, binocular interaction and functional architecture in the cat's visual cortex' *J. Physiol.*, 160 106–154.

Hubel, D. H. and Wiesel, T. N. (1979). 'Brain Mechanisms of Vision' *Scient. Am.*, 241 130–144.

Hurlbert, A. (2001). 'Trading faces' *Nat Neurosci*, 4 3–5.

Hurlbert, A. C. and Ling, Y. (2007). 'Biological components of sex differences in color preference' *Curr. Biol.*, 17 R623–R625.

Hürlimann, F., Kiper, D. C., and Carandini, M. (2002). 'Testing the Bayesian model of perceived speed' *Vision Research*, 42 2253–2257.

Hurvich, L. M. and Jameson, D. (1960). 'Perceived Color, Induction Effects, and Opponent-Response Mechanisms' *J. Gen. Physiol.*, 43 63–80.

Husain, M. and Rorden, C. (2003). 'Non-spatially lateralized mechanisms in hemispatial neglect' *Nature Reviews Neuroscience*, 4 26–36.

Huston, S. J. and Krapp, H. G. (2008). 'Visuomotor Transformation in the Fly Gaze Stabilization System' *PLoS Biology*, 6 e173.

Ione, A. and Tyler, C. (2003). 'Was Kandinsky a Synesthete?' *Journal of the History of the Neurosciences*, 12 223–226.

Irtel, H. (2000). 'Farbatlanten' *Spektrum der Wissenschaft Spezial*, 4 22–27.

Itti, L. and Koch, C. (2000). 'A saliency-based search mechanism for overt and covert shifts of visual attention' *Vision Research*, 40 1489–1506.

James, W. (1890) *The Principles of Psychology* (New York: Henry Holt & Co).

Jameson, D. and Hurvich, L. M. (1964). 'Theory of brightness and color contrast in human vision' *Vision Research*, 4 135–154.

Jastreboff, P. J. and Hazell, J. W. P. (1993). 'A neurophysiological approach to tinnitus: Clinical implications' *British Journal of Audiology*, 27 7–17.

Jenkins, J. S. (2001). 'The Mozart effect' *JRSM* 94 170.

Johansson, R. S., Landstrom, U., and Lundstrom, R. (1982). 'Responses of mechanoreceptive afferent units in the glabrous skin of the human hand to sinusoidal skin displacements' *Brain Res*, 244 17–25.

Johnson, G. A. (2005). *Renaissance Art: A Very Short Introduction* (Oxford: Oxford University Press).

Johnson, K. O. and Phillips, J. R. (1981). 'Tactile spatial resolution. I: Two-point discrimination, gap detection, grating resolution, and letter recognition' *Journal of Neurophysiology*, 46 1177.

Johnston, A., McOwan, P. W., and Benton, C. P. (1999) 'Robust velocity computation from a biologically motivated model of motion perception' *Proceedings of the Royal Society London*, B 266 509–518.

Julesz, B. (1971). *Foundations of Cyclopean Perception* (Cambridge, MA: MIT Press).

Julesz, B. and Miller, J. E. (1962). 'Automatic stereoscopic presentation of functions of two variables' *Bell System Technical Journal*, 41 663–676.

Kandel, E. R. and Squire, L. R. (2001). 'Breaking down scientific barriers to the study of brain and mind' *Annals of the New York Academy of Sciences*, 935 118–135.

Kanizsa, G. (1976). 'Subjective Contours' *Scient. Am.*, 234 48–52.

Kanizsa, G. (1979). *Organization in Vision: Essays on Gestalt Perception* (New York: Praeger Publishers).

Katz, D. B., Nicolelis, M. A. L, and Simon, S. A. (2002). 'Gustatory processing is dynamic and distributed' *Current Opinion in Neurobiology*, 12 448–454.

Kaufman, L. and Rock, I. (1962). 'The Moon Illusion' *Scientific American*, 207(1) 120–132.

Kelling, S. T. and Halpern, B. P. (1983). 'Taste flashes: Reaction times, intensity, and quality' *Science*, 219 412–414.

Kelly, D. H. (1962). 'Visual Responses to Time-Dependent Stimuli. III: Individual Variations' *Journal of the Optical Society of America*, 52 89–95.

Kelly, D. H. (1972). 'Flicker', in D. Jameson and L. M. Hurvich (Eds) *Handbook of Sensory Physiology VII/4 Visual Psychophysics* (Berlin, Heidelberg, New York: Springer Verlag) pp. 273–302.

Kennedy, J. S. (1983). 'Zigzagging and casting as a programmed response to wind-borne odour: A review' *Phys. Entom.*, 8 109–120.

Kennett, S., Spence, C., and Driver, J. (2002). 'Visuo-tactile links in covert exogenous spatial attention remap across changes in unseen hand posture' *Perception and Psychophysics*, 64 1083–1094.

Kersten, D. Mamassian, P. and Knill, D. C. (1997). 'Moving cast shadows induce apparent motion in depth' *Perception*, 26 171–192.

King, A. J. and Calvert, G. A. (2001). 'Multisensory integration: Perceptual grouping by eye and ear' *Curr. Biol.*, 11 R322–R325.

King, A. J. and Nelken, I. (2009). 'Unraveling the principles of auditory cortical processing: Can we learn from the visual system?' *Nat Neurosci*, 12 698–701.

King, A. J., Schnupp, J. W. H., Doubell, T. P. (2001) 'The shape of ears to come: dynamic coding of auditory space' *Trends in Cognitive Sciences*, 5 261–270.

Kitaoka, A. (2002). *Trick Eyes* (Tokyo: Kanzen).

Koch, C. and Crick, F. (2001). 'The zombie within' *Nature*, 411 893.

Koch, K., McLean, J., Segev, R., Freed, M. A., Berry Ii M. J., Balasubramanian, V., and Sterling, P. (2006). 'How Much the Eye Tells the Brain' *Current Biology*, 16 1428–1434.

Koelsch, S. and Siebel, W. A. (2005). 'Towards a neural basis of music perception' *Trends in Cognitive Sciences*, 9 578–584.

Koffka, K. (1935). *Principles of Gestalt Psychology* (London: Routledge).

Kohler, I. (1962). 'Experiments with Goggles' *Scient. Am.*, 206 62–72.

Köhler, W. (1947). *Gestalt Psychology* (New York: Liveright Publishing Corporation).

Konishi, M. (1986) 'Centrally synthesized maps of sensory space' *Trends in Neuroscience*, 4/86 163–168.

Koulakov, A., Gelperin, A., and Rinberg, D. (2007). 'Olfactory Coding With All-or-Nothing Glomeruli' *J Neurophysiol*, 98 3134–3142.

Kuffler, S. W. (1953). 'Discharge patterns and functional organization of mammalian retina' *J Neurophysiol*, 16 37–68.

Kuhn, G., Amlani, A. A., and Rensink, R. A. (2008). 'Towards a science of magic' *Trends Cogn Sci.* 12(9) 349–54.

Kuhn, G. and Land, M. F. (2006). 'There's more to magic than meets the eye' *Current Biology*, 16 950–951.

Kuhn, G. and Tatler, B. W. (2005). 'Magic and fixation: Now you don't see it, now you do' *Perception*, 34 1155–1161.

Kuhn, T. S. (1962). *The Structure of Scientific Revolutions* (Chicago: University of Chicago Press).

Lachman, R., Lachman, J. L. and Butterfield, E. C. (1979). *Cognitive Psychology and Information Processing: An Introduction* (Lawrence Erlbaum Associates Hillsdale, NJ).

Land, E. H. (1977). 'The Retinex Theory of Color Vision' *Sci. Am.*, 237(6) 108–129.

Land, M. (2008). 'Biological Optics: Circularly Polarised Crustaceans' *Current Biology*, 18 R348–R349.

Land, M. F. (2001). 'Does Steering a Car Involve Perception of the Velocity Flow Field', in *Motion Vision – Computational, Neural, and Ecological Constraints* (Eds) J. M. Zanker and J. Zeil (Berlin Heidelberg New York: Springer-Verlag) pp. 227–235.

Land, M. F. (2006). 'Eye movements and the control of actions in everyday life' *Progress in Retinal and Eye Research*, 25 296–324.

Land, M. F. and McLeod, P. (2000). 'From eye movements to actions: How batsmen hit the ball' *Nature Neuroscience*, 3 1340–1345.

Langton, S. R. H., Watt, R. J., and Bruce, V. (2000). 'Do the eyes have it? Cues to the direction of social attention' *Trends in Cognitive Sciences*, 4 50–59.

Lappe, M., Bremmer, F., and Van den Berg, A. V. (1999). 'Perception of self-motion from visual flow' *Trends in Cognitive Sciences*, 3 329–335.

Laugerette, F., Passilly-Degrace, P., Patris, B., Niot, I., Febbraio, M., Montmayeur, J. P., and Besnard, P. (2005). 'CD36 involvement in orosensory detection of dietary lipids, spontaneous fat preference, and digestive secretions' *Journal of Clinical Investigation*, 115 3177.

Lavie, N. (1995). 'Perceptual load as a necessary condition for selective attention' *Journal of Experimental Psychology*, 21 451–468.

Lavie, N. (2005). 'Distracted and confused?: Selective attention under load' *Trends in Cognitive Sciences*, 9 75–82.

Le Bihan, D. (2003). 'Looking into the functional architecture of the brain with diffusion MRI' *Nature Reviews Neuroscience*, 4 469–480.

Lee, D. N. (1976). 'A theory of visual control of braking based on information about time-to-collision' *Perception*, 5 437–459.

Lee, T. S. (1995). 'A Bayesian Framework for Understanding Texture Segmentation in the Primary Visual Cortex' *Vision Research*, 35 2643–2657.

Leibowitz, H. W., Brislin, R., Perlmutter, L., and Hennessy, R. (1969). 'Ponzo Perspective Illusion as a Manifestation of Space Perception' *Science*, 166 1174–1176.

Levitin, D. J. and Rogers, S. E. (2005). 'Absolute pitch: Perception, coding, and controversies' *Trends in Cognitive Sciences*, 9 26–33.

Lewin, R. (1992). 'The great brain race' *New Scientist*, Dec. 1992 2–8.

Limb, C. J. and Braun, A. R. (2008). 'Neural Substrates of Spontaneous Musical Performance: An fMRI Study of Jazz Improvisation' *PLoS ONE*, 3 e1679.

Livingstone, M. S. and Hubel, D. H. (1988). 'Segregation of Form, Color, Movement, and Depth: Anatomy, Physiology, and Perception' *Science*, 240 740–749.

Longuet-Higgins, H. C. (1979). 'The perception of music' *Proceedings of the Royal Society London*, B 205 307–322.

Loomis, J. M. (1981) 'Tactile pattern perception' *Perception*, 10 5–27.

Macaluso, E. and Driver, J. (2005). 'Multisensory spatial interactions: A window onto functional integration in the human brain' *Trends in Neurosciences*, 28 264–271.

Mack, A. and Rock, I. (1998). 'Inattentional blindness: Perception without attention' *Visual Attention*, 8 55–76.

Macknik, S. L., King, M., Randi, J., Robbins, A., Teller, Thompson, J., and Martinez-Conde, S. (2008). 'Attention and awareness in stage magic: Turning tricks into research' *Nat Rev Neurosci*, 9 871–879.

Maffei, L. and Fiorentini, A. (1973). 'The visual cortex as spatial frequency analyser' *Vision Research* 13 1255–1267.

MagicEyeInc. (1993). *Magic Eye: A New Way of Looking at the World*. Kansas City, MO: Andrews and McMeel, a Universal Press Syndicate Company.

Mamlouk, A. M. and Martinetz, T. (2004). 'On the dimensions of the olfactory perception space' *Neurocomputing*, 58 1019–1025.

Manger, P. R., Woods, T. M., and Jones, E. G. (1996). 'Plasticity of the Somatosensory Cortical Map in Macaque Monkeys after Chronic Partial Amputation of a Digit' *Proceedings: Biological Sciences*, 263 933–939.

Marr, D. (1982). *Vision: A Computational Investigation into the Human Representation and Processing of Visual Information* (San Francisco: Freeman & Co.).

Marr, D. and Poggio, T. (1979). 'A computational theory of human stereo vision' *Proceedings of the Royal Society London*, B 204 301–328.

Marshall, J. C. (1987). 'Is seeing believing?' *Nature*, 325 583–584.

Martinez-Conde, S. and Macknik, S. L. (2007). 'Windows on the Mind' *Scientific American*, August 2007 56–63.

Mather, G. and Harris, J. P. (1998). 'Theoretical Models of the Motion Aftereffect', in G. Mather, F. A. J. Verstraten and S. M. Anstis (Eds) *The Motion Aftereffect: A Modern Perspective* (Boston: Boston) pp. 157–185.

May, J. J. (2000). 'Occupational hearing loss' *American Journal of Industrial Medicine*, 37 112–120.

McCollough, C. (1965). 'Color adaptation of edge-detectors in the human visual system' *Science*, 149 1115–1116.

McGurk, H. and MacDonald, J. (1976). 'Hearing lips and seeing voices' *Nature*, 264 746–748.

Mellado Lagarde, M. M., Drexl, M., Lukashkina, V. A., Lukashkin, A. N., and Russell, I. J. 2008 'Outer hair cell somatic, not hair bundle, motility is the basis of the cochlear amplifier' *Nat Neurosci*, 11 746–748.

Merzenich, M. M., Nelson, R. J., Stryker, M. P., Cynader, M. S., Schoppmann, A., and Zook, J. M. (1984). 'Somatosensory cortical map changes following digit amputation in adult monkeys' *The Journal of Comparative Neurology*, 224 591–605.

Metelli, F. (1974). 'The Perception of Transparency' *Scient. Am.*, 4/74.

Middlebrooks, J. C. and Green, D. M. (1991). 'Sound Localization by Human Listeners' *Annual Reviews in Psychology*, 42 135–159.

Millan, M. J. (1999). 'The induction of pain: An integrative review' *Progress in Neurobiology*, 57 1–164.

Millar, S. (1971). 'Visual and haptic cue utilization by preschool children: The recognition of visual and haptic stimuli presented separately and together' *J Exp Child Psychol*, 12 88–94.

Miller, G. A. (1956). 'Information and Memory' *Scientific American*, 195(2) 42–46.

Minsky, M. L. and Papert, S. A. (1988). *Perceptrons: Expanded edition* (Cambridge, MA: MIT Press).

Mishkin, M., Ungerleider, L. G., and Macko, K. A. (1983). 'Object vision and spatial vision: Two cortical pathways' *Trends in Neuroscience*, 6 414–417.

Möller, M., Sintek, M., Buitelaar, P., Mukherjee, S., Zhou, X. S., and Freund, J. (2008). 'Medical image understanding through the integration of cross-modal object recognition with formal domain knowledge', in A. Fred, J. Filipe, and H. Gamboa (Eds) *Best papers of BIOSTEC 2008* (Berlin Heidelberg: Springer-Verlag).

Moore, B. C. J. (2003). *An Introduction to the Psychology of Hearing* (San Diego: Academic Press).

Moore, D. R. and Shannon, R. V. (2009). 'Beyond cochlear implants: awakening the deafened brain' *Nat Neurosci*, 12 686–691.

Moray, N. (1959). 'Attention in dichotic listening: Affective cues and the influence of instructions' *The Quarterly Journal of Experimental Psychology*, 11 56–60.

Mostin, M. (2001). 'Taste disturbances after pine nut ingestion' *European Journal of Emergency Medicine*, 8 76.

Movshon, J. A., Adelson, E. H., Gizzi, M. S., and Newsome, W. T. (1985). 'The analysis of moving visual patterns', in C. Chagas, R. Gattass, and C. Gross (Eds) *Pattern Recognition Mechanisms: Pontificiae Academiae Scientiarum Sripta Varia 54* (Ex Aedibus Academicis In Civitate Vaticana, Civitate Vaticana) pp. 117–151.

Munger, S. D. (2009). 'Olfaction: Noses within noses' *Nature*, 459 521–522.

Munsell, A. H. (1912). 'A Pigment Color System and Notation' *The American Journal of Psychology*, 23 236–244.

Munsell, A. H. and Farnum, R. B. (1941). *A Color Notation: An Illustrated System Defining All Colors and their Relationships* (Baltimore, MD: Munsell Color Company).

Nahum, M., Nelken, I., and Ahissar, M. (2008). 'Low-Level Information and High-Level Perception: The Case of Speech in Noise' *PLoS Biology*, 6 e126.

Neisser, U. (1968). 'The Processes of Vision' *Scient. Am.*, 219 204–214.

Nelson, G., Chandrashekar, J., Hoon, M. A., Feng, L., Zhao, G., Ryba, N. J. P., and Zuker, C. S. (2002). 'An amino-acid taste receptor' *Nature*, 416 199–202.

Nelson, M. E. and MacIver, M. A. (1999). 'Prey capture in the weakly electric fish Apteronotus albifrons: Sensory Acquisition strategies and elctrosensory consequences' *Journal of Experimental Biology*, 202 1195–1203.

Neuweiler, G. (1984). 'Foraging, Echolocation and Audition in Bats' *Naturwissenschaften*, 71 446–455.

Newman, E. A. and Hartline, P. H. (1982). 'The infrared vision of snakes' *Scientific American*, 246 116–127.

Newton, I. (1704). *Opticks* (London: Smith & Walford).

Nishimura, H., Hashikawa, K., Doi, K., Iwaki, T., Watanabe, Y., Kusuoka, H., Nishimura, T., and Kubo, T. (1999). 'Sign language "heard" in the auditory cortex' *Nature* 397 116.

Norman, J. (2002). 'Two visual systems and two theories of perception: An attempt to reconcile the constructivist and ecological approaches' *Behavioral and Brain Sciences*, 25 73–144.

Nowlan, S. J. and Sejnowski, T. J. (1994). 'Filter selection model for motion segmentation and velocity integration' *Journal of the Optical Society of America* A11 3177–3200.

O'Regan, J. K., Rensink, R. A., and Clark, J. J. (1999). 'Change blindness as a result of "mud-splashes"' *Nature*, 398 34.

Ochs, A. L. (1979). 'Is Fourier analysis performed by the visual system or by the investigator' *Journal of the Optical Society of America*, 69 95–98.

Osorio, D. and Vorobyev, M. (1996). 'Colour vision as an adaptation to frugivory in primates' *Proceedings of the Royal Society London*, B 263 593–599.

Paradiso, M. A., Shimojo, S., and Nakayama, K. (1989). 'Subjective contours, tilt aftereffect, and visual cortical organization' *Vision Research*, 29 1205–1213.

Patterson, R. D., Nimmo-Smith, I., Weber, D. L., and Milroy, R. (1982). 'The deterioration of hearing with age: Frequency selectivity, the critical ratio, the audiogram, and speech threshold' *The Journal of the Acoustical Society of America*, 72 1788.

Payne, K. B., Langbauer, W. R., and Thomas, E. M. (1986). 'Infrasonic calls of the Asian elephant (Elephas maximus)' *Behav. Ecol. Sociobiol.*, 18 297–301.

Pelah, A. and Barlow, H. B. (1996). 'Visual illusion from running' *Nature*, 381 283.

Penfield, W. and Rasmussen, T. (1950). *The Cerebral Cortex of Man: A Clinical Study of Localization of Function* (New York: Macmillan Co.).

Pessoa, L., Mingolla, E., and Neumann, H. (1995). 'A Contrast- and Luninace-driven Multiscale Network Model of Brightness Perception' *Vision Research*, 35 2201–2223.

Peterhans, E. and von der Heydt, R. (1991). 'Subjective contours – bridging the gap between psychophysics and physiology' *TINS*, 14 112–119.

Petitto, L. A., Zatorre, R. J., Gauna, K., Nikelski, E. J., Dostie, D., and Evans, A. C. (2000). 'Speech-like cerebral activity in profoundly deaf people processing signed languages: Implications for the neural basis of human language' *Proceedings of the National Academy of Sciences of the United States of America*, 97 13961–13966.

Pfaffmann, C. (1955). 'Gustatory nerve impulses in rat, cat and rabbit' *J Neurophysiol*, 18 429–440.

Pierce, J. R. (1992). *The Science of Musical Sound* (New York: Freeman & Co).

Pinna, B., Werner, J. S., and Spillmann, L. (2003). 'The watercolor effect: A new principle of grouping and figure-ground organization' *Vision Research*, 43 43–52.

Pitchford, N. J. and Mullen, K. T. (2005). 'The role of perception, language, and preference in the developmental acquisition of basic color terms' *Journal of Experimental Child Psychology*, 90 275–302.

Plack, C. J. (2005). *The Sense Of Hearing* (Mahwah, NJ: Lawrence Erlbaum Associates).

Porter, J., Craven, B., Khan, R. M., Chang, S-J., Kang, I., Judkewitz, B., Volpe, J., Settles, G., and Sobel, N. (2007). 'Mechanisms of scent-tracking in humans' *Nat Neurosci*, 10 27–29.

Posner, M. I. (1980). 'Orienting of Attention' *The Quarterly Journal of Experimental Psychology*, 32 3–25.

Price, C. J. (2000). 'The anatomy of language: Contributions from functional neuroimaging' *Journal of Anatomy*, 197 335–359.

Ramachandran, V. S. (1988). 'Perceiving Shape from Shading' *Sci. Am.* 259 76–83.

Ramachandran, V. S. and Anstis, S. M. (1986). 'The perception of apparent motion' *Sci. Am.*, 254 80–87.

Ramachandran, V. S. and Hubbard, E. M. (2003). 'Hearing colors, tasting shapes' *Scientific American*, 288 52–59.

Ramachandran, V. S. and Rogers-Ramachandran, D. (2000). 'Phantom Limbs and Neural Plasticity' *Archives of Neurology*, 57 317–320.

Rauscher, F. H., Shaw, G. L., and Ky, K. N. (1993). 'Music and spatial task performance' *Nature*, 365 611.

Rayner, K. (1998). 'Eye movements in reading and information processing: 20 years of research' *Psychological Bulletin*, 124 372–422.

Reed, D. R. (2008). 'Birth of a New Breed of Supertaster' *Chem. Senses*, 33 489–491.

Rees, G., Wojciulik, E., Clarke, K., Husain, M., Frith, C., and Driver, J. (2000). 'Unconscious activation of visual cortex in the damaged right hemisphere of a parietal patient with extinction' *Brain*, 123 1624–1633.

Reichardt, W. (1961). 'Autocorrelation, a principle for the evaluation of sensory information by the central nervous system', in W. A. Rosenblith (Ed.) *Sensory Communication* (Cambridge, MA: MIT Press) pp. 303–317.

Rensink, R. A., O'Regan, J. K., and Clark, J. J. (1997). 'To see or not to see: The need for attention to perceive changes in scenes' *Psychol. Sci.*, 8 368–373.

Revonsuo, A. and Newman, J. (1999). 'Binding and Consciousness' *Consciousness and Cognition*, 8 123–127.

Rieke, F., Warland, D., de Ruyter van Steveninck, R., Bialek, W. (1996). *Spikes: Exploring the Neural Code* (Cambridge, MA: MIT Press).

Riley, B. (1995). *Dialogues on Art* (London: Zwemmer).

Roberts, D. R. (2002). *Signals and Perception: The Fundamentals of Human Sensation* (Houndmills, Basingstoke: Palgrave Macmillan).

Robinson, D. A. (1965). 'The mechanics of human smooth pursuit eye movement' *J Physiol* 180 569–591.

Robinson, R. (2009). 'Feedback System Protects Inner Ear' *PLoS Biology*, 7 e12.

Rock, I. and Harris, C. S. (1967). 'Vision and Touch' *Scientific American*, 216(5) 96–104.

Rogers, B. J. and Graham, M. E. (1984). 'Motion parallax and stereoscopic aftereffects', in L. Spillmann and B. R. Wooten (Eds) *Sensory Experience, Adaptation, and Perception: Festschrift for Ivo Köhler* (Hillsdale, NJ: Lawrence Erlbaum Ass.) pp. 606–619.

Rolls, E. T. (2000). 'The Orbitofrontal Cortex and Reward' *Cereb. Cortex*, 10 284–294.

Ross, J., Morrone, M. C., and Burr, D. C. (1989). 'The conditions under which Mach bands are visible' *Vision Research*, 29 699–715.

Russ, M. (2004). *Sound Synthesis and Sampling* (Oxford: Focal Press).

Russell, M. J. (1976). 'Human olfactory communication' *Nature*, 260 520–522.

Sacks, O. W. (1998). *The Man Who Mistook His Wife For A Hat* (New York: Touchstone).

Salvador, R., Suckling, J., Coleman, M. R., Pickard, J. D., Menon, D. and Bullmore, E. (2005). 'Neurophysiological Architecture of Functional Magnetic Resonance Images of Human Brain' *Cereb. Cortex*, 15 1332–1342.

Sanfey, A. G. (2007). 'Social Decision-Making: Insights from Game Theory and Neuroscience' *Science*, 318 598–602.

Scharf, B. (1971). 'Fundamentals of auditory masking' *Audiology*, 10 30–40.

Scheibert, J., Leurent, S., Prevost, A., and Debregeas, G. (2009). 'The Role of Fingerprints in the Coding of Tactile Information Probed with a Biomimetic Sensor' *Science*, 1166467.

Schnupp, J. W. H. and Carr, C. E. (2009). 'On hearing with more than one ear: Lessons from evolution' *Nat Neurosci*, 12 692–697.

Schober, H. and Munker, H. (1967). 'Untersuchungen zu den Übertragungseigenschaften des Gesichtssinns für die Farbinformation' *Vision Research*, 7 1015–1026.

Scholl, B. J., Pylyshyn, Z. W., and Feldman, J. (2001). 'What is a visual object? Evidence from target merging in multiple object tracking' *Cognition*, 80 159–177.

Schrauf, M., Lingelbach, B., and Wist, E. R. (1997). 'The Scintillating Grid Illusion' *Vision Research*, 37 1033–1038.

Scott, T. R. and Chang, F-C. T. (1984). 'The state of gustatory neural coding' *Chem. Senses*, 8 297–314.

Sekuler, R., Nash, D., and Armstrong, R. (1973). 'Sensitive, objective procedure for evaluating response to light touch' *Neurology*, 23 1282.

Sekuler, R., Sekuler, A. B., and Lau, R. (1997). 'Sound alters visual motion perception' *Nature*, 385 308.

Sergent, J. (1993). 'Music, the brain and Ravel' *Trends in Neurosciences*, 16 168–172.

Shannon, C. E. and Weaver, W. (1949). *The Mathematical Theory of Communication* (Urbana & Chicago: University of Illinois Press).

Shannon, R. V., Zeng, F. G., Kamath, V., Wygonski, J., and Ekelid, M. (1995). 'Speech Recognition with Primarily Temporal Cues' *Science*, 270 303.

Sharpe, L. T., Stockman, A., Jägle, H., and Nathans, J. (2001). 'Opsin genes, cone photopigments, color vision, and color blindness', in K. R. Gegenfurtner and L. T. Sharpe (Eds) *Color Vision: From Genes to Perception* (Cambridge: Cambridge University Press) pp. 3–51.

Shepard, R. N. (1964). 'Circularity in Judgments of Relative Pitch' *The Journal of the Acoustical Society of America*, 36 2346.

Sherrington, C. S. (1907). 'On the proprio-ceptive system, especially in its reflex aspect' *Brain*, 29 467–482.

Shimojo, S. and Shams, L. (2001). 'Sensory modalities are not separate modalities: plasticity and interactions' *Current Opinion in Neurobiology*, 11 505–509.

Siebeck, U. E. (2004). 'Communication in coral reef fish: The role of ultraviolet colour patterns in damselfish territorial behaviour' *Animal Behaviour*, 68 273–282.

Simner, J., Mulvenna, C., Sagiv, N., Tsakanikos, E., Witherby, S. A., Fraser, C., Scott, K., Ward, J. (2006). 'Synaesthesia: The prevalence of atypical cross-modal experiences' *Perception*, 35 1024–1033.

Simons, D. J. and Chabris, C. F. (1999). 'Gorillas in our midst: Sustained inattentional blindness for dynamic events' *Perception*, 28 1059–1074.

Smith, A. T. and Snowden, R. J. (1994). *Visual Detection of Motion* (London: Academic Press).

Smith, J. (2006). 'Bodily Awareness, Imagination and the Self' *European Journal of Philosophy*, 14 49–68.

Snowden, R. J. and Hess, R. F. (1992). 'Temporal frequency filters in the human peripheral visual field' *Vision Research*, 32 61–72.

Soto-Faraco, S., Lyons, J., Gazzaniga, M., Spence, C., and Kingstone, A. (2002). 'The ventriloquist in motion: Illusory capture of dynamic information across sensory modalities' *Cognitive Brain Research*, 14 139–146.

Stein, B. E., Meredith, M. A., and Wolf, S. (1993). *The Merging of the Senses* (Boston, MA: MIT Press).

Steinbeis, N. and Koelsch, S. (2008). 'Comparing the Processing of Music and Language Meaning Using EEG and fMRI Provides Evidence for Similar and Distinct Neural Representations' *PLoS ONE*, 3 e2226.

Stevens, J. C., Foulke, E., and Patterson, M. Q. (1996). 'Tactile acuity, aging, and braille reading in long-term blindness' *Journal of Experimental Psychology: Applied*, 2 91–106.

Stevens, S. S. (1936). 'A scale for the measurement of a psychological magnitude: Loudness' *Psychological Review*, 43 405–416.

Stevens, S. S. (1956). 'The Direct Estimation of Sensory Magnitudes: Loudness' *The American Journal of Psychology*, 69 1–25.

Stevens, S. S. (1957). 'On the psychophysical law' *Psychological Review*, 64 153–181.

Stevens, S. S. (1961). 'To Honor Fechner and Repeal His Law: A power function, not a log function, describes the operating characteristic of a sensory system' *Science*, 133 80–86.

Stevens, S. S. (1970). 'Neural Events and the Psychophysical Law' *Science*, 170 1043–1050.

Stevens, S. S. and Newman, E. B. (1934). 'The Localization of Pure Tones' *Proceedings of the National Academy of Sciences of the United States of America* 20 593–596.

Stevenson, R. J., Boakes, R. A., and Prescott, J. (1998). 'Changes in Odor Sweetness Resulting from Implicit Learning of a Simultaneous Odor-Sweetness Association: An Example of Learned Synesthesia' *Learning and Motivation*, 29 113–132.

Stewart, D., Cudworth, C. J., and Lishman, J. R. (1993). 'Misperception of time-to-collision by drivers in pedestrian accidents' *Perception*, 22 1227–1244.

Stoffregen, Thomas A. and Pittenger, John B. (1995). 'Human Echolocation as a Basic Form of Perception and Action' *Ecological Psychology*, 7 181–216.

Strait, D. L., Kraus, N., Skoe, E., and Ashley, R. (2009). 'Musical experience and neural efficiency – effects of training on subcortical processing of vocal expressions of emotion' *European Journal of Neuroscience*, 29 661–668.

Stratton, G. M. (1931). 'Brain Localization by Albertus Magnus and Some Earlier Writers' *The American Journal of Psychology*, 43 128–131.

Swade, D. (2000). *The Cogwheel Brain* (London: Little, Brown & Co).

Terhardt, E. (1974). 'Pitch, consonance, and harmony' *The Journal of the Acoustical Society of America*, 55 1061–1069.

Tootell, R. B., Reppas, J. B., Kwong, K. K., Malach, R., Born, R. T., Brady, T. J., Rosen, B. R., and Belliveau, J. W. (1995). 'Functional Analysis of Human MT and Related Visual Cortex Areas Using Magnetic Resonance Imaging' *J. Neurosci.*, 15 3215–3230.

Tootell, R. B., Silverman, M. S., and DeValois, R. L. (1981) 'Spatial Frequency Columns in Primary Visual Cortex' *Science*, 214 813–815.

Tootell, R. B. H., Hadjikhani, N., Hall, E. K., Marrett, S., Vanduffel, W., Vaughan, J. T., and Dale, A. M. (1998). 'The retinotopy of visual spatial attention' *Neuron*, 21(6) 1409–1422.

Treede, R. D., Apkarian, A. V., Bromm, B., Greenspan, J. D., and Lenz, F. A. (2000). 'Cortical representation of pain: Functional characterization of nociceptive areas near the lateral sulcus' *Pain*, 87 113–119.

Treisman, A. (1986). 'Features and Objects in Visual Processing' *Sci. Am.*, 255 106–115.

Treisman, A. (1998). 'Feature binding, attention and object perception' *Philosophical Transactions of the Royal Society B: Biological Sciences*, 353 1295–1306.

Treisman, A. and Gelade, G. (1980). 'A Feature-Integration Theory of Attention' *Cognitive Psychology*, 12 97–136.

Tresilian, J. R., Mon-Williams, M., and Kelly, B. M. (1999). 'Increasing confidence in vergence as a cue to distance' *Proceedings of the Royal Society of London. Series B: Biological Sciences*, 266 39–44.

Treue, S., Hol, K., and Rauber, H-J. (2000). 'Seeing multiple directions of motion – physiology and psychophysics' *Nature Neuroscience*, 3 270–276.

Ts'o D. Y. and Gilbert, C. D. (1988). 'The Organization of Chromatic and Spatial Interactions in the Primate Striate Cortex' *J. Neurosci.*, 8 1712–1727.

Tsakiris, M. and Haggard, P. (2005). 'The Rubber Hand Illusion Revisited: Visuotactile Integration and Self-Attribution' *Journal of Experimental Psychology: Human Perception and Performance*, 31 80–91.

Tyler, C. W. and Clarke, M. B. (1990). 'The Autostereogram', in *SPIE Stereoscopic Displays and Applications 1256*, pp. 182–196.

Ullman, S. (1979). 'The interpretation of structure from motion' *Proceedings of the Royal Society London*, B 203 405–426.

Uttal, W. R. (2003). *The New Phrenology: The Limits of Localizing Cognitive Processes in the Brain* (Cambridge, MA: MIT Press).

Valentine, E. R. (1992). *Conceptual Issues in Psychology* (London, New York: Routledge).

Van Bergeijk, W. A. (1966). 'Evolution of the Sense of Hearing in Vertebrates' *Amer. Zool.*, 6 371–377.

Van Essen, D. C., Anderson, C. H., and Felleman, D. J. (1992). 'Information processing in the primate visual system: An integrated systems perspective' *Science*, 255 419–423.

Van Hateren, J. H., Srinivasan, M. V., and Wait, P. B. (1990). 'Pattern Recognition in Bees: Orientation Discrimination' *Journal of Comparative Physiology A: Neuroethology, Sensory, Neural, and Behavioral Physiology*, 167 649–654.

Vladusich, T. and Broerse, J. (2002). 'Color constancy and the functional significance of McCollough effects' *Neural Networks*, 15 775–809.

Von Bekesy, G. (1949). 'The Moon Illusion and Similar Auditory Phenomena' *The American Journal of Psychology*, 62 540–552.

Von Bekesy, G. (1964). 'Olfactory analogue to directional hearing' *J Appl Physiol*, 19 369–373.

Von Békésy, G. (1949). 'The Structure of the Middle Ear and the Hearing of One's Own Voice by Bone Conduction' *The Journal of the Acoustical Society of America*, 21 217.

Von Békésy, G. (1961). 'Concerning the Pleasures of Observing, and the Mechanics of the Inner Ear', in *Nobel Lectures, Physiology or Medicine 1942–1962* (Amsterdam: Elsevier Publishing Company) pp. 519–532.

Von Békésy, G. (1967a). 'Mach Band Type Lateral Inhibition in Different Sense Organs' *J. Gen. Physiol.* 50 519–532.

Von Békésy, G. (1967b). *Sensory Inhibition* (Princeton, NJ: Princeton University Press).

Von Helmholtz, H. (1852). 'Über die Theorie der zusammengesetzten Farben', *Archiv für Anatomie, Physiologie und wissenschaftliche Medizin* 461–482.

Von Helmholtz, H. (1924). *Treatise on Physiological Optics* (New York: Dover).

Wade, N. J. (1994). 'A selective history of the study of visual motion aftereffects' *Perception*, 23 1111–1134.

Wade, N. J. (1998). *A Natural History of Vision* (Cambridge, MA: MIT Press).

Wade, N. J. (2003). 'Movements in art: From Rosso to Riley' *Perception* 32 1029–1036.

Wade, N. J. (2007). 'Image, eye, and retina (invited review)' *Journal of the Optical Society of America*, A 24 1229–1249.

Wade, N. J., Spillmann, L., and Swanston, M. T. (1996). 'Visual Motion Aftereffects: Critical Adaptation and Test Conditions' *Vision Research*, 36 2167–2175.

Wade, N. J. and Tatler, B. W. (2005). *The Moving Tablet of the Eye: The Origins of Modern Eye Movement Research* (Oxford: Oxford University Press).

Wall, M. B. and Smith, A. T. (2008). 'The Representation of Egomotion in the Human Brain' *Current Biology*, 18 191–194.

Wallach, H. (1935). 'Ueber visuell wahrgenommene Bewegungsrichtung' *Psychologische Forschung* 20 325–380.

Wandell, B. A. (1995). *Foundations of Vision* (Sunderland, MA: Sinauer Associates, Inc.).

Wandell, B. A. (2008). 'What's in your mind?' *Nat Neurosci*, 11 384–385.

Ward, J., Huckstep, B., and Tsakanikos, E. (2006). 'Sound-Colour Synaesthesia: to What Extent Does it Use Cross-Modal Mechanisms Common to us All?' *Cortex*, 42 264–280.

Watson, A. B. (1993). *Digital Images and Human Vision* (Cambridge, MA: MIT Press).

Watson, A. B., Barlow, H. B., and Robson, J. G. (1983). 'What does the eye see best?' *Nature*, 302 119.

Webster, M. A. and Mollon, J. D. (1995). 'Colour constancy influenced by contrast adaptation' *Nature*, 373 694–698.

Wegel, R. L. and Lane, C. E. (1924). 'The Auditory Masking of One Pure Tone by Another and its Probable Relation to the Dynamics of the Inner Ear' *Physical Review*, 23 266–285.

Wertheimer, M. (1912). 'Experimentelle Studien über das Sehen von Bewegung' *Z. Psychol.*, 61 161–278.

Wertheimer, M. (1923). 'Untersuchungen zur Lehre von der Gestalt' *Psychol. Forschg.*, 301–350.

Westerkull, P. (2002). 'BAHA: The Direct Bone Conductor' *Trends in Amplification*, 6 45–52.

Westheimer, G. (1984). 'Spatial Vision' *Annual Reviews of Psychology*, 35 201–226.

Westheimer, G. (2008). 'Was Helmholtz a Bayesian?' *Perception*, 37 642–650.

Wheatstone, C. (1838). 'Contributions to the Physiology of Vision. Part the First: On Some Remarkable, and Hitherto Unobserved, Phenomena of Binocular Vision' *Philosophical Transactions of the Royal Society of London*, 128 371–394.

White, M. (1979) 'A new effect of pattern on perceived lightness' *Perception*, 8 413–416.

Wiener, N. (1948). *Cybernetics: Or the Control and Communication in the Animal and the Machine* (Cambridge, MA: MIT Press).

Wilson, H. R. (1991) 'Pattern discrimination, Visual Filters, and Spatial Sampling Irregularity', in M. S. Landy and J. A. Movshon (Eds) *Computational Models of Visual Processing* (Cambridge, MA: Cambridge MA) pp. 153–168.

Wong, P. C. M., Skoe, E., Russo, N. M., Dees, T., and Kraus, N. (2007). 'Musical experience shapes human brainstem encoding of linguistic pitch patterns' *Nat Neurosci*, 10 420–422.

Wyszecki, G. and Stiles, W. S. (1982). *Color Science – Concepts and Methods, Quantitative Data and Formulae* (New York: John Wiley & Sons).

Yarbus, A. L. (1967). *Eye Movements and Vision* (New York: Plenum Press).

Yonas, A., Pettersen, L., and Granrud, C. E. (1982). 'Infant's Sensitivity to Familiar Size as Information for Distance' *Child Dev.*, 53 1285–1290.

Young, T. (1802). 'The Bakerian Lecture: On the Theory of Light and Colours' *Philosophical Transactions of the Royal Society of London*, 92 12–48.

Zanker, J. M. (1994). 'Modeling Human Motion Perception. I: Classical Stimuli' *Naturwissenschaften*, 81 156–163.

Zanker, J. M. and Harris, J. P. (2002). 'On temporal hyperacuity in the human visual system' *Vision Research*, 42 2499–2508.

Zanker, J. M. and Walker, R. (2004). 'A new look at Op art: Towards a simple explanation of illusory motion' *Naturwissenschaften*, 91 149–156.

Zanker, J. M. and Zeil, J. (2001). 'Motion Vision: Computational, Neural and Ecological Constraints', (Berlin, Heidelberg, New York: Springer Verlag).

Zatorre, R. J., Chen, J. L., and Penhune, V. B. (2007). 'When the brain plays music: auditory-motor interactions in music perception and production' *Nat Rev Neurosci*, 8 547–558.

Zeil, J. and Hemmi, J. (2006). 'The visual ecology of fiddler crabs' *Journal of Comparative Physiology A: Neuroethology, Sensory, Neural, and Behavioral Physiology*, 192 1–25.

Zeki, S. (1993). *A Vision of the Brain* (Oxford: Blackwell Scientific Publications).

Zhao, L. and Chubb, C. (2001). 'The size-tuning of the face-distortion after-effect' *Vision Research*, 41 2979–2994.

Zola-Morgan, S. (1995). 'Localization of Brain Function: The Legacy of Franz Joseph Gall (1758–1828)' *Annual Review of Neuroscience*, 18 359–383.

Index